THE AGONY OF ALGERIA

The Agony of Algeria

MARTIN STONE

Columbia University Press
New York

DT
295.5
.S75
1997

Columbia University Press
Publishers since 1893
New York

Copyright © 1997 by Martin Stone

First published in the United Kingdom by
C. Hurst & Co. (Publishers) Ltd., London

Library of Congress Cataloging-in-Publication Data

Stone, Martin
    The agony of Algeria / Martin Stone.
      p.   cm.
    First published: London : C. Hurst.
    Includes bibliographic references.
    ISBN 0-231-10910-5 (cloth). -- ISBN 0-231-10911-3 (pbk.)
      1. Algeria--Politics and government--1962- 2. Algeria--Social
conditions. 3. Islam and state--Algeria. 4. Islam and politics-
-Algeria. 5. Democracy--Algeria. I. Title.
DT295.5.S75 1997
965.05--dc21   97-24402
                                        CIP

Printed in England

C 10 9 8 7 6 5 4 3 2 1

PREFACE AND ACKNOWLEDGEMENTS

There are few countries as little studied and as much misunderstood as modern Algeria, at least in the English-speaking world. Although French control of North Africa's largest country ended in 1962, the French language and, it can be argued, the French intellectual tradition remained the primary vehicle of international enquiry into the country for more than thirty years, with a few honourable exceptions. Despite Algeria's avowed commitment to the non-aligned movement, British and North American observers, with their traditional focus on the eastern Arab world, were often content to leave the country as a scholarly chasse gardée of France. Mostly, Algeria was explained to the world through French (or French-educated) eyes and articulated in a French intellectual idiom.

Algeria's history between 1962 and 1989 reinforced this state of affairs. The early interest in the country from the Anglo-Saxon dominated international oil and gas industry collapsed in the face of the Boumedienne government's decision largely to nationalise the sector in 1972. By the early 1980s the country had a disproportionately small English-speaking expatriate community: most foreign residents were French, southern European or from the communist Eastern bloc. Thus by the time that Algeria was propelled once again to the forefront of international affairs from 1988 onwards, the range of works on it in English – at least ones published from the late 1960s – was generally inadequate.

This book attempts to introduce Algeria to English-speaking readers who may be unfamiliar with it, and has eschewed some of the more rigorous academic structures to maximise accessibility to students, analysts, businesspeople and general readers. My prime objective is to provide a comprehensive explanation of how Algeria reached its multiple crises in the 1990s, while at the same time whetting the appetite for further study of what I consider the most fascinating, complex and contradictory society in the Arab world.

I wish to express my appreciation to Hans-Heino Kopietz who first suggested that I tackle this subject, and to John Bray, who at the time I began writing was Head of Research at Control Risks Information Services. I would also like to record how much my appreciation of the complexities and fascination of Algeria has been inspired by the work of Hugh Roberts, whose influence will be easily detected in this book. I am also grateful for the encouragement of Gary Duffield, Saad Djebbar and the Algerian Embassy in London.

Even more than most Arab countries, Algeria presents the writer with serious problems of transliteration. Wherever possible I have selected the forms for place and personal names that are most commonly used in English journalistic and academic writing about Algeria. In most cases these arrived in English via French, resulting in widely accepted anomalies such as the use of dj- for j- and occasionally c- for s-. Others reflect a version of an Algerian dialectical pronounciation, such as l- for al-. I have tried to avoid using some of the most ungainly arabicisms insisted upon by some authorities.

London, August 1997   MARTIN STONE

CONTENTS

MAPS

TABLES

ABBREVIATIONS

ABERC	Académie Berbère de l'Échange et de la Recherche Culturel
AIS	Armée Islamique du Salut
ALN	Armée de Libération Nationale
AML	Amis du Manifeste et de la Liberté
ANP	Armée Nationale Populaire
CCN	Conseil Consultatif National
CEC	Comité des Enfants de Chouhada
CNRA	Conseil National de la Révolution Algérienne
CRUA	Comité Révolutionnaire d'Unité et d'Action
FAF	Fraternité Algérienne en France
FFS	Front des Forces Socialistes
FIS	Front Islamique de Salut
FLN	Front de Libération Nationale
GIA	Groupes Islamiques Armées
GPRA	Gouvernement Provisoire de la République Algérienne
HCE	Haut Comité d'État
LADDH	Ligue Algérien pour la Défense des Droits de l'Homme
MCB	Mouvement Culturel Berbère
MDA	Mouvement por la Démocratie en Algérie
MIA	Mouvement Islamique Armé
MNA	Mouvement National Algérien
MSP	Mouvement pour la Société de la Paix
MTLD	Mouvement pour le Triomphe des Libertés Démocratiques
OAS	Organisation de l'Armée Secrète
ONM	Organisation Nationale des Moudjahidine
OS	Organisation Spéciale
PAGS	Parti de L'Avant-Garde Socialiste
PPA	Parti du Peuple Algérien
PT	Parti des Travailleurs
RCD	Rassemblement por la Culture et la Démocratie
RND	Rassemblement National Démocratique

RPN	Rassemblement Patriotique National
SM	Sécurité Militaire
UNFA	Union Nationale des Femmes Algeriennes
UDMA	Union Démocratique du Manifeste Algérien
UNJA	Union Nationale de la Jeunnesse Algérienne
UOIF	Union des Organisations Islamiques de France
UGTA	Union Générale des Travailleurs Algériens
VERA	Volontariat des Étudiants pour la Révolution Agraire

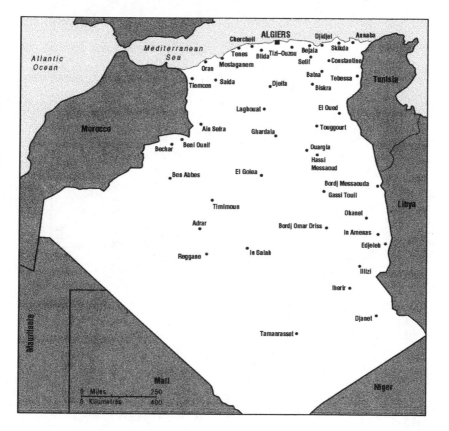

Algeria

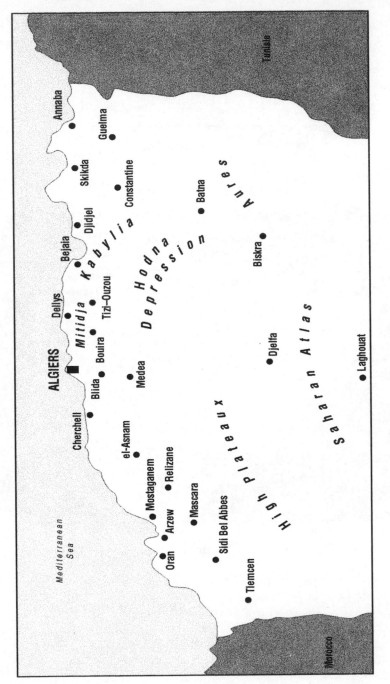

The North

INTRODUCTION

3.30 p.m. Monday 30 January 1995: a car loaded with
TNT explodes in front of the Algiers headquarters of the
Sûreté Nationale on the boulevard Amirouche. At this
time of day carnage is inevitable. An overcrowded bus
passes in front of the car at the moment of detonation,
and the street is crowded with shoppers buying food for
the start of the holy fasting month of Ramadan, which
starts later in the evening. Blood, limbs, clothes and
papers litter the pavement; severed limbs have to be
removed from the roofs of nearby buildings. Forty-two
people are killed, more than 250 injured. Although this is
the worst single bombing in the history of independent
Algeria, it has taken place in an unexceptional week: in
addition to at least thirty members of the security forces
being killed, gunmen have kidnapped and killed the four
children of a hero of the war of independence and
murdered a French resident in Algiers.

Algeria in the mid-1990s was in a desperate condition.
Between 1992 and 1997 some 120,000 people were killed
in a terrorist insurgency characterised by staggering
cruelty on both sides. Fanatical Islamist insurgents
pursued a dirty war to topple the state, fighting fearlessly
against their numerically superior foe and literally
terrorising the population. In the mountains and the
countryside, an informal guerrilla army laid ambushes for
a security apparatus reliant mainly on conscripts; in the
cities and towns killers, some in their teens, assassinated
thousands of 'liberals' who were considered supporters of
the state: schoolteachers, doctors, lawyers, journalists,
academics, civil servants and former fighters in the war of
independence against France. More than 100 foreigners
were killed, mostly French, of whom more than thirty

1

were men and women of religion – priests, nuns, monks. The Bishop of Oran was among them.

Algerians grew accustomed to unexplained explosions and bursts of gunfire at night; to news of yet another colleague or relative being knifed to death or gunned down while on the way to work or out shopping; to constantly coming across security force roadblocks and checkpoints that could always turn out to be a dreaded *faux barrage*, a 'false checkpoint'. Across northern Algeria, guerrillas raped and murdered women, some merely for refusing to wear the veil. In certain villages guerrillas even tried to enforce the highly questionable practice of *muta'* (temporary) marriage, which is tantamount to legalised prostitution. Individuals who considered themselves at risk were forced to live the life of a fugitive, furtively staying with friends or in protected compounds surrounded by the security forces. Those who could afford it left to live and work abroad, mostly in France.

Algerians had learned to read between the lines of the terse reports of security encounters published in the government-monitored press. They had become accustomed to reports of startling military successes against the guerrillas in the mountains and of 'key' terrorist leaders being killed in raids, understanding that, in reality, summary justice had been meted out. Many Algerians, even members of the security forces, accused members of the state itself of being behind the terrorist actions as a means of prolonging the violence for their own ends. Policemen secretly complained of being ordered to participate in death squads, shoot-to-kill raids and the torture of suspects.

The factors that underlie this appalling situation are complex and hotly disputed. Having lost virtually all legitimacy, Algeria's military-backed regime clung to power in the face of a savage terrorist war. Thirty years of rural depopulation had resulted in overcrowded cities where unemployment was rampant and the living conditions of the majority were intolerable. From being an elegant colonial port in 1962, Algiers had developed into a sprawling overcrowded metropolis. Most of the population were under thirty years of age, their parents having moved from the more socially conservative rural areas to the city in the 1960s and 1970s. Thousands of families were crammed into crumbling old apartment blocks or into modern soulless high-rises, with children often forced to sleep in beds by shifts. Unemployment and under-employment were high; the quality of life poor for most; and a sense of hope absent. The pattern was repeated in most towns across northern Algeria - Blida, Medea, Constantine, Skikda. Economically Algerians were paying the price for the mistakes of the past: the grand industrialisation schemes of the 1970s; over-reliance on oil and gas revenues; and the effects of a crippling foreign debt.

The argument of this book is that issues left unresolved after Algeria won independence from France in 1962 were at the root of the country's predicament in the mid-1990s, what I refer to as the 'post-Chadli crisis'. A nation-state in Algeria as defined in European terms came into being during the latter half of the nineteenth century. In the first six decades of the twentieth century the indigenous Muslim populations re-evaluated their own societies and over time determined to suppress their inherent divisions and coalesce together to eject the occupying colonial power. This suppression of social segmentations spawned new factions and frictions within society that re-emerged immediately after independence in 1962, only to be swept aside as a small westernised élite seized power.

This élite used the imperatives of nation-state building, the assertion of political independence, national development and stability to suppress debate about the political, cultural, religious, social and even linguistic identities and directions of the independent state. One of the key questions left unaddressed in the early 1960s was the religious orientation of the Constitution. The regime's adoption of a blend of Third World socialism, Western European social democracy, pan-Arabism and Islam was a compromise designed to appeal to all sectors of society, but which in fact was rejected by all. The first two Algerian regimes designated the country as a purely Arab nation, thereby ignoring the wishes of the Kabyle Berber minority, which constitutes up to 20 per cent of the population.

From 1965 to 1979 the country enjoyed a period of stability and economic growth, but this was exceptional and is unlikely to be witnessed again until the issues left unresolved in the immediate post-independence period are addressed. Rapid industrialisation and ill-managed agricultural collectivisation in the 1970s fatally ignored the importance of Algeria's agricultural sector and exacerbated the constant process of rural depopulation and the drift to the cities. This development further undermined traditional society, which was based on the family and the tribe, while the government's ideology first ignored and then tried to control the one remaining constant, Islam. The efforts of the so-called 'reformers' of the 1980s once again failed to address the real problems, and in the latter half of the decade the people turned against those whom they perceived as the hijackers of the spirit of the bloody war of independence. As in many other post-colonial Muslim societies, radical Islam was bound to be the beneficiary of the regime's failure. And because the economic successes of the 1970s and early 1980s had taught Algerians to expect reasonable living standards, the worsening situation after the oil price crash of 1986 brought about a crisis of expectations.

Since independence, Algerian politics has been dominated by the interaction between various factions, clans, interest groups and ideological tendencies. Until 1989 the official ruling organisation, the Front de Libération Nationale (FLN) was merely a political façade behind which these various groups vied for power and influence. Although the one-party state was formally demolished in 1989, the four main political tendencies within the FLN – the dirigistes, the liberals, the secularists and the Islamists, each of which held conflicting conceptions of Algerian society – became locked in a bitter rivalry. This dangerous interplay grew apace with the introduction of political pluralism and the legalisation of the Front des Forces Socialistes (FFS) and the establishment of the Front Islamique de Salut (FIS) in 1989. As with previous groups, there was considerable blurring and flexibility of the groups' memberships and ideologies, with some public figures considering themselves as belonging to more than one camp. Although the FFS and FIS had supporters in government and in the political parties, their efforts were principally directed at gaining the ear of the ultimate power in Algeria, the military. The military was itself divided over the Islamist 'problem', broadly forming two camps – the 'eradicators', who favoured liquidation of the Islamists and the 'conciliators', who sought to bring them into the establishment.

In 1962 the FLN's role as a vehicle of mass mobilisation to achieve the liberation of Algeria ended. From then on its various constituent tendencies – conservative/traditionalist, liberal, social-democrat, communist, and so on – were obliged either to separate from the one permitted political organisation or to work within it, a situation further complicated by Kabyle ethnic awareness. Between 1962 and 1989 these various tendencies either vied for influence within the state and the FLN, or remained marginalised. The emergence in 1965 of the initially clandestine FFS marked the separation from the state of much of the Kabyle social-democratic and liberal strand within the pre-1962 FLN; while the establishment in 1989 of the FIS acted as a focus for the conservative and traditionalist strand. As such, the FIS perpetuates rather than subverts Algeria's post-1992 political tradition and, as is often remarked, the party is an authentic heir of the nationalist project launched by the FLN in the 1950s. This project was subverted by the pre-eminence of Western, mainly French, political models up till the 1970s, a process that delayed Algeria's recognition of the nation's religious and cultural bases. As François Burgat has remarked, the advent of Islamism is perhaps a further stage in the disengagement of post-colonial societies from their former rulers. In Algeria, this phenomenon was complicated by a desire to forge a genuine and relevant national identity in reponse to the lingering cultural imperialism of French rule.

One of the effects of the post-Chadli crisis was to re-focus international attention on Algeria after some twenty years of neglect, particularly outside France. The apparent threat of 'another Iran' on the very doorstep of southern Europe concentrated government minds in Europe and North America on Algiers to a higher degree than at any time since the 1960s. France exploited these fears, including the spectre of a flood of Algerian 'boat people' pouring into southern Europe, to rally support for its own Algeria policy, leading to ill-conceived and ineffective European Union initiatives such as the Euro-Med Partnership talks held in Barcelona in November 1995. However, Algeria's enormous oil and gas wealth had already placed it at the forefront of Western governments' concerns, with several major US and European companies involved in the construction of the Algeria-Spain gas pipeline that will make Algeria the major supplier of gas to three European countries by early in the next century. The outcome of the post-Chadli crisis is of prime importance. At stake is the cultural and social identity of a state that, for all its chronic problems, remains capable of one day emerging as one of the richest and most powerful in the Arab world.

The Algerians

At the 1987 census, Algeria's population was a little over 25 million though with a 2.6 per cent annual demographic increase rate it was estimated that it would rise to at least 27 million by 1993.[1] Even conservative predictions forecast a population of nearly 33 million by 2000. The population is distributed remarkably unevenly, reflecting the relatively benign climate and soils of the coastal plains as opposed to the harsh terrain of the mountains, plateaux and desert. Some 94 per cent of the population inhabits northern Algeria, which constitutes only 14 per cent of the country's land area, with population densities ranging from 30 people per sq. km. to 1,100. In contrast, figures for the Sahara are quoted in sq. km. per person. The rural depopulation and urbanisation that began in the 1940s have accelerated sharply since independence: 50

[1] Source: The Economist Intelligence Unit Country Report, Algeria, 1993.

per cent of Algerians live in towns and cities and some 100,000 people migrate to the cities every year in search of employment. Algeria is also a remarkably youthful society: 75 per cent of the population is under 30.

Apart from tiny residual Christian and Jewish communities in Algiers and other northern cities, nearly all Algerians are Muslims. But this apparent homogeneity belies the enormous geographical, linguistic, ethnic and other local divisions among Algerians; indeed, one of the central themes of successive Algerian regimes since 1962 has been the goal of forging a 'national' identity as a means of overcoming the profound problems caused by these cleavages. Instead, it is perhaps more profitable and less confusing to examine the Algerian ethnic picture in terms of language, though this too is fraught with inconsistency and confusion. In broad terms, Algerians belong to one of two ethno-linguistic groups: Arabs or Berbers. As the overwhelming majority of the inhabitants of what is now Algeria are racially Berber in origin, the terms are immediately inadequate, but for the purposes of this book we will use 'Arab' to refer to Algerians whose first language is Arabic, while 'Berber' denotes those whose mother-tongue is a Berber dialect. However, first-time visitors to Algeria may well feel that they have arrived in a Francophone country, so entrenched is the use of the French language among large sectors of the population.

An understanding of the Berber question is a key to the study of modern Algeria. The presence of Berber communities is one of the most important characteristics that distinguish Maghrebi (that is, North-West African) Arab countries, particularly Algeria and Morocco, from the Mashreqi ones. Although almost all Algerians have some Berber blood, only 20-30 per cent – the figure is hotly disputed – would describe themselves as Berbers. Indeed, many Algerians – both secularist and Islamist – would oppose the very use of the term 'Berber', arguing that it undermines national unity or is inimical to Islam. The term Berber is derived from the Latin *barbarus*, barbarian. The Berbers have no collective name for themselves, and later European civilisations have described them as Numidian, Getulian and Mauritanian.

Their origins are uncertain, but it is clear that Berber civilisations have existed in North Africa since at least the Bronze Age. Today Berbers are found in a wide arc extending from southern Morocco, through Algeria (particularly in Kabylia) and into parts of Tunisia; there also are residual Berber communities in Libya and Egypt. Throughout history Berbers have adapted well to successive foreign invasions – Phoenician, Roman, Arab, Turkish and French – and retained much of their distinctive civilisation based on clan loyalties. Many Berber communities converted to Judaism before the arrival of the Arabs in the seventh century, and large numbers of Kabyles became Christians during the 130-year French occupation.

There are four major Berber groups in Algeria, though there are numerous smaller tribal groups speaking Berber dialects that are often barely intelligible to other related groups and who often display different cultural and physical characteristics. The principal feature that unites them all in as much as they are united is their common distrust of and, frequently, hostility to the Arab majority. This leads in turn to a sense of common ethnic solidarity. A further shared feature is that most Berbers are viewed (with some justification) by the government in Algiers as a potential wellspring of unrest.

Algerian Berbers live in a number of ill-defined areas: the Kabyles in the mountains of Kabylia, the Chaouias in the Aurès mountains around Biskra and Batna, the M'zabites in the Ghardaia area, and the nomadic Touareg (singular Targui) of the Ahaggar region in the deep Sahara. Smaller Berber communities, living in villages among settled Arabs but maintaining a separate cultural identity, are found in the hill country to the north of the Chélif river, in the Ouarsenais, in the Djebel Amour, and to the south of Djelfa. Kabyles have a reputation as the most geographically dispersed Berber group; the presence of many thousands of Kabyles in Algiers has earned it a reputation as a Kabyle city. The Berber language, of which there are innumerable dialects, belongs to the Hamitic group and is thus a distant relative of Arabic and even ancient Egyptian. Until the twentieth century,

Berber dialects were spoken rather than written (the Punic, Latin, Arabic, Turkish and then French scripts were used for written communication), though the Touareg dialect Tamanhaq had developed an ancient and elegant writing system called Tifinagh for special or principally religious, purposes. The main Kabyle dialect is known variously as Tamazigh, Tmazigh or Tamazirte; the Chaouia dialect is closer to that spoken by Berbers in Tunisia.

The Kabyles, numbering over four million and representing around 20 per cent of the total population, are by far the most important Berber group. They have inhabited the beautiful uplands of Kabylia since fleeing the encroaching Roman and Arab invaders. The ridge villages of Kabylia lie in one of the most fertile and hence over-populated regions of Algeria, and it was to escape such conditions that thousands of Kabyles first migrated to France in the latter part of the nineteenth century. This process continues, though it has been much reduced since the French government took steps to limit all immigration from Algeria in the mid 1980s. Nevertheless, Kabyles comprise the majority of Algerian immigrants in France, both as unskilled workers and as professionals, and they continue to send back remittances to their families. Many Kabyle workers in France return home each summer to build a comfortable house or farm, giving many villages and towns a surprising air of prosperity. Algiers-based Kabyles maintain strong links with their home towns and villages and look upon their adopted city as exile.

Kabyles have the reputation of being Algeria's most successful professionals and entrepreneurs, a distinction that provokes envy, distrust and hatred from their Arabised compatriots. Fiercely proud of their regional heritage and of the customs that distinguish them from other Algerians, Kabyles have proved unruly to successive invaders, but they have had little success in ruling themselves on more than a village basis. To an outsider they can appear dour, reserved and unwelcoming, but this masks a hospitality and a *joie de vivre* that is often expressed in enthusiastic consumption of alcohol and a love of music. Kabyles make up a disproportionate number of Algeria's intellectuals, academics and journalists, though they are to some extent discriminated against in the allocation of public sector jobs. Despite the deep and enduring links between Kabyles and the French, Kabylia was at the forefront of the nationalist movement during the war of independence; today it is almost entirely opposed to the illiberal repression preached by the FIS. Kabyle women, who are usually unveiled, have traditionally enjoyed greater freedom within the family and in public than their arabised sisters.

The Chaouias inhabit the rugged and remote Aurès mountains, where the first shots in the Algerian war of independence were fired on All Saints' Day 1954. Traditionally more isolated than their Kabyle neighbours due to their even more remote location and irregular contact with the outside world, the Chaouias have been less affected by the culture and language of the ruling power than the Kabyles. Chaouias are particularly subject to clan in-fighting, leading some observers to draw parallels with Corsica. Although Chaouias were among the fiercest of the *mudjahidine* (referring, in this context, to freedom fighters) in the war against the French, clan rivalry diluted their impact. The M'zabites are the descendants of a Kharidjite [2] kingdom displaced to the Ghardaia region in the tenth century. The M'zabite community, which numbers around 50,000 people, is strictly theocratic and is often described as 'puritan'. The local dialect is related to that spoken by Berber enclaves in western Algeria. Although the five M'zabite towns are known for their unique architecture and are often visited

---

[2] Kharidjism is a Muslim heresy that developed in Arabia in the mid-seventh century. Among other doctrines it rejected the Arabs' automatic assumption of leadership of the Islamic community. This doctrine appealed to the independent-minded Berbers, who first revolted in 740 throughout North Africa in the name of Kharidjism, and in 776 a kingdom was established at Tahert (near present-day Tiaret), where the local rulers (known as Rustumids or Ibadites) gained a reputation for integrity and asceticism. The Tahert kingdom was destroyed by 911, after which the first Ibadites settled in the M'Zab.

by tourists, the community has little influence on the politics of Algeria as a whole.

Touareg communities are found mainly in the remote Tamanrasset and Djanet areas, and have more connection with related communities in Niger and Mali than with the Kabyles or Chaouias. Strongly based on tribal structures, the Touareg, who call themselves *Imohagh* (the free) converted to Islam only in the ninth century, having rejected it on fourteen occasions. Touareg nomads are a constant irritant to the government in Algiers, which views with concern the activities of the Niger-based Army for the Liberation of Azawad and el-Air (ALAA) in the vast desert areas near the Malian and Nigerian borders. However, the Touareg people have a very peripheral role in Algerian politics and retain a stronger psychological connection with the countries to the south.

Arabs comprise around 80 per cent of the population and thus are the dominant ethno-linguistic group. The vast majority of Algerians spoke Berber dialects until the invasion in the eleventh century of the Arab Banu Hillal and Banu Sullaym tribal confederacies from Egypt and Syria. As these gradually replaced the local Islamised Berber dynasties, their language over time supplanted Berber dialects, particularly in the accessible coastal regions and parts of the Tellian Atlas. The process was assisted by the flourishing trade between northern Algeria and the Arab east, and the dominant contemporary Algerian Arabic dialect has directly developed from the Banu Hillal and the Banu Sullaym. However, some areas of northern Algeria – including parts of the Petite Kabylie, south of Bejaia, and in the Trara mountains near the Moroccan border – continue to speak Berber dialects. Since independence, Algerian regimes have tried hard to impose Modern Standard Arabic (MSA) as the national language while rejecting local Algerian Arabic and Berber dialects as somehow inferior. This has caused serious disruption to the country: Modern Standard Arabic is largely unintelligible to speakers of Algerian Arabic dialects and is roundly rejected by Berber-speakers.

Society

There are two dominant elements in Algerian society: Islam and the tribe. Islam has been central to the Algerian way of life since its arrival in North Africa in the seventh century. Under the rule of the Arabs, the local Berber kingdoms and later the Turks, the inhabitants of what is now Algeria fused their own pre-Islamic beliefs with the mainstream Sunni rite to create their own particular brand of Islam. Later the doctrines of Kharidjism and Shiism arrived. The first appealing mainly to local independent-minded Berber dynasties, but, notwithstanding the Kharidjite communities that remain to this day, it was shortlived. In the eleventh century the Fatimid dynasties adopted Shia Islam, but by the twelfth century Sunni doctrine had reasserted itself and remains predominant. Sufism was well received in Algeria, particularly among unsophisticated rural communities and in Kabylia where the concept of spiritual power, important in Sufism, was already well entrenched among the local tribes

An important feature of Algerian Islamic tradition is that of the *marabout* (plural *murabitin*), individuals generally perceived to have a special religious status in the community. Acts and attributes that conferred such status ranged from justice, charity and the ability to work miracles, to madness or merely being designated by other *murabitin*. In many ways *murabitin* correspond to the Christian saints of the Middle Ages – their shrines and sanctuaries were the objects of pilgrimage. *Murabitin* often founded brotherhoods based in monasteries that followed a particular *tariqa* (plural *turuq*) or 'way'. Each *tariqa* claimed to offer a superior route to divine favour, often involving the use of trances and sometimes drugs. *Murabitin* also acted as local temporal leaders and conciliators, in some ways anticipating the spiritual leaders of the Islamist movements such as Abbasi Madani. Although many *marabout* brotherhoods had been dissolved by independence, the *murabitin* remain active in rural areas and have held local positions such as that of mayor. But the *marabout* system conflicts with the radical

Islam of the FIS, and *murabitin* or their descendants have
been increasingly targeted by Islamic extremists. A
further important feature of Algerian Islamic tradition
were the religious foundations known as *habous*; under
Islamic law, *habous* lands are held in perpetuity. Such
distinctive features, which although present in the towns
and cities more commonly reflect the conservative
traditions of the countryside, distinguish Maghrebi
Islamic tradition from that of the eastern Arab world.

Contemporary perceptions of Islam in Algeria are
dominated by the rise of so-called Islamic fundamentalism since the mid-1980s. While religion undeniably plays
a central role in contemporary Algerian politics, the
picture is in fact considerably more complex than at first
meets the eye. At independence, Islamic observance was
generally weak in the towns and cities but strong elsewhere. The massive displacement of rural populations to
the rapidly expanding cities in the 1960s and 1970s
subverted these centuries-old traditions, engendering
tensions between the conservative and generally poor
newcomers and the urban, liberal élite. This situation was
compounded by the government's attempts to comman-
deer Islam as a means of mobilising the population against
its enemies, and by the general drift to conservative Islam
that swept the Islamic world after the Iranian revolution
of 1980. By the early 1980s Islamic resurgence had given
birth to political Islam and later the exploitation of Islam
as a political vehicle, which in turn spawned Islamic
extremism in the early 1980s. Algeria has in many
respects been at the vanguard of political and social
movements in the Arab world. Since the collapse of
communism, political Islam is now the most inspiring
political/social movement in Algeria. Most Algerians are
practising Muslims but only a few are fundamentalists;
those who are prepared to fight for the establishment of
an 'Islamic state' remain the minority.

Tribal relationships played a key role in pre-
independence rural Algeria. In 'Arab' areas the primary
unit was the *ayla* (family), whose members claimed
descent through the male line from a single grandfather
and who enjoyed a form of collective ownership of

agricultural land or pastoral territories. A collection of *aylas* constituted a wider lineage traceable back to a more distant common male ancestor. Clans are a collection of lineages descended from an even more remote common ancestor; clans joined together to form tribes based on common or related ancestors or for their mutual benefit. Tribes for most of the time operated as independent units, forming larger confederations in time of war, invasion or other external threat. Heads of clans submitted to the authority of a *caid* (local official) in affairs of common interest, typifiying the highly stratified nature of Arab tribal society where social prestige and honour were the key components. By contrast, the organisation of society among settled Berber populations has always been characterised by a degree of democracy. Settlements comprise a collection of clans from which all adult males participate in the *djemaa*[3] (council). The most influential men within the *djemaa* are the heads of lineages, the *taman*, who elect the council's head, the *amin*. Historically, the role of the *djemaa* was to create and administer local laws (*qanuns*) and settle disputes.

Successive post-1962 Algerian regimes have tacitly adhered to the myth of an Arab Algerian identity that subverted and overturned the traditional role of the clans and tribes in Algeria. The extent to which this is true is mainly an accident of history: the French colonial policy of *regroupement*, or the resettlement of rural populations and the enormous displacement caused by the war of independence in some cases removed the traditional dynamic of kin against non-kin, promoting for the first time a genuine sense of solidarity based on a common predicament. More recently, rural depopulation and the drift to the cities have consolidated this process, with clan distinctions fused in the melting pot of the cities. However, outside the big urban centres, and particularly in Kabylia, the traditional tribal culture persists, a good example being the position of politician Hocine Aït Ahmed in Kabyle society. Moreover, new 'tribes' have emerged, perhaps most clearly demonstrated by the

---

[3] Alternative form is *tajma'a*, plural *tajma'aat*.

cohesion of the senior military officer class. And most recently, there has been an efflorescence of armed Islamic groups across northern Algeria. While these were initially under something approaching a unified command, by mid-1994 there were scores of groups, each with its own *emir* (prince or leader), and each expending almost as much effort on neutralising rival groups as overturning the regime in Algiers.

Despite the many features that distinguish Algeria from the rest of the Arab-Islamic complex, the role of the family, the individual and the sexes positions the country firmly within it. For the vast majority of Algerians, life remains centred on the family unit, though there are of course significant variations between the more modernised north and the more traditional south in the degree to which these units interplay with extended families, clans, lineages and tribes. Family numbers tend to be large: lower-income nuclear families in urban areas may have as many as ten children, perhaps reflecting the belief that more children eventually mean more income. Unfortunately the infrastructure cannot support the large size of families that predominates in lower-income urban areas, and many families are forced to live six, ten or even twelve to a room; the practice of sleeping in beds by shifts is not uncommon. A corollary of this is overloaded sanitation and utilities, turning districts previously considered well-to-do into slums. To combat this the government has pledged to build hundreds of thousands of new family dwellings, although even if the money is found to build them many of these almost inevitably will themselves turn into high-rise overcrowded slums. The situation is made significantly worse by the high annual rate of population increase that started as early as the late 1960s as Algeria began to recover from the holocaust of the war of independence. Even in rural areas, the family-lineage-clan-tribe system has been seriously undermined since the 1950s.

Relations between the sexes is a controversial area that modern Islamism has exploited to the full. The so-called socialist – and by implication modernising – ideologies espoused during the Boumedienne era reinforced the challenge to traditional social structures in place before the mid to late nineteenth century. As in all Arab-Islamic countries there is a strong conviction that men are socially, psychologically and, of course, physically stronger than women. Fathers generally rule their households while their wives are expected to take care of the (preferably male) children. Male family members jealously guard the 'honour' of 'their' females (and thus the family), and women are required to behave modestly and decorously in public. This situation changed little, if at all, during the 1960s, '70s and early '80s, and indeed was reinforced by the Islamic resurgence and consequent rise of political Islam; while in the 1970s the sight of a veiled woman in Algiers was comparatively rare, many men now force their wives and daughters to wear the veil in public. In rural communities, where women have always engaged in heavy work and are less likely be seen by non-kin, veiling has traditionally been less common.

The position of women in Algeria is a highly complex and emotional issue. Thousands of women fought as *mudjahidaat* (freedom fighters) alongside their Muslim brothers in the war of independence, and this experience, combined with exposure to European, and specifically French, culture showing a freer role for women, imbued them with the desire to overturn the traditional female role in Algeria. Almost immediately it became clear that the new rulers of Algeria were intent on restoring the traditional patriarchal system, and little progress was made in the subsequent three decades. The situation depends much on location, class and ethno-linguistic orientation. Although many Algerian women work – both in the rural and urban sectors – the advent of the Islamist movement is encouraging many men to forbid their wives and daughters to go out to work. The combination of the country's dire economic situation and the political-social crisis has frustrated many women, who have benefitted from Algeria's impressive education system and who have raised their aspirations accordingly. That said, many thousands of women are enthusiastic Islamists, although again they are divided between those who favour employment for women and the traditionalists.

Sex is a battleground that, some observers have suggested, is an important explanation for the psychological appeal of Islam. Pre-marital relations are strictly forbidden, even in 'liberal' homes. Teenage boys and girls almost never meet socially outside the immediate family and co-education has done little to subvert the strict segregation of the sexes at universities; the resumption of single-sex education is a cornerstone of the Islamist political platform. In many urban areas the crowds of young men – characterised as wall-leaners, *hittistes* – inevitably become frustrated with the taboos surrounding sex and take refuge in political Islam. Marriage is generally by arrangement, though the Western notion of 'romantic love' has made some inroads into social consciousness, principally among the middle classes. Girls typically marry in their early twenties a man in his late twenties to mid-thirties and go to live in the man's family household, sometimes joining a group of six to eight other young wives. There is no perception of homosexuality as a lifestyle.

As in most Arab-Islamic societies, the concept of a civil society is weak; the family and lineage are much more important. But Algerians do differ from other Arab cousins in the distinct sense of egalitarianism evident in most areas of life. At independence in 1962, there was no real élite; Europeans and Europeanised Muslims alike had fled the country as the FLN took over. The appalling experience inflicted on the Muslim population by the colonial authorities imbued it with a genuine sense of solidarity and this has to a large extent remained intact among the older generation into the 1990s. Indeed, it was this egalitarianism that played a large part in the popular disgust at the abuses of power and privilege committed by the ruling élite during the 1980s. However, the coherence of society has weakened as new generations of Algerians become increasingly remote from the experience of the war.

Language

Language is a primary political, ideological, social and psychological issue in Algeria. It is closely connected with the country's search for its identity and is a unifying force in a land of enormous regional and ethnic diversity. Classical Arabic is the official language of Algeria, and French, Maghrebi Arabic and Berber dialects are not even mentioned in the country's constitution. The language which an Algerian chooses to speak is often tantamount to a political statement: no Islamist would like to be heard peppering his speech with French borrowings or hybrid words, and Algerian Maghrebi Arabic is only rarely heard in Kabylia. The question of language also is closely associated with the issue of Algerianisation and Arabisation; with the renaissance of the country's Arab-Islamic-Berber heritage; and with responses to colonialism and the French occupation. Arabisation has always been the locus for various conflicts within Algerian society, reflecting the different political, social, ethnic and economic imperatives.

The linguistic map of Algeria is complex and subject to variations based on region and class. In 1962 the city-dwellers of the northern regions largely spoke French, though overlaid with Maghrebi Arabic. Rural populations of the north and in the Sahara used Maghrebi Arabic while French and Berber dialects predominated in Kabylia. Although the situation remains largely the same in Kabylia, Arabic is much more widely used in the northern littoral. This can be traced to the arabisation policies first developed during the Ben Bella and Boumedienne regimes and which are still employed in the 1990s. To the Islamists, the use of Arabic is proof of the speaker's Arabo-Islamic credentials and evidence of Koranic study. To modernist *arabisants*, Arabic represents national independence from the West, and in particular France. As John Entelis has remarked: 'The government's official policy of Arabisation, Algerianisation and Islamisation gives additional expressive and symbolic meaning to Arabic language used by all concerned.'[4]

However, despite thirty years of government pressure to Arabise, the use of French remains entrenched everywhere in Algeria. Everyone has some knowledge of, or competence in, French – even the illiterate. Unlike in neighbouring Morocco and Tunisia, this is not a result of a widespread feeling that French culture is superior to the Arab: Algerians are suspicious and often hostile to French civilisation due to the bitterness engendered by the years of French occupation and the often negative experiences of hundreds of thousands of Algerians working in France. An indication of this is the appelation *'roumiya'* used more often in Algeria to refer to the French language than *'français'* or the Arabic *'fransiyya'*. The term is derived from the Ottoman Turkish name for Europe – Rum, or 'Rome' – and carries connotations of Christianity and the infidel.

The incoherence of successive government Arabisation programmes, most notably the first established in 1963, is the principal reason for the endurance of the French language. In order to carry out its promise of 'education for all' (90 per cent of the contemporary population were illiterate), the Ben Bella regime imported thousands of often third-rate and unenthusiastic teachers from the Arab east, principally Egypt, Iraq and Syria. These further confused a bewildered population by teaching their own local version of Modern Standard Arabic in an idiom almost incomprehensible to the local population and with foreign cultural references. The importation of foreign teachers alienated many young people, educated by arabophones, from the older generation who had been brought up in the francophone tradition. Boumedienne's acceleration of the policy as an integral part of the major reforms of the early 1970s unintentionally fuelled the early growth of political Islam and ultimately the FIS. The policy, which Arabised local administration, the courts and much of central government, was ill-conceived and

---

[4]'Elite political culture and socialisation in Algeria: tensions and discontinuities', *Middle East Journal* (1981).

often directed by those with only a middling command of Arabic who continued to think in French. (In the 1970s there were numerous translation agencies in Algiers and other major cities.) The government slowed the pace of Arabisation after 1975, when President Boumedienne declared, 'When Arabic becomes the tool of work and communication in the petrochemical plant of Skikda and the steel plant of el-Hadjar, it will be the language of iron and steel.' This implied that notwithstanding the ideological imperatives of Arabisation, the government continued to view French as the most viable operational language. Within the central government only the justice and religious affairs ministries continue to operate entirely in Arabic in the mid-1990s.

Education was the one area where the state's Arabisation programme was successful, though there were drawbacks. The government had Arabised secondary and higher education by the mid-1990s, often at the demand of the students themselves; the last bilingual *baccalauréat* was taken in 1988. All primary education had been entirely in Arabic since the 1960s: French is taught as a 'foreign' language'. However, the shortage of suitably qualified Arabic-speaking teachers and the government's failure to provide Arabic typewriters and computers meant that many students in Arabised institutes received a second-rate education. Arabisation also limited their employment opportunities, and this on occasion led to students reversing their previous adherence to Arabisation for fear that their degrees would prove worthless. Candidates who spoke French and English were often preferred for sought-after posts in the diplomatic service or in management. It is important to remember, however, that although opposition to the policy was widespread, few dared openly to question the government's Arabo-Islamic motivation for fear of being branded a member of the 'party of France'. In 1988 the Chadli government forbade Algerians from attending francophone *lycées*, provoking a small exodus of well-off pupils to schools in France, Belgium and Switzerland. Many of the majority left behind are known as '*analphabètes bilingues*', unable to master either Arabic or French. Although the promotion of Modern Standard Arabic was seen as a desirable policy, its main flaw was the insistence on its use to the detriment of all other languages: Maghrebi Arabic, Berber dialects and French.

The December 1990 Arabisation law illustrated that the impetus behind the programme remained healthy. The controversial law, which was drawn up by the Mouloud Hamrouche administration, aimed to make Arabic the only language used in official and commercial documents by the thirtieth anniversary of Algerian independence in July 1992. Even educational institutions originally exempted from Arabisation – teaching medicine, technology and information science – were to Arabise by 1997. Television broadcasts already were entirely in Arabic – both Modern Standard and the local Algerian dialect. The law prompted enormous controversy. Hocine Aït Ahmed criticised it as a 'coup against democracy' and led tens of thousands in a demonstration against the law in December 1990. Ever eager to sustain the concept of a Francophone community of nations, the French government also urged Algerians to 'make their voices heard' against the law. Foreign investors in Algeria also expressed concern that obligatory use of Arabic would disrupt their operations. There was much relief when the Abdessalam administration postponed implementation of the law amid the tensions that followed the assassination of Mohamed Boudiaf in July 1992.

The Arab tradition of separate written and spoken language forms to some extent accounts for the educated Algerian's predilection to read in French and speak in the curiously mixed Algerian dialect. The proliferation of newspapers and weekly magazines in the 1990s illustrated the situation regarding the written language. There were nineteen daily newspapers, most of them published in French. The most respected of these were the Algiers-based *El Watan, Le Matin* and *Horizons*, all of which earned a reputation for often courageous reporting. The arabophone young and the Islamists not surprisingly favoured the Arabic journals, and in the mid-1990s these were the fastest growing section of newspaper readership. As Mina

Rezzouk, editor of a woman's magazine, observed: 'Seventy-five per cent of the population are under thirty years of age; the vast majority of young people are educated in Arabic, do not speak French – or only speak it very badly. If a francophone reader dies, he will not be replaced.' There was also a noticeable anti-French current in the Arabic press, often extending to an editorial line opposed to the government and characterised as the *courant franco-laïco-communiste*.

The language spoken in the home and on the street is, despite the meddling of the politicians and the imams, a rich and unique mix of Classical and Maghrebi Arabic, various local Berber dialects and *roumiya*. This hybrid is a relatively recent development: before the French occupation, all inhabitants of the coastal littoral (though not all Kabyles) would have been proficient in Maghrebi Arabic as well as Classical Arabic. Maghrebi Arabic itself is spoken across North Africa, and developed in the late Middle Ages from Classical Arabic with a few borrowings from Spanish, Berber dialects and Turkish. As with all spoken languages, it is constantly changing but has a special ability to seize French words and mutate them into acceptably Algerian-sounding forms. Algerians speak of '*trandji*' instead of '*étranger*' (foreigner), and have created Arabic-sounding plurals for words. Examples are: '*djouatna*' (cigarettes, from *gitanes*) and '*zouafra*' (worker, from the French '*ouvrier*', that generates the hybrid singular word '*zoufri*').The language also occasionally adopts and modifies French verbs and verbal phrases, for instance '*ma portaliché*', a Maghrebi Arabic bastardisation of '*peu m'importé* (I don't care).

In contrast, the language of broadcasting and official speeches is stilted and reflects the speaker's political or socio-economic status. Government ministers often lapse into French in the middle of a speech, frequently replying to questions put to them in French. Moreover, many Algerians have enormous difficulty understanding the Classical Arabic used in television news broadcasts, and prefer to watch the French satellite channels beamed from across the Mediterranean. In the political and social crises of the 1990s satellite dishes became a frequent target for Islamic extremists in heavily Islamist-influenced areas such as Blida and parts of Algiers.

Another important factor behind the dissonance of society is the emergence in the 1960s of a local élite, most of whom had been educated in French but which generally espoused the Arabo-Islamic development credo of the Boumedienne era. While the regime ordered Algerians to speak Modern Standard Arabic and use Islam as their reference for socialism, the privileged political and middle classes continued to function in a more or less Europeanised context, with French remaining their *lingua franca* and the West their training ground. In the 1990s the situation has not changed enormously: while the regime conducts more of its business in Arabic, the merchant and technocratic classes continue to be educated in French (often in France itself) and inevitably become well-versed in European culture. This, with its implied class structure, is anathema to Islamists, who stress the brotherhood of all Muslims and the primacy of Islam and Arabic culture.

It is against this background that any attempt to sketch the Algerian 'character' will almost inevitably be flawed. Outsiders visiting the country for the first time may be struck by the markedly reserved nature of the locals – they may find them taciturn and indifferent where the reverse is the case in the countries of the Arab east. Some visitors have complained of the Algerian's suspicious nature, the near impossibility of navigating the complex webs of family, local and linguistic relationships. Indeed, it is often true that Algerians are introverted and sometimes appear sullen and this can lead to an impression of xenophobia (this would hardly be surprising given the country's horrendous colonial experience and, more recently, concerns over the treatment of Algerian immigrants in France). Algerians are often held to be secretive, uncommunicative and deeply suspicious of everyone ranging from the Western powers to their own brothers. This contrasts with the rigorous loyalty that exists among clan members, and on a national level this sometimes translates into excessive pride, independence and self-reliance. In the modern context it can be best illustrated perhaps by the regime's refusal until 1994 to contemplate rescheduling the country's crippling debt repayments and to encourage mass tourism as in neighbouring Morocco and Tunisia. There is also a passion for belonging: intense pride in being Algerian, being an Arab or being a Kabyle, and more recently an almost tribal adherence to political party. This passion can be brutal; instances of astonishing cruelty pepper the history of the central Maghreb from pre-Roman times to the present: reports of murders by Islamic extremists and their enemies frequently include ritualistic and barbarous details, recalling the butcheries perpetrated by both sides in the war of independence. While there is a strong resistance to personality leadership, as both Ahmed Ben Bella and Chadli Bendjedid found to their cost, Algerians appreciate ceremony and rigid hierarchies. As the leader Abderrazak Chentouf once explained, 'The Algerian mentality is characterised by the right-angle. There are no contours or compromises.'

1

ALGERIA BEFORE 1962

A detailed history and analysis of Algeria before the departure of the French in 1962 is beyond the scope of a book outlining the history of post-1962 Algeria. However, the reader would be rash to attempt an examination of Algeria since independence without at least a brief glance at the country in antiquity and, more important, in colonial times.

In the fifth century BC the inhabitants of a chain of Berber states in the central part of North Africa began to engage in farming, pastoralism, crude manufacturing and trade. By the third century BC there were two Berber kingdoms – Masaesyles in the west and Massyles in the east. In 203 BC King Massinissa of Massyles defeated his rivals from Massaesyles to found Numidia, with its capital at Constantine (then called Cirta) and a population estimated at 100,000. This state eroded the highly tribalised nature of Berber society and attained a high degree of civilisation. It soon attracted the attention of Rome, which defeated Massinissa's son Jugurtha and divided Numidia among three of his sons under their own sovereignty. By the first century AD Numidia had fallen under the direct rule of Rome, although this extended only as far as the Tellian Atlas, from where the Berber tribes gradually reasserted their control over the western coast after the fall of Rome in AD 429. By the mid-seventh century Berber society had been largely retribalised under the control of tribal confederations, and these were able to put up stout resistance to the invading Arabs, who took thirty-five years to take control of the entire central Maghreb. The Arabs followed their military

invasion with the forced conversion of most local Berbers
to Islam; from the eighth century the central Maghreb
became predominantly Muslim, and Islam represented
virtually the only cohesive factor in a society prone to
tribal and factional fighting. However, acceptance of
Islam did not mean assent to Arab rule. Berber tribes in
the west rose up in the name of Kharidjite Islam in 740,
and by 756 Arab rule had been shaken off in many areas
of Algeria for good.

The following eight centuries have been called the
golden age of the Maghreb. In the first three centuries
there was a series of disputes between Arab dynasties in
the west and Berber tribal states in the east. The most
noteworthy of the latter was the Kharidji kingdom of the
Rustamids based at Tahert, whose leaders maintained
religious links with the Ibadi Shia Muslims at Basra in
southern Mesopotamia (Iraq). To the east lay the lands of
the Fatimids, who in 910 destroyed the Rustamids and
eventually went on to found a state in Egypt. The Zirids,
who were nominally under the suzerainty of the Fatimids,
founded the cities of Algiers, Medea and Miliana and
brought the region out of its traditional obscurity. The
Zirids in turn gave control of their western domains to the
Hammadids, who founded Bejaia, but eventually broke
with the Zirids and established their own dynasty in the
north-east. However, once installed in Cairo the Fatimids
refused to sever all ties with their Maghreban origins. In
1050 the Fatimid Caliph used two tribes of Syrian origin
then settled in the Nile Delta, the Banu Hillal and the Banu
Sullaym, to move westwards to reconquer the lost lands.
After a rapid sweep across Libya, the tribes defeated the
Zirids at Gabes, in modern Tunisia, in 1052, precipitating
several decades of anarchy during which the Banu Hillal's
descendants, the Hillalians, reversed the steps towards
political organisation that had been made under the
Fatimids and the Zirids. The advent of the Hillalians also
marked the beginning of the decline of Berbero-Arabic
society, in which Berber languages had been dominant:
henceforth Hillalian Arabic was the predominant vernacular.

The fundamentalist Almoravid house was the next dynasty to make its mark on the region. The name is a Latinate corruption of the *dar al-Murabitoun*, the House of the People of the Ribat, roughly equivalent to a monastery. The Almoravids emerged in the central Moroccan Atlas in the tenth century and by the late eleventh century they had restored order in Algiers and Oran, though they in turn were succeeded by another dynasty from the Moroccan Atlas, the Almohads (another Latinate corruption from *al-Muwahhidoun*, the unitarists). The Almohads were highly civilising despite their strong tribal background. Their defeat of the Almoravids in 1145 allowed the Almohads steadily to gain control of most of the Maghreb and Muslim Spain by the end of the twelfth century, although the vast size of their dominions exposed them to constant attack from Almoravid strongholds in the Balearic Islands and by Bedouin tribes in the Sahara.

The decline of the Almohad dynasty around 1250 ended the last era of self-rule in the central Maghreb until 1962 and accelerated the decline of the entire region that had been underway since the time of the Hillalians. The region fell into two parts, to the east and to the west of the Grande Kabylie. The Hafsids, an Almohad successor dynasty based in Tunis, controlled the eastern half until their own defeat by the Ottoman Turks in 1574. The Hafsids saw themselves as the legitimate successors to the Almohads and claimed for themselves the title of Caliph, the supreme Islamic office that had been swept away by the Mongol invasions of Mesopotamia and the consequent demise of the Abbasid dynasty in Baghdad. The western half fell under the control of a loose alliance of Zenata Berber tribes under the leadership of the Banu Abd al-Wad, alternatively known as the Zayyanids, who established their capital in the western city of Tlemcen. Both the Hafsid and Zayyanid states suffered from continuous faction-fighting; the loss of the Saharan trade routes; and a growing threat from the Christian states to the north of the Mediterranean, which culminated in the Spanish *reconquista* of the late fifteenth century. Many refugees from southern Spain settled in a string of city

states – Oran, Algiers, and Bejaia among them – along the
central Maghreban littoral and these, together with the
resurgent tribes of the interior, constituted a significant
challenge to the Hafsid and Zayyanid dynasties.

The Ottoman conquest of the Central Maghreb in the
early sixteenth century was precipitated by two Turkish
privateers, the brothers Aruj and Khair al-Din
(Barbarossa, or 'red beard'). The brothers appeared off
the coast of Algiers in 1504, and in 1516 the beleaguered
citizens requested Aruj to assist them against the Spanish.
Aruj seized the opportunity to take control of the city and
declare himself Sultan. His brother Khair al-Din expelled
the Hafsids from the north-east by 1525 and the Zayyanids from the west by 1545, resulting in the Ottoman
Sultan bestowing on him the title of *beylerbey* – governor-
general. By 1571, all of the central and eastern Maghreb,
from Tlemcen to Benghazi in eastern Libya was nominally
an Ottoman province, a state of affairs which persisted, at
least in theory, for 270 years.

The Turks ruled a relatively stable and economically
successful state in the central Maghreb until 1830. In the
principal city, Algiers, power was exercised by a succession of officers initially entitled *taifas,* and later *aghas.* After
1671 the title *dey* came into use, originally to denote an
Ottoman officer commanding around one hundred
troops. The *dey* ruled according to the wishes of a corps of
Janissaries – soldiers largely recruited from among
Anatolian Turks – and of the corsairs, the local pirates
operating along the North African coast. The Janissaries
dominated the *divan,* the council which selected the *dey,*
and ensured that one of their own number always
emerged. Corsair activities in the Mediterranean provided
the source of finance for the government in Algiers, as
agricultural production had been in decline since the
fourteenth century. Although Algiers paid tribute to the
Ottoman Sultan in faraway Constantinople, its own
financial viability ensured a large degree of independence.
The rest of the central Maghreb was divided between
semi-independent *beyliks* (states ruled by beys) at Oran,
Medea and Constantine, though many areas of the Tellian
Atlas and the High Plateaux remained more or less

independent of outside interference until well into the nineteenth century, with *tariqa* leaders influential among many tribal populations. During the Ottoman era urban society in the coastal cities evolved into a fascinating ethnic mix of Turks, Arabs, Berbers, *Kouloughlis* (people of mixed Turkish and central Maghrebi blood), Moors (descendants of Muslim Spanish refugees) and Jews. The interior, meanwhile, remained largely unchanged.

Ottoman rule in the central Maghreb went into decline in the second half of the eighteenth century, as the increasingly strong British and Dutch navies hampered the corsairs' privateering activities in the western Mediterranean and Algiers lost its traditional trading markets in France. The result was financial, political and social crisis throughout most of region. In Algiers itself there were ten years of political turmoil during which local resentment against Turkish influence prompted a series of rebellions led by religious leaders in the nineteenth century. The twelve-year rule of Hussein Dey, the last *dey* to rule in Algiers, was the first to rely on local troops rather than Turkish Janissaries as had been done for over two centuries. It has been argued that this short period set in train a process of transforming an overwhelmingly oligarchical ruling institution into something ressembling a centralised monarchy and possibly even an 'Algerian nation'. At the same time the *beyliks* of Oran and Constantine had also begun to rely increasingly on indigenous – at any rate *Kouloughli* – military support, thereby distancing themselves further from Ottoman Turkish authority. Many late twentieth-century nationalist Algerians have focused on this period as 'evidence' of the existence of an 'Algerian nation' before the colonial period, although modern Islamists reject the significance of a nation-state.

Under the French

The French occupation of Algeria, which began with the seizure of Algiers in 1830 and ended with the Evian Accords of 1962, is of incalculable importance in a study of modern Algeria. The period serves as a central reference point to all citizens of the modern republic: nationalists and Islamists, modernists and traditionalists, Arabs and Berbers. The history, or perhaps more often the mythology, of this period underpins the conscious- ness of every Algerian over the age of thirty and contin- ues to shape the unconscious of the country's vast youth. In a country so divided on almost every aspect of political, social, cultural and economic life, the French occupation constitutes more or less the one point of agreement and the common denominator. This is all the more important given that the 'glorious' episode of Algeria's eight-year struggle for liberation contains grounds for dissent and disagreement, and that the history of independent Algeria has become discredited in the perceptions of so many of its citizens.

The immediate pretext for the French conquest was the comical and trivial episode of 29 April 1827 in which Hussein Dey struck the French Consul, Pierre Deval, three times on the arm with a fly-whisk. Hussein had been provoked by Deval's refusal to answer his request for information on an oustanding French debt of some 8 million francs. The episode would have remained little more than an anecdote in diplomatic history had the French King Charles X and his Prime Minister, the Prince de Polignac, in 1829 not seen in a campaign against Algiers to avenge France's honour a useful means of restoring their waning popularity. French forces landed at Sidi Ferruch, to the north-west of Algiers, on 14 June 1830, and the city officially passed under French control on 5 July. The French invaders ignored their govern- ment's orders to behave as a 'civilising force' to rid Algiers of Turkish influence and indulged in countless acts of base savagery and religious vandalism which shocked France. Thousands of Turks and *Kouloughlis* were expelled.

The French invasion did not go unresisted. The most famous obstacle to French ambitions was the great Algerian hero, Emir Abd al-Kader, who first came to prominence in 1832 as the head of a Moroccan force trying to dislodge the French from Oran. Between 1832 and 1839 the deeply religious Abd al-Kader headed a state founded on egalitarian Islamic principles formed of local Berber tribes and based in Mascara. He brought into the administration a far greater range of the population than had been the case under the Ottomans and has provided a key reference point for later generations of Algerian Muslim historians and nationalists. By concluding a series of treaties with the French and defeating all local rulers in his path, Abd al-Kader was able to extend his rule from the present Moroccan border as far as the Grande Kabylie. Ahmad Bey, who favoured the establishment of a local aristocratic rule to step into the shoes of the departing Turks, was the third power in the central Maghreb of the 1830s until the French took his capital Constantine in 1837.

Initially, France pursued a policy of restricted occupation, negotiating a complicated series of treaties with local rulers designed to extend its influence but not its direct control. In 1834 French rule comprised only the Algiers hinterland and an archipelago of enclaves around Bougie (Bejaia) and Bone (Annaba) in the east, and around Mostaganem and Oran in the west. The fall of Constantine, however, marked the end of the French policy of restricted occupation. In 1839 Abd al-Kader declared a *jihad* (holy war) on France to which the French Marshal Bugeaud responded by employing ruthless tactics against the local populations in areas controlled by the Emir. Eight years of all-out war ensued, forcing the Emir at one point to operate from Moroccan territory. He managed to hold out until 1847 by which time the French forces had extended their rule into the High Plateaux and the margins of the Sahara; the tribal federations of the Grande Kabylie surrendered to France in 1857. Tribal and religious leaders, however, continued to lead periodic rebellions against the French into the 1890s. More than 2,600 Europeans and many times that number of Algerians died when a tribal leader from Constantine, Mohamed al-Hadj al-Muqrani, encouraged thousands of dispirited Muslims from Algiers to Constantine to rise against the French in 1871.

The French conquest of Algeria was one of the most ignominious examples of systematic colonisation that the world has ever seen. By the end of the nineteenth century

the once relatively prosperous Muslim population of
Algeria had been rendered second-class and dispossessed.
The French colonial authorities initially discouraged
colonisation but by 1836 more than 14,000 Europeans
had settled in and around the occupied cities; this figure
had risen to more than 100,000 by 1847. By 1851 Paris
had established three civil territories – Algiers, Oran and
Constantine – which were declared integral parts of
France and ruled by an entirely European administration.
Outside these areas the indigenous Arab and Berber
populations were theoretically allowed to continue
undisturbed under French military rule, but this plan soon
ran aground as the growing number of colonists clam-
oured for more land, their demands eventually receiving
the official sanction of Napoleon III who enthusiastically
granted land concessions. However, the growing power of
the colonists was disrupted between 1860 and 1871 when
Napoleon III, who had latterly begun to favour the
concept of an 'Arab kingdom' for Algeria over which he
would reign as Emperor, sought to protect the rights of
the indigenous population by granting French nationality
to the Muslims. He also attempted to restrict European
colonisation into the coastal littoral. However, these plans
ignored traditional tribal structures and effectively
required Muslims to renounce their recognition of Islamic
law. Both Muslims and European colonists alike rejected
the measures.

European colonists briefly established a revolutionary
commune in Algiers amid the disruption of the Franco-
Prussian war of 1870, but in the following two decades
France steadily strengthened local European control over
Algeria. Europeans from the three French *départements* of
Algiers, Oran and Constantine were granted nominal
representation in parliament while the amount of land
under military control steadily decreased. This became
easier following the Muqrani uprising of 1871; a further
rebellion in 1872 prompted the French authorities to take
stricter measures against Muslim integration into the
French system in Algeria by appropriating vast areas of
tribal lands for sale or grant to the colonists. Kabylia itself
was designated an area under 'extraordinary rule', where

Muslims could be subject to punishments without referral to the courts.

The extraordinary economic expansion in Algeria during the last thirty years of the nineteenth century was almost entirely at the expense of the native Muslim population. Immigration, particularly from Italy and Spain, increased with the promise of lands seized from their rightful owners. The colonial community developed to such an extent that there emerged a small élite of wealthy and powerful *grands colons* (leading colonists) who established thriving agricultural and industrial enterprises. The *grands colons* led the European community in obstinately blocking any reforms proposed by Paris to weaken their power over the Muslim majority. Meanwhile, scores of Muslim tribes were effectively destroyed; thousands of Muslim Algerians were forced to migrate to the European-dominated coastal cities or, from the 1870s onwards, to France; and the traditional economy was devastated. One example of this was the introduction of wine-making to replace cereal production for the domestic market. The only significant benefit to the native population – passionately disputed by many Algerian scholars – was the creation of a tiny French-speaking, Western-educated Muslim élite. In 1892 the Algerian population comprised some 300,000 French citizens, 200,000 non-French Europeans and at least 4 million Muslim second-class citizens.

Nationalism

The First World War can be taken as the true starting point of nationalist aspirations among the Muslim community in Algeria. It was around this time that Muslims who had been forced to emigrate to France became aware of democratic and egalitarian principles vigorously suppressed in Algeria, and of the emergent Arab nationalist movements in states of the Arab east. A Muslim emigrant, Messali al-Hadj, founded the first Algerian nationalist journal in France in 1924; a year later he formed the Étoile Nord-Africaine movement in Paris,

which advocated full independence from France. Other
Muslim figures, particularly Sheikh Abdelhamid Ben
Badis, Ferhat Abbas and Mohamed Bendjelloul, were
more moderate in their thinking, although in 1935 Ben
Badis quarrelled with Abbas over demands articulated by
his Federation of Muslim Councillors for full and equita-
ble integration of the Muslim community into the
European society in Algeria. While the European Algerians remained consistently opposed to early nationalist
stirrings, the reaction in Paris was divided. In 1936 fierce
colonialist opposition in Algeria obliged the left-leaning
government of Léon Blum to abandon plans, drawn up
with a former Governor General of Algeria, Maurice
Viollette, to grant full equality to a substantial number of
educated Algerian Muslims. Although Abbas and
Bendjelloul welcomed the plans, Messali al-Hadj denounced them. The embryonic nationalist tendency
increasingly became divided during the 1920s. There
were three camps: those who supported the integration of
Algeria (and all its inhabitants) into France, led by Ferhat
Abbas; those who advocated full independence, led by
Messali al-Hadj; and a conservative religious strand
championed by Ben Badis's conservative Association of
Reformist Ulema. Messali was one of the key figures
behind the foundation in 1937 of the Parti du Peuple
Algérien (PPA), which continued to demand full independence for Algeria. Ferhat Abbas later shifted his
position away from integration into France towards a
loose association of Europeans and Muslims in Algeria
based on full equality for both communities.

World War II was another turning point in the development of Algerian nationalism. Most European colonists
in Algeria enthusiastically supported the establishment of
the pro-Nazi German Vichy regime in 1940, which
resulted in Algeria's sizeable Jewish population being
subject to the same discrimination as the Muslims. After
the Allied liberation of Algeria in 1942, Ferhat Abbas
offered his community's support for the ejection of the
Axis forces from the remainder of North Africa in return
for the establishment of an elected Algerian assembly, but
without calling for full independence. Supported by fifty-

six nationalists, Abbas in February 1943 presented a 'Manifesto for the Algerian People' calling for the introduction of Arabic as the official language; a subsequent proposal reiterated the demand for a constituent assembly and looked forward to the establishment of a Maghreb union of Morocco, Algeria and Tunisia. The document illustrates the dominance of secular Arab nationalist thinking in the separatist movement at the time: the conservative Islamic strand of Ben Badis became more or less subsumed until the early 1980s. In spite of harbouring some sympathy for the manifesto, the Free French administration responded by passing a modified version of the Blum-Viollette plan, in which some 32,000 Muslims were granted full French citizenship compared with 450,000 European Algerians. Frustrated, Ferhat Abbas altered his position once again towards that of the still-imprisoned Messali Hadj and the Ulema, with whom he founded the Amis du Manifeste et de la Liberté (AML). The AML tended to enjoy most support among the Muslim middle classes while the urban working classes tended to support the banned PPA.

Brutal riots in May 1945 shattered hopes that these groups would be able to effect peaceful change. AML and PPA demonstrations marking Victory in Europe Day in Setif evolved into armed clashes with the police and perhaps as many as 15,000 Muslims died in violence which spread to several towns in the Constantine region. The authorities outlawed the AML and ordered the arrest of more than 14,000 Muslims, including Ferhat Abbas. The Setif riots are usually taken as marking the real beginning of the Algerian nationalist movement and the final cleavage between the minority European and majority Muslim populations. On his release Abbas established the Union Démocratique du Manifeste Algérien (UDMA) which advocated the establishment of a secular autonomous state linked to France. The UDMA won 11 of the 13 seats reserved for a Muslim second college of the Second Constituent Assembly in Paris but Abbas withdrew in September 1946. For his part, Messali formed a more radical organisation demanding a fully independent sovereign Algerian state, the Mouvement pour le Triomphe des Libertés Démocratiques (MTLD). A clandestine terrorist Organisation spéciale (OS) supported its activities; it was initially headed by Hocine Aït Ahmed and later by Ahmed Ben Bella. The group launched its first attack in Oran in 1949 and went on to establish a core group in Kabylia.

France attempted to effect a compromise in September 1947 with a new constitition, the enfranchisement of all Algerians and the recognition of Arabic as the official language alongside French. The Algerian Assembly comprised two sixty-member colleges, one for the 1.5 million Europeans and the other for 9 million Muslims. However, the Europeans, using a combination of intimidation, vote-rigging, arrests and other illegal practices, managed to prevent the UDMA and the MTLD from ever attaining their true electoral strength in elections for the Algerian Assembly and in local and French Assembly elections over the following six years. All attempts by Ferhat Abbas and the more liberal European elements to open official enquiries into the gerrymandering all came to nothing, fuelling the influence of advocates of total independence over the nationalist trend. However, the MTLD was riven by increasing factionalism, particularly after Messali's arrest and deportation to France in 1952. In March 1954 five MTLD members, Mohamed Boudiaf, Mohamed Larbi Ben M'Hidi, Moustafa Ben Boulaid, Mourad Didouche and Rabah Bitat, established the Comité Révolutionnaire d'Unité et d'Action (CRUA); Krim Belkacem, Ben Bella, Mohamed Khider and Aït Ahmed joined in the following two years. These two groups, who are usually referred to collectively as the nine 'historic chiefs', between March and October 1954 laid down plans for the rebellion against French rule. On 1 November 1954 the CRUA changed its name to the Front de Libération Nationale (FLN), the political wing of the Armée de Libération Nationale (ALN).

The War of Independence

Algeria's struggle for independence lasting eight years was one of the most bitter and bloody wars of self-determination in history. To describe the war as merely a struggle between colonisers (the French) and colonised (the Muslims) would be misleading and incorrect. Parallels with South Africa are more appropriate as the conflict was principally between the *pieds noirs* (Algerians of French descent) who wanted to remain in their native land under French protection, and the indigenous Muslims, who demanded initially an end to their second-class status but ultimately full statehood and complete control over the reins of power. The war also involved feuds and disputes between rival Muslims and between the *pieds noirs* and the French authorities. Acts of barbarism were committed on all sides.

The first shots of the war of independence were fired in the Aurès mountains at midnight on 31 October 1954. By early 1955 the uprising had spread to Kabylia, the Constantinois hinterland and the Moroccan border areas west of Oran, and all of northern Algeria was affected by the end of 1956. The ALN and its clandestine terrorist groups engaged in direct attacks against the French army and security forces as well as assassinations, economic sabotage and intimidation of the FLN's opponents within both the Muslim and European communities. By 1956 the initially makeshift ALN had evolved into a well-disciplined force of some 20,000 armed men with a well-developed terrorist capability. The FLN also by this time had managed to draw in virtually all nationalist leaders and groups, including Ferhat Abbas, the UDMA and the Ulema. Only Messali's Mouvement Nationale Algérien (MNA), a successor to the collapsed MTLD largely active among Algerian immigrants in France, where it engaged in street battles with FLN supporters, remained independent. In August 1956 the FLN held a secret congress at Soummam in Kabylia, where it appointed a central committee and the 34-member Conseil National de la Révolution Algérienne (CNRA) and adopted an explicitly socialist political programme. The French authorities had dissolved the Algerian National Assembly in April 1956.

The colonial authorities placed most of northern Algeria under a state of emergency and increasingly resorted to brutal repression of the Muslim population in response to the FLN's successes in the field and a wave of urban terrorism in 1956 and 1957. Repeated French initiatives to find a compromise solution foundered on the weakness of successive coalition governments in Paris and the strength of resolve of the European colonists, who stubbornly insisted that aid from abroad, particularly Arab nationalist regimes such as that of President Gamal Abdel Nasser in Egypt, was the mainstay of the FLN rebellion. However, the FLN received a significant setback in October 1956 when Governor-General Robert Lacoste's military aide staged the successful kidnapping of five of the nine historic FLN chiefs – Ben Bella, Aït Ahmed, Khider, Bitat and Boudiaf – while they were travelling by aeroplane from Morocco to Tunis. The five were forced to sit out the remainder of the war in France.

From November 1956 until early 1958 the French army divided Algeria into small sectors in an attempt to reduce the level of FLN terrorism. However, this strategy had the drawback of preventing major offensives against the ALN, and the electrified fences, known as the Morice Line, erected along the borders with Morocco and Tunisia failed substantially to reduce the ALN's capabilities. Many remote and mountainous areas across the north steadily fell under the control of the ALN, although the French army's grip on the Sahara was never weakened. In 1957 the army began resettling whole rural communities in military camps to deny the ALN support, while General Jacques Massu directed a ruthless campaign to eradicate the FLN terrorists from the main coastal cities.

The Algerian war now began directly to affect the course of government and politics in Paris. *Colon* extremist groups began to emerge in 1957, and in May 1958 they organised a coup d'état in Algiers designed to bring to power General Charles de Gaulle who, they believed, would defeat the FLN. However, the plotters' designs were frustrated when de Gaulle, on his accession to the presidency on 1 June, proposed a new constitution under which Algeria would be a partner with rather than an integral part of a new Fifth French Republic. Increasingly confident of victory, the FLN responded to the French government's plans to organise a free referendum on the new constitution by launching a campaign of intimidation against voting, and in September it established a provisional government (Gouvernement Provisoire de la République Algérienne – GPRA) in Tunis under Ferhat Abbas. This drew official recognition from a number of countries in the developing world, including Morocco and Tunisia, as well as several communist states. Meanwhile, de Gaulle was increasingly convinced of the strength of Algerian nationalism and the inevitability of Algerian independence. Notwithstanding the fact that 60 per cent of Muslims had braved the FLN to vote in the referendum, and despite the 90 per cent vote in favour of his proposed constitution, de Gaulle abandoned his plans and in September 1959 made his first public statement adhering to Algeria's right of self-determination.

The stage was set for the sure collision between de Gaulle and the increasingly marginalised European Algerian community. After an abortive *colon* uprising in January 1960 the authorities carried out a year-long purge of disloyal Europeans from the colonial administration. Amid renewed atrocities by both *colons* and Algerian nationalists, de Gaulle opened secret negotiations with the FLN in France in June 1960, leading up to a referendum in January 1961 intended to provide a new mandate to carry through his programme of self-determination. A massive abstention rate rendered the results questionable and de Gaulle instead opened a new channel to the FLN through President Bourguiba of Tunisia. However, the *colon* extremists had not yet given up the struggle: in April four hardline officers, Generals Challe, Zeller, Jouhaud and Salan, staged a new uprising against de Gaulle's plans and formed a new clandestine terrorist group, the Organisation de l'Armée Secrète (OAS), to sabotage a negotiated settlement and to coordinate the uprising. The majority of army units rallied to de Gaulle and the revolt failed to last longer than four days, although General

Salan's OAS continued to stage terrorist atrocities in both Algeria and France right up to the eve of independence. New secret talks between the French government and the FLN opened in Evian on 20 May and moved to Lugrin in July, and despite a last burst of FLN guerrilla activity in the last months of 1961, the war had effectively come to an end. The discussions stalled in August over the question of the Sahara, where important oil and gas reserves had recently been discovered, as well as an FLN protest against a French attack on the Tunisian town of Bizerte. After renewed meetings in December 1961 in Geneva, contacts resumed at a higher level in Paris in February 1962. The final cease-fire agreement was concluded at Evian on 18 March 1962.

The Evian Accords officially ended more than 130 years of French rule in Algeria and recognised the FLN as the sole legal representative of the Algerian people. Algeria was to become an independent republic subject to a 'yes' vote in a referendum and after a brief transitional period. A provisional GPRA executive chaired by Abderrahman Fares, a former president of the Algerian Assembly, was charged with organising the referendum and administering the country until full independence. The Evian Accords also guaranteed the freedom and property of Algeria's European population, and France's right to maintain the strategic Mers el-Kebir naval base and other military installations for fifteen years in return for guarantees of French aid to the new state. Ninety-one per cent of French voters agreed to the terms of the Evian Accords in the referendum held on 18 April 1962.

However, the hurdle of the OAS remained. During the spring of 1962, in a last desperate attempt to prevent the inevitable by goading the FLN into breaching the cease-fire, OAS terrorists stepped up their terrorist campaign against the Muslim population and tried to establish an independent enclave around el-Asnam. A combination of an efficient police reponse and internal divisions within the OAS, particularly after the capture of General Salan on 22 April 1962, thwarted the organisation's plans. Meanwhile the trickle of terrified Europeans fleeing Algeria became a flood between April and June 1962, particularly when the FLN resumed terrorist activities in retaliation for the OAS action. However, terrorism on both sides did not delay the final act of Algerian independence: 91 per cent of the 6.5 million Algerian electorate on 1 July voted in favour of self-rule, which de Gaulle officially declared two days later.

It is difficult to assess accurately the cost in human lives of the eight years of the Algerian war. Official figures put the figure in excess of one million, while some European observers estimate it at between 300,000 and 400,000. The true number probably lies in the region of 800,000. Around two million Muslims had been placed in French internment camps and around 500,000 had fled to refugee camps in Tunisia and Morocco. The displacement of more than three million Muslims from their homes resulted in a sharp increase in the urban population, especially in Algiers, in the immediate post-war period. Hundreds of villages had been destroyed or looted; whole districts of towns and cities had been damaged; and the country's second city, Oran, was a virtual ghost town. Almost all governmental institutions that had existed before the French occupation had been dismantled or were non-functioning; those which remained were based on the traditional collective village or tribal councils, the *djamaas*. Furthermore, the victorious nationalist organisation, the FLN, was disunited and there were fissures: between 'internals', who had fought inside Algeria, and 'externals', who had supported the struggle outside the country; between Arabs and Berbers; between French-educated and French-thinking intellectuals and those oriented towards the Arab east; and even between ALN officers who had defected to the nationalist cause from the French army and those who had joined directly.

Naturally the war's death toll included the *pieds noirs*. In what has been described as one of the greatest mass migrations of the twentieth century, approximately 90 per cent of the one-million-strong European settler community fled their native land in the few hectic months leading up to independence in July 1962. These were almost all of Algeria's bureaucrats, teachers, doctors, engineers and skilled workers, though many were as poor as the Muslims whom they had struggled so hard to keep as second-class citizens. Thus it was that the population of newly-independent Algeria was overwhelmingly disoriented, bewildered, displaced and hopelessly ill-equipped for the task ahead.

2

ALGERIA UNDER BEN BELLA AND BOUMEDIENNE

The history of independent Algeria can be conveniently divided into four chronological periods. The first corresponds with the three-year presidency of Ahmed Ben Bella from 1962 until 1965; the second with the thirteen years of Houari Boumedienne's presidency from 1965 until his death in 1978; the third is another thirteen-year period under Chadli Bendjedid from 1979 until 1992; and the fourth the years following the military's intervention in January 1992, years which this book refers to as the post-Chadli crisis, presided over first by the Haut Comité d'État (HCE) and then by President Lamine Zeroual.

The Struggle for Power

The factionalism that the seven years of war had suppressed re-emerged in the months leading up to independence and immediately threw the FLN into disarray over the question of leadership of the new republic. Even as the CNRA was meeting in Tripoli in May and June 1962 to decide on its initial political and economic strategy, the extent of the persistent power struggles between the numerous interest groups and individuals, and the absence of political and ideological direction, was becoming clear. The leading contenders were the five 'historic chiefs' who had been released from detention in France on the day that the Evian Agreement was signed; the provisional government (GPRA) under Benyoucef Ben Khedda; moderate Muslim politicians; the military, itself divided between 'internals' and 'externals'; the six

43

commanders of the *wilayat* (the military provinces, or districts, organised by the FLN during the war of independence); the trade unions; and leaders of France-based Algerian Muslims. However, the most prominent of the historic chiefs, Ahmed Ben Bella, gained the advantage in Tripoli when he engineered the establishment of a Political Bureau to replace the GPRA comprising the five former prisoners, one *wilaya* leader and only one member of the GPRA. Ben Bella claimed that most CNRA members approved of the Bureau though it was never officially ratified, and it served primarily as a vehicle for Ben Bella to outmanoeuvre the GPRA.

Ben Bella was now set on a collision course with the GPRA. In the weeks following the official declaration of independence on 5 July, its leader Ben Khedda established the GPRA at Tizi Ouzou, the capital of Kabylia, in a move that illustrates the Kabyle origins of many of the executive's members. Ben Khedda then attempted to impose his authority over the powerful ALN by dismissing its commander-in-chief, Houari Boumedienne. However, this encouraged Boumedienne to defect to the opposition, and in July Boumedienne joined up with Ben Bella in making it clear that he supported the candidacy of Ben Bella over that of Ben Khedda. Ben Khedda realised that this axis was irresistible and, beset by deepening divisions within his own ranks, he formally recognised the primacy and composition of the Political Bureau on 28 July. The Bureau and the GPRA then agreed upon elections for a National Assembly based on a list of 196 candidates.

However, Ben Bella faced continued resistance from his own former independent-minded military commanders. The commanders of *wilaya*s II (Constantine), III (Kabylia) and IV (Algiers) opposed the government's plan to entrust Boumedienne and the 'externals' (many of whom had no combat experience) with transforming the ALN into an Armée Nationale Populaire (ANP) claiming that the plan contravened the spirit of the revolution. 'Internal' military commanders resented Boumedienne's 'Army of the Exterior' for failing to assist them during the war and were anxious to preserve their own authority and privileges that they had established during the previous seven years. After negotiations between the Bureau and the commanders broke down, the Bureau on 30 August called on the population to help it crush the dissident commanders and ordered the ALN to move on Algiers from Oran. Full-scale civil war was only averted by the speed and ease of the ALN's conquest of Algiers and by the population's clear disgust at this new period of violence so early in the existence of the newly-independent state. The power struggle, in which it has been estimated that perhaps 15,000 Algerians died, was over when Ben Bella arrived in Algiers on 4 September; Boumedienne arrived five days later after some heavy clashes with *wilaya* IV forces. The defeat of the commanders allowed the Bureau to draw up a new list of 180 candidates for the National Assembly elections and at the same time to further marginalise the GPRA: Ben Bella ordered the removal from the lists of one-third of the candidates, including Ben Khedda himself, before the elections took place on 20 September. A suspicious 99.5 per cent of participants in the election voted in favour of the list, and the first session of the Assembly opened on 25 September. The Assembly elected Ferhat Abbas as president and Ben Bella prime minister. Ben Bella's constitutional proposals became law following a national referendum on 8 September. Algeria was designated a socialist one-party state with the FLN the sole permitted political body. The status of the National Assembly was reduced to that of essentially a rubber-stamp body, with the executive and the FLN assuming policy making functions. The language of the republic was to be Arabic, though French was to be retained provisionally; Islam was defined as the religion of the state.

Ben Bella

Ben Bella was dogged by challenges, both real and imagined, throughout his relatively brief period in office. His position was fragile and was dependent on the continued support of figures with their own ambitions. His principal supporters were the Political Bureau, whose members he had nominated; the 'Tlemcen Group' (Boumedienne, Khider and Abbas); and the ANP, particularly the 'Oujda clan'. This comprised the five senior officers who had served with Boumedienne's Army of the Exterior at the Moroccan border city of Oujda: Ahmed Kaid, Ahmed Medeghri, Cherif Belkacem, Abdelaziz Bouteflika and Mohamed Tayebi. Support from the Tlemcen Group was fragile as its leading members were all potentially serious challengers for his position – Abbas only allied himself with the Tlemcen group to avenge his replacement as President of the GPRA by Ben Khedda the previous year. All this was played out against the background of deep divisions among the Algerian population itself, most importantly between the more liberal, generally French-educated bourgeoisie and the politicised ex-revolutionaries who were increasingly gravitating towards socialism as the path the new republic should follow. These tensions were overlaid with the ambitions of resentful *wilaya* commanders, Kabyle activists and the influential trade union federation, the Union Générale des Travailleurs Algériens (UGTA).

Ben Bella believed that the establishment of a presidential regime would be the most effective method of ensuring his own authority, marginalising his opponents and guaranteeing the adoption of his favoured ideologies. To this end Ben Bella skilfully removed all the leading figures who had posed a serious challenge to him in 1962, blunted the aspirations of all the major factions that had emerged at independence, and filled key cabinet positions with his own supporters. The first casualty was the head of the Political Bureau, Mohamed Khider, who opposed some of Ben Bella's consitutional proposals. In March 1963 Ben Bella arranged for Khider to be forced into exile in Switzerland, clearing the way for him to accelerate the process of drafting the constitution. Next was the foreign minister, Mohamed Khemisti, who was assassinated in April, and Mohamed Boudiaf, who was arrested in June and his Parti Révolutionnaire Socialiste (PRS), which he had founded after his resignation from the Political Bureau, banned. Ferhat Abbas resigned as president of the National Assembly on 12 August in protest at the unrepresentative power of the Political Bureau and the sidelining of the FLN, which in any case had yet to be legally constituted as a separate entity. The regime banned embryonic political parties and abolished the *wilaya* system, though the term was later used to replace the French *département* system of local government, and on 13 September Ben Bella assumed the offices of president, prime minister and commander-in-chief of the armed forces. However, Hocine Aït Ahmed, who had resigned from the Political Bureau along with Boudiaf, proved a more determined opponent. He joined with the *wilaya* III (Kabylia) commander Mohand Ou el-Hadj in June to declare a unified resistance against Ben Bella before founding the Front des Forces Socialistes (FFS) on 29 September. As Ait Ahmed was a leading Kabyle and the FFS was from the beginning perceived as primarily a vehicle for Kabyle regionalist aspirations, despite its ideology derived from European socialist and social democratic traditions. The FFS became like a *maquis* in Kabylia and eventually the regime was obliged to send in a police force and offer a compromise when the unrest threatened to develop into an insurrection.

Ben Bella even used a short border war with Morocco to accuse Aït Ahmed of being a Moroccan agent and thus an enemy of the Algerian revolution. In 1962 Morocco had pressed a claim to vast parts of the western Algerian Sahara, including the iron-ore-rich area of Ghara Djebillet. The government refused to negotiate on the grounds that surrender of the land would have required an unacceptable betrayal of Algeria's hard-won sovereignty, nationalist ideology and prestige. Small-scale clashes broke out in October 1963 near the frontier posts of Hassi-Beida and Tinjoub but mediation by Ethiopia and Mali brought the hostilities to an end after three weeks. Although there was a considerable thawing of relations between Morocco and Algeria throughout the 1960s – a twenty-year cooperation treaty was signed in 1969 – the border was not finally demarcated until June 1972, when Algeria and King Hassan agreed to the Tindouf area remaining in Algerian hands and its iron-ore resources being exploited by a joint Algerian-Moroccan company.

The short Moroccan war produced a fresh wave of Algerian nationalism and support for the FFS subsided. Nevertheless, in February 1964 FFS supporters embarked on a new series of low-level attacks against symbols of authority in Kabylia and the Algiers region, including an unsuccessful assassination attempt against Ben Bella. At around the same time Colonel Mohamed Chaabani, the former *wilaya* VI (Sahara) commander and member of the Political Bureau took up arms against the regime in the Biskra region, though Boumedienne's troops managed to regain the upper hand in Kabylia and against Chaabani by mid-October despite valuable support from Aït Ahmed and Mohamed Khider. Aït Ahmed was arrested in October 1964 and sentenced to death the following year, though Ben Bella subsequently commuted the sentence to life imprisonment; Chaabani, however, was executed in September 1964. These revolts obliged Ben Bella to rely even more on the support of the Oujda clan and the ANP, though this subsequently proved a miscalculation. In treating them as merely one of many factions whose members were to be courted, exploited, rewarded and occasionally rejected rather than favouring them especially, Ben Bella further strengthened Boumedienne's authority.

Ben Bella also sought to impose his personal authority over the FLN, an organisation perceived by his opponents as the last forum in which to promote political pluralism. The President manoeuvred Khider, Aït Ahmed and Boudiaf out of preparations for the first post-independence congress of the FLN held in April 1964, and although he was not powerful enough to prevent Boumedienne and the Oujda clan playing a central role, the resulting Charter of Algiers reflected more or less entirely the views and ideologies of Ben Bella and his socialist supporters: Mohamed Harbi, the Frenchman Michel Raptis and the Egyptian Souliman Lotfallah. The charter declared that socialism was entirely appropriate to the Algerian 'revolution' and analysed the FLN's previous errors, defined relations between the three central pillars of society – state, party and army – and expounded the theoretical and practical bases for *autogestion* (worker self-management). Drawing extensively on revolutionary idiom it called on the party to 'purge itself of non-revolutionary elements'. This clearly ignored the party's growing middle-class membership which was joining principally to ensure its own advancement in the growing bureaucracy. The Charter also reiterated the regime's intention to impose Modern Standard Arabic as the official national language to replace French, while acknowledging that the process would be protracted and difficult. This was an attempt to appease the growing number of nationalists and traditionalist critics, notably the traditionally-educated Boumedienne, who saw Arabisation as essential for the 'Islamic' character of the revolution and who opposed the central role played by foreigners in the drafting of the Charter. Left-leaning radicals, who were fluent in the vocabulary of French political theory, favoured the French language as an engine of genuine democracy, modernity and secularism. There was not universal support for the Charter, but the number of those in a position to resist was decreasing.

By late 1964 Ben Bella had constructed a regime that relied almost entirely on himself and a small group of supporters. Despite the grand revolutionary discourse the function of the FLN's central committee, the Political Bureau, and the National Assembly was to rubber-stamp policy decisions and laws drawn up by Ben Bella and his clique. This centralisation of power in the hands of such a small group of people and the lack of any viable political base left Ben Bella dangerously exposed, particularly to the single faction over which he had so far been unable to assume control – the general staff. In the autumn of 1963 Ben Bella began to move against Boumedienne's supporters, who controlled roughly as many government positions as the President's clique, by appointing his own supporters, or at least those who did not support Boumedienne, to key posts. Ben Bella appointed the *wilaya* commander Tahar Zbiri as chief of staff in October 1963 and then turned his attention to Boumedienne's core support, the Oujda Clan. During 1964 he gradually eased out clan members (Ahmed Kaid, Belkacem and Medeghri) from cabinet positions and by the end of the year only Boumedienne, as minister of war, and Abdelaziz Bouteflika, as foreign minister, remained in place. Ben Bella alienated Boumedienne still further when he forwarded plans to replace the ANP with popular militias while at the same time he adopted a more leftist political tone.

Boumedienne began to plot a coup d'état to overthrow Ben Bella in late 1964. Relations between the two plummeted further when Ben Bella threatened to dismiss Bouteflika over his complaint that the President was undermining his authority during the preparations for the second Afro-Asian conference scheduled to take place in Algiers in June 1965. But the last straw came with leaks that Ben Bella planned to revive Kabyle support for the President against Boumedienne by replacing Bouteflika with the imprisoned Aït Ahmed. In the early hours of 19 June 1965 Boumedienne's troops quietly and efficiently arrested Ben Bella and took control of key buildings in Algiers; many Algiers residents believed that the tanks in the streets were being used as props in Pontecorvo's celebrated film *The Battle of Algiers*. Apart from a few dedicated left-wingers, few Algerians mourned Ben Bella's overthrow. · The ex-President remained in prison until President Chadli Bendjedid finally released him in 1979, after which he decamped to voluntary exile in France.

Houari Boumedienne

The small group of military officers that engineered the coup made up the core of a new 26-member ruling Council of the Revolution. Boumedienne effectively neutralised potential opposition from the various factions by skilfully co-opting them into his government. In addition to the core group of officers, the Council included the general staff, nine current and former *wilaya* commanders and two former members of the Ben Bella clan. Boumedienne's awareness that his authority continued to rely in a large measure on the support and co-operation of the factions, particularly the still-strong *wilaya* commanders, explained the broad base of the council. Although the Council's function in theory was advisory and consultative, it also acted as a mechanism for control and represented the stable body from which Boumedienne derived his legitimacy. Boumedienne formed a new twenty-member cabinet on 10 July, in which Bouteflika retained the foreign ministry and nine ministers who had served under Ben Bella were reshuffled. This line-up of ministers continued in power, with a few exceptions, until the President began gradually to marginalise and ease out the members of the Oujda clan and key conservatives from the cabinet. Boumedienne himself held the triple post of president, prime minister and minister of defence.

Despite Boumedienne's skill in dealing with the factions, his authority did not go unchallenged. Colonel Zbiri, who had personally arrested Ben Bella during the 19 June coup and had remained in his post as chief-of-staff, was the first challenger. The relationship between the two men steadily deteriorated throughout 1965 and 1966 due to disagreements over the military's role in politics. Zbiri feared that the clique loyal to Boumedienne was gradually establishing a dictatorship as a replacement for the theoretically collective leadership of the Council of the Revolution, and imputed the last formal meeting of the Council in 1967 (though it continued to meet informally until 1976) as proof of this. Zbiri, in common with a handful of leftist cabinet ministers, the UGTA and the students, also resisted the regime's ideological gravitation towards state socialism as opposed to the syndicalist concepts promulgated under Ben Bella. Zbiri and a small force marched on Algiers from the Mitidja in December 1967 but they were decisively defeated after only two days, mainly because Boumedienne loyalists continued to hold the key posts in the military. Amid a hasty purge of the UGTA and the government Zbiri fled to the Aurès where he was subsequently linked to plots to kill Ahmed Kaid in January 1968 and an assassination attempt against Boumedienne himself in April of the same year, in which the President was injured. The regime also faced opposition from student activists originally mobilised by the Ben Bella regime. Students and staff at Algiers University in

February 1968 staged a long strike against the government's attempts to impose a student committee loyal to the FLN. However, Boumedienne had by the end of the year neutralised or marginalised most potential opposition leaders, such as the *mudjahidine* leader Ali Kafi and the Kabyle Mohand Ou el-Hadj, by appointing them to peripheral posts. By 1969 most former opposition leaders had been forced to flee abroad or languished in prison, confining the internal expression of opposition to student activists.

The incoming regime altered the most controversial parts of the constitution imposed by Ben Bella and began to construct mechanisms for local government. In theory, these structural changes were intended to deliver Algeria back into the realm of constitutional government and re-establish public participation in political life. The 1963 constitution, the FLN Political Bureau and the APN were all abolished, though the process of constructing replacements took far longer than originally envisaged: consultation on the new constitution, the National Charter, began in 1967 but was not completed until 1976. The regime reorganised and held elections for the bodies controlling communes (the *assemblées populaires communales* (APCs) in 1967, and it organised elections for new *assemblées populaires des wilayat* (APWs) in 1969. However, the degree of real power and genuine decision-making authority devolved to the APCs and APWs was small, and their primary function was largely to implement decisions from above and to provide a channel for political advancement and mobilisation at local level. All members of the assemblies were members of the FLN.

The regime also proceeded with the Arabisation programme established under Ben Bella, the objective of which was the full transformation of a Maghrebi-European society into a purely Arab one. The architects of the programme believed that this would transcend the enduring ethnic, tribal, clan and geographical fragmentation that traditionally inhibited the creation of a nation-state conceptualised in largely European terms. The use of the French language was to be minimised while the use of Modern Standard Arabic was encouraged as far as

possible. However, the major flaw in the plan was the
presence of a sizeable minority that entirely rejected its
adherence to Arab nationalism and denial of the country's
Berber character. Moreover, the implementation of the
programme was haphazard and ineffective from the start.
One serious problem lay in the quality of the Arabic-
speaking teachers, many of whom were inferior graduates
from eastern Arab states such as Syria, Iraq and Egypt,
whose type of Arabic was confusing and disorienting to
speakers of Maghrebi Arabic and French. This, combined
with too rapid and insufficient preparation of technical
textbooks, produced two tiers of educated Algerians, one
educated mostly in Arabic (the *arabisants*), the other
largely in French (the *francisants*). As industry and
commerce continued to operate mostly in French,
Arabic-speakers were effectively denied jobs, resulting in
a persistent predominance of the *francisant* middle classes.

The ideology that shaped the formulation of the
Arabisation programme, the 'agrarian revolution' and the
developmental initiatives of the Boumedienne regime,
such as industrialisation and nationalisation, is referred to
variously   as   'Arabo-Islamic   socialism'   or
'Boumediennism'. It was in reality a culmination of the
policies adopted by the FLN during the war of independence, by the Tripoli conference of 1962 and by Ben
Bella's 1964 Charter of Algiers. And it was a synthesis of
diverse political, social and cultural influences and
ideologies ranging from the teachings of Islam to the
nationalisms of the *mudjahidine* and the Arab east, and the
socialism and Marxism of Algerian intellectuals educated
in France and later in the Soviet bloc. Boumedienne,
however, was a pragmatist and acutely aware of the
realities of the faction-ridden Algerian political landscape.
Government policy was often steered towards dilution
and compromise, and the ideologies of nationalism,
populism and developmentalism invoked by his regime to
justify its programmes were often merely totemic.
Boumediennism's main strength was the breadth of its
appeal; in general, the educated urban population, both
arabisant and *francisant*, identified more with the secular

elements of its programme, while conservative 'Islamic' values remained pre-eminent for the rural population.

The results of this attempt at ideological synthesis were more negative than positive. Where Boumedienne's stated aim had been to create a state based on the interplay between the rulers and the ruled, where political education and mobilisation were to be channelled from the base upwards, Algeria in fact developed into a remarkably depoliticised society in which the rulers not surprisingly had taken total control. Boumedienne's political manoueuvrings were the initial stimulation for this process, but an increasingly influential class of bureaucrats and technocrats, the compliance of the FLN which more and more functioned as a means for career advancement, the docility of trade unions and the *volontariats* (organisations for popular mobilisation) also contributed. Although the various factions and their clients paid lip-service to the rhetoric and political vocabulary of Boumediennism, their support for the revolution, and in particular the agrarian reforms, was motivated more by self-interest than ideology. This was underlined by the way in which the regime had ensured the tractability of the unions and political organisations before embarking on the reforms.

Boumedienne's policies also favoured a more direct role for the army in politics and other areas of public life. The process of transformation of the old ALN into the professional ANP, which continued apace throughout the early stage of Boumedienne's rule, brought to the fore a class of French-educated officers who had spent the war outside Algeria and thus did not have supportive clienteles developed by common experience in the field. By the mid-1970s the armed forces had developed into a separate faction that perceived itself as the supreme embodiment of the spirit of the Algerian war of independence and of Algerian national identity. To a large extent, the military, despite the clannishness that existed within it, was one of the few institutions that had managed to transcend Algeria's enduring factionalism and clientelism and develop as a 'national' entity. The mythologisation of the war carried out by the regime's internal propaganda machine and through the channel of the educational system assured public respect for the military.

Also crucial was the Boumedienne regime's failure to decentralise government to the provinces: promoting the formation of local élites who represented the state to the local populations, rather than the reverse as it had envisaged. Despite the official rhetoric to the contrary, the state concentrated more on building itself and laying the foundations of a modern industrialised economy than effectively developing the country at large, and the ordinary Algerian was largely denied access to the decision-making process.

There were some achievements. There were ambitious and wide-ranging attempts at introducting economic reforms. Between 1966 and 1971 the Boumedienne government took major steps towards taking control of Algeria's economy by nationalising the minerals, banking, insurance and manufacturing sectors, a process that culminated in 1971 with the nationalisation of the oil and gas sectors. The influential minister of industry, Belaïd Abdessalam, oversaw the imposition of a strategy of rapid industrialisation, based on the concept of *industries industrialisantes* formulated by the French economist Gérard Destanne de Bernis, which privileged industrial over agricultural production. The education system, too, was improved and the initially massive demand for foreign teachers and advisors during the 1960s was gradually reduced to provide work for the rapidly growing number of Algerian graduates. The total number of enrolments at educational establishments increased from around 800,000 at independence to more than 3.5 million in 1977. The regime also made some advances towards greater political and social freedoms for women, and there were relatively high proportions of working women in cities such as Algiers and Oran in the late 1970s. Generally, however, the results of the regime's initiatives were disappointing as the government grappled with the problems of over-rapid industrial development, low productivity, a soaring foreign debt and, worst of all in the 1970s, the colossal demographic growth.

The National Charter

Boumedienne did not really feel secure in his own authority until ten years after his coming to power. Crucial was the marginalisation of the Oujda clan in which Boumedienne had previously suspected a source of opposition. The clan's value to the President diminished during the progress of the 'agrarian revolution', and in any case, the implied élitism of its position obliged the President to reverse its privileged status after 1971 as part of his 'leftist' strategy. Henceforth, Boumedienne increasingly relied upon new individuals to replace former ill-qualified ALN cadres to manage key areas of the bureaucracy and state sector. The most important of these was the industry minister Belaïd Abdessalam, Ahmed Taleb Ibrahimi at the Higher Education Ministry and Mohamed Liassine. The regime also relied upon younger technocrats, many of them educated in France, though these were less influential.

In June 1975 the President was able to announce a package of key political changes that reflected the greater security of his personal position. The programme included the reconvening of the National Assembly; the drawing up of a new constitution, the National Charter; and the organisation of a single-candidate presidential election. The regime published the draft Charter in early 1976, and in a move that indicated the regime's growing confidence, for the first time encouraged broad public debate, both in meetings and in the press, over its contents. The Charter, which was overtly socialist in conception and content, proposed plans for the renewal of the FLN and defined the organisational structures and internal relationships of the Algerian state. Among other stipulations, the Charter guaranteed protection of private property that was not used to exploit others and the basic rights of expression and assembly. It also limited the much-abused practice of *garde à vue* (remand) detention to forty-eight hours. The Assembly was to sit for five years and comprise 261 members chosen by universal suffrage from a list of 783 FLN candidates drawn up by the party. A national referendum would ratify the appointment of the president by a full congress of the FLN. Although the President retained the defence portfolio, he was now encouraged to appoint a prime minister and/or vice-president. In a referendum on 27 June 1976, 98.5 per cent of voters approved the Charter proposals, and in the subsequent presidential elections held the following December, official results put the number of votes for Boumedienne at 95.23 per cent. After eleven years of 'transitional' arrangements, Algeria adopted a new constitution, its second, on 22 November 1976.

It is likely that Boumedienne would have continued in office for many more years had he not rapidly succumbed to a rare blood disease in November 1978. The fact that no successor had been chosen suggests that the President himself was intending to remain in power for the foreseeable future. In the absence of a vice-president, prime minister or even defence minister, the running of the country was assumed by the Council of the Revolution for a 45-day period under the chairmanship of Rabah Bitat. The last of the series of reforms initiated by Boumedienne in 1975 came in January 1979, when the delayed FLN congress created a new central committee of between 120 and 160 members and between 30 and 40 advisory members, which would meet every six months and constitute the supreme decision-making body of both the FLN and the country.

It is ironic that the indictments against the Boumedienne regime bear so much resemblance to those against the regime of his predecessor, Ahmed Ben Bella. Both were hamstrung by the ever-present factionalism and by a constant striving to impose a 'national' identity where none existed. Boumedienne, however, managed to remain in power and win a large degree of political legitimacy by deft manipulation of the various interest groups, clans and factions that comprised the Algerian political and social landscape. Where Ben Bella had neutralised all opposition except the most powerful faction, Boumedienne skilfully identified the major players and juggled his own position accordingly, carefully not depending on any one group and relying on himself rather than a *cercle présidentiel*.

3

ALGERIA UNDER CHADLI BENDJEDID

Two leading candidates had emerged as potential successors Boumedienne during his short final illness. The first, Mohamed Salah Yahiaoui, who since 1977 had served as the co-ordinator of the FLN , was seen as the choice of the radical socialists, the 'Boumediennists', the avant-garde, the *arabisants* and the powerful trade union, the UGTA. He proposed the continued political mobilisation of the masses through the medium of a genuinely 'vanguard' FLN over which he wished the élite to further extend its control. His opponent was foreign minister Abdelaziz Bouteflika, the choice of the technocrats, the bourgeoisie and those opposed to the Arab-socialist orientation of the regime since 1971. Bouteflika, who had been one of the original Oujda clan, favoured marginalising the role of the FLN and promoting economic liberalisation as the means of addressing administrative inefficiency. In the event, however, the senior military establishment prevented either camp securing its man. On 31 January 1979 the FLN party congress selected the military's own candidate, Colonel Chadli Bendjedid, the commander of the Oran military district and the highest-ranking officer in the army. The army presented Chadli as a compromise candidate between the two extremes represented by Yahiaoui and Bouteflika; his nomination was approved by 94 per cent of voters in a referendum on 7 February.

Chadli's primary objective was to consolidate his own authority within the military and the FLN. He reorganised the military establishment in 1980-1 by moving key figures into positions over which the presidency had more control, and introduced key changes to the FLN party structure to reinforce his personal authority. The high point of this came in July 1981 when the FLN Political Bureau's membership was reduced to ten and both Bouteflika and Yahiaoui were excluded. Chadli was re-elected as FLN secretary-general in December 1983 with 95.4 per cent of the electorate approving his, the only, candidacy in presidential elections on 12 January 1984. He also replaced moderates at the ministries of information and culture with *arabisant* ideologues while skilfully exploiting the rivalry between Bouteflika and Yahiaoui which had persisted despite their removal from the centre of politics. The President also moved to stamp out the stirrings of political independence among the population at large, which, despite the repression of the Boumedienne years, was not yet fully responsive to the wishes of the ruling élite as embodied in, and directed by, the FLN. Members of the Parti de l'Avant-Garde Socialiste (PAGS), which, despite its officially illegal status, was allowed to organise in quasi-autonmous institutions such as the UGTA, were now ordered to join the FLN or lose their posts.

Chadli wished to place the presidency above the day-to-day running of the administration but without losing any of his overall authority. To this end he appointed the reliable administrator Colonel Mohamed ben Ahmed Abdelghani as Algeria's first prime minister since 1962 not to serve simultaneously as president. Chadli also reorganised the FLN cabinet and the administration, reshuffling the cabinet on the pretext of an anti-corruption initiative. Among the casualties were two men who would go on to serve as prime minister in the post-Chadli crisis years, Sid Ahmed Ghozali and Belaïd Abdessalam. By removing Bouteflika and Yahiaoui from the FLN central committee, the new President created a situation where no faction was predominant in the government though all were represented. Although the President declared that doctrinaire Arab-socialism was an 'irreversible' course for Algeria, he almost immediately showed signs of breaking with the past by carrying out a number of popular reforms. Initially he even adopted a

less dictatorial personal style than Boumedienne. Ultimately his objectives were to redefine the relationship
between state and government and population; to
overhaul the structure of the FLN to the advantage of the
presidency; and to remove the last political vestiges of
Boumediennist socialism while retaining some of its
autocratic architecture. The reorientation allowed Chadli
to make gestures towards public opinion and the opposition, something which had been impossible under
Boumedienne. Thus he lifted the unpopular exit visa
requirement and, in July 1979, ordered the release of Ben
Bella from prison. Chadli exploited the high price of oil to
make tentative steps towards economic liberalisation and
the establishment of a free market, including the lifting of
restrictions on the import of goods that had been
unavailable during the years of austerity under Boumedienne.

At the beginning of his second five-year term in 1984
Chadli made more moves to strengthen the economic
liberalisers in the regime and to consolidate his own
position. Abdelhamid Brahimi, a leading economic
liberaliser who had served as minister of planning and the
head of the US office of Sonatrach, the state hydrocarbons monopoly, was appointed as the second prime
minister of the Chadli term. The President then moved
two men who had constructed their own power-bases, the
former commander of the Blida military region, Abdallah
Belhouchet, and the head of military security, Kasdi
Merbah, into less threatening positions. After months of
consultation and debate orchestrated by Chadli and
almost ten years after Boumedienne's National Charter a
special congress of the FLN in February 1985 adopted a
new charter. Although this retained the curious blend of
Islam and socialism that the 1976 Charter had defined as
Algeria's 'state ideology', the new document included
elements that further shifted the country away from the
dirigiste and doctrinaire socialism of the Boumedienne
era. More than 98 per cent of voters approved the new
Charter at yet another referendum in January 1986.

These tentative moves towards liberalisation inevitably
alienated the left, and in order to counterbalance this

Chadli courted the support of the *arabisants* and the conservatives. The regime accelerated Arabisation at all levels of the educational system, appointed *arabisants* to government posts, Arabised the judiciary and encouraged the FLN Central Committee to commit to the Arabisation of all newspapers. It also introduced Arabic place names instead of the French: Algiers officially reverted to its Arabic name of *el-Djezaïr*, Constantine to *Qacentina* and Blida to *el-Boulaïda*, though most of the previous names remained in common usage. However, Chadli's alliance with the *arabisants* proved dangerous: by the mid-1980s the Islamist tendency, encouraged by their official promotion, had taken over the agenda of the conservative and *arabisant* wing and as early as 1979 *arabisant* students at the University of Algiers felt sufficiently confident to organise a long strike and numerous demonstrations in protest at the better career opportunities available to French-speaking graduates, and to press for more rapid and more coherent Arabisation. Similar protests erupted among high-school students in various places.

Of more concern to the Chadli regime in the early 1980s, however, was the effects of the Arabisation programme upon the Kabyle minority. The Kabyles held many positions within the administration and made up much of the intelligentsia, and by virtue of their greater historical connection and exposure to France and French intellectual traditions continued to tend towards the left and, paradoxically, to the Boumediennist political tradition. They had lobbied unsuccessfully for the recognition of the Berber language Tamazigh as a national language alongside Arabic since the 1960s, when a handful of Kabyle cultural organisations were established among the Kabyle community in France. On 10 March 1980 years of resentment at a series of repressive measures introduced in the previous decade erupted into violence in Tizi Ouzou province after its governor banned Mouloud Mammeri, Kabylia's most distinguished intellectual and the figure considered to be the father of the Berberist movement, from giving a lecture on ancient Berber pottery at the University Centre there. Students went on strike in protest, occupied university buildings and encouraged demonstrations elsewhere in Tizi Ouzou. In Algiers, the authorities used violence to disperse large pro-Berberist student demonstrations there on 16 March and 7 April. In a bid to halt the unrest the authorities unconvincingly pledged to consider the students' grievances at the next FLN Central Committee meeting, but this only prompted the Berberists to call a general strike in Tizi Ouzou on 16 April. When the authorities sent in the security forces on the 19th to end sit-ins at the University Centre, the hospital and industrial plants, rioting students from throughout Kabylia attacked scores of symbols of authority and privilege, including FLN offices and a tourist hotel. The unrest was the worst since independence; unconfirmed reports estimated the number of dead at 32 with nearly 200 injured. Hundreds of Berberist militants were arrested, including many supporters of the Front des Forces Socialistes (FFS), fuelling further riots in Tizi Ouzou and elsewhere, and the region was isolated from the rest of Algeria for four days.

The unrest, which became known as 'the Tizi Ouzou Spring', had some positive effects in that it was one of the principal stimuli for the political liberalisation of the mid-1980s. The *mudjahid* and lawyer Abdennour Ali Yahia, who in June 1985 founded the Ligue Algérienne pour la Défense des Droits de l'Homme (LADDH), did much to draw international attention to the causes of Berberists and Islamists alike, and he was instrumental in pushing the Chadli regime towards political liberalisation. The process was assisted by the fact that many of the incoming deputies in the Assembly elections of February 1987 were young reformists who were more likely to support the reformism of Chadli and his advisors. In July 1987 the regime passed legislation permitting the formation of local associations, though it explicitly forbade those deemed to pose a threat to the security of Algeria.

However, Chadli went much further towards reforming Algeria's economy and bureaucracy than its political system. In July 1987 the Assembly began to consider the removal of state control over agricultural co-operatives and in the following November it abolished the ministry of planning, which previously had overseen most aspects of the country's economic life, and placed the ministry's remaining functions under the direct control of Prime Minister Brahimi. The government also created a new ministry of education and training. In December 1987 it announced legislation aimed at removing the largest obstacle to Brahimi's planned economic reforms by improving Algeria's labyrinthine administration and bureaucracy. Private enterprise was allowed more freedom and public sector managers were given the right to take some decisions without reference to the bureaucracy. A national commission to prepare for the Sixth FLN congress was appointed in February 1988 to work on the country's second Five-Year Plan, and more technocrat ministers were appointed later that year. Chadli in June 1988 took the bold step of reorganising the public sector by establishing theoretically autonomous state-sponsored trust companies, *fonds de participation*, to which managers would be responsible.

The hesitant steps towards economic liberalisation prompted episodes of social unrest which became increasingly frequent from 1985 onwards. In the first instance of economic unrest since independence, spontaneous protests erupted in April 1985 against appalling housing conditions, and specifically against a number of deaths caused by the collapse of houses in the Algiers casbah. These developed into a large demonstration and march on the FLN headquarters in central Algiers. There was a wave of strikes and protests in Algiers, Oran, Skikda and Constantine in November 1986 and tensions deepened further when the military used excessive force to suppress a student protest against changes to the *baccalauréat* examination in Constantine. Subsequent protests in the city against military repression prompted fresh violence in which an estimated four people were killed and more than 180 arrested as protesters attacked a wide range of symbols of the state. Growing frustration with the government's economic policies and resentment of the military's use of force ensured that the spate of sporadic student protests and labour unrest persisted into 1987 and 1988. By September 1988 strikes were paralysing cities throughout the country, particularly the industrial suburbs around Algiers. The crisis came to a head on 2 October 1988 with a strike by post office workers in Algiers and rumours of a national general strike due to begin two days later. The stage was set for the riots of October 1988: 'Black October'.

'Black October'

On the evening of 4 October as many as 5,000 youths went on the rampage in Bab el-Oued, a notoriously overcrowded and underprivileged suburb of Algiers. The trouble spread to the city centre during the following day when rioters ran amok in the main shopping street, rue Didouche Mourad, ransacking symbols of wealth and privilege such as the notorious Blue Note nightclub and the offices of Air Algérie and Lufthansa. They also attacked symbols of the state – the ministry of sports and youth, government offices, state-owned shops, buses, police stations and even telephone booths. Protesters ransacked the Ryad el-Feth shopping centre, the favoured meeting place of the sons and daughters of the élite (the '*chi-chis*'), and torched the office of Polisario, the Western Saharan liberation organisation which Algeria had generously funded since the Moroccan invasion in 1975. After three days of continuous violence the government imposed a state of siege on 7 October and granted the army the right to shoot on sight, and ultimately to use automatic weapons. Nevertheless, disturbances spread to Oran, Annaba, Mostaganem, Blida and many other towns and cities across the country. Estimates of those killed in the disturbances range from 200 to 500 people, with the higher figure being the more likely. At least 3,500 people were arrested, many of them children; a large number were tortured.

The worst single incident of the unrest occured on 10 October when more than 100 protesters gathered in the Place des Martyrs in central Algiers to hear Ali Belhadj, a charismatic young preacher. The authorities deemed the meeting to be an illegal Islamist gathering and ordered the security forces to fire on the crowd. Forty people were killed, most of whom were from Belhadj's stronghold of Bab el-Oued. Aware that the massacre threatened to propel the country into an even more violent period, Chadli went on television the same day to deliver a twenty-minute address in which he pledged to introduce a programme of wide-ranging reforms and to 'remove the abuse of power'. Two days later the President made further concessions by lifting the state of siege and called a referendum for November on proposals to produce a 'greater organisation of political action', involving 'a new organisation of the executive'.

Algerians were stunned both by the unrest itself and by the brutality displayed by the armed forces, in particular the Sécurité Militaire (SM). For the first time, not only did the state repression fail to silence the opposition; it empowered it instead. Opposition groups of all hues – students, trade unionists, communists and Islamists – exploited the unrest to demand substantial political reform and the dismantling of the state apparatus which had allowed a tiny élite and the military to abuse Algeria in the name of the people. The regime was shaken and over the next nine months hastily set about reforming the apparatus on which it had depended for two decades. The first casualties were Mohamed Cherif Mesaadia, the unpopular FLN secretary-general and effectively the second-most powerful figure in Algeria, and the hated chief of the Sécurité Militaire, Medjoub Lakhal-Ayat, who had both been dismissed by the end of October. On 3 November 92.27 per cent of a high (83 per cent) turnout approved Chadli's reform programme. This incalculably increased the independence of the prime minister by for the first time making him and his cabinet answerable to the Assembly rather than the FLN; hitherto the position had been no more than the President's executive aide. The President also lost his constitutional designation as the 'embodiment of the party-state union' becoming instead the 'embodiment of the unity of the nation'.

'Black October' was the most significant upheaval since Algerian independence and a turning point in the country's history. It permanently altered the role of the FLN and its relationship to the regime and finally demolished the myth of the military as the honourable guarantor of the revolution. A combination of economic, social and political factors, many of which can be traced back to mistakes made in the 1960s, can be identified as the causes of the explosion, though a convenient starting point is a meeting of OPEC in Geneva in December 1985 where Iran, Iraq and Saudi Arabia refused to maintain low production quotas. The decision caused a sudden decline in the price of oil and subsequently gas, and eventually resulted in Algeria's hydrocarbon earnings falling by 40 per cent and its foreign debt surpassing $24 billion. Stubbornly refusing to default on its debt obligations, the regime introduced a wide-ranging austerity package to cover the shortfall. The government was forced to reduce subsidies on staple foodstuffs; order inefficient co-operative farms to sell off land; drastically cut back on imports; and impose a freeze on wages. All these measures provoked widespread resentment of the government's economic policies, particularly when party and state officials, who often participated in black market activities, were allowed access to special state shops. While the ordinary citizens of Algiers suffered from persistent water shortages, the élite were able to fill their swimming pools and their children – the detested '*chi-chis*' – ostentatiously drove foreign cars and wore Parisian clothes. Officials who controlled foreign currency reserves were often unable to resist the temptation to extort bribes. Although levels of corruption were probably lower than in other Arab states, the practice disgusted Algerians, whose sense of egalitarianism had been sharpened during the war of independence. Particular opprobrium was reserved for the *millionaires du légume* – the food traffickers whose activities caused permanent but unnecessary food shortages. Such charges were borne out when semolina, flour and cooking oil appeared in state-owned shops in the aftermath of the October riots.

There also were demographic factors at work. The boom birth-rate of the 1970s had doubled the population to around 23 million in 1988 and, because about 65 per cent of Algerians were under 25, this placed an intolerable strain on the country's education system and infrastructure. In crowded city areas, where hundreds of thousands of immigrants from the countryside had swollen the population, families typically lived eight to a room in unsanitary conditions. An inevitable corollary of this was a high rate of unemployment, officially 15 per cent in 1988 but in reality much higher. Agricultural production had fallen because of rural depopulation, inefficient management and repeated droughts, and even basic food items were scarce and expensive. On the eve of the riots, a kilo of meat cost around $35.

These factors combined strongly suggest that the unrest was a spontaneous eruption in protest at the abuses of government and economic adversity. There is evidence, however, that Chadli's opponents within the élite took advantage of popular dissatisfation to engineer the riots. The extraordinarily candid speech that Chadli delivered two weeks before the unrest, in which he strongly criticised state officials for incompetence and complacency and the 'profiteering' within the private sector, supports this argument. He also urged a thorough review and increased decentralisation of state industries and administration (*autonomie d'entreprises*), which threatened the positions and privileges of numerous officials. The advocates of this programme have claimed that Chadli's opponents were behind the strikes of early September and the general strike scheduled for 5 October, and that at the last minute the plotters had also encouraged youths in Bab el-Oued to take to the streets in the hope that Chadli would be forced to abandon his reformist programme because of the unrest. The scale and subsequent course of the violence were apparently unintended, and the plotters reportedly tried to conceal their part in the unrest by issuing a bogus claim of responsibility for the riots in the name of a previously unheard-of pro-democracy organisation, the Movement for Algerian Renewal.

The Constitution of 1989

Whatever their causes, there is no doubt that 'Black October' brought about the most promising and inspiring phase of political life since Algerian independence. Civil society burst into life for the first time since 1962 and the world watched fascinated as Chadli appeared set to establish the first genuinely pluralistic society in the Arab world. However, the President's most pressing task was to reform the regime itself. Probably at the insistence of the FLN, which had lost confidence in the President's ability to introduce the necessary reforms, on 5 November Chadli replaced Brahimi as prime minister with the former chief of military security, Kasdi Merbah. More important still was the Sixth FLN party congress in Algiers in late November 1988, which marked the beginning of the end of the Algerian one-party state. During the congress Chadli argued for the separation of political and administrative functions of the FLN and, making frequent use of the word 'democracy', he overcame determined resistance from the old guard to persuade the delegates to allow non-FLN members to stand in local and Assembly elections. The congress also passed proposals for reform of media law and the internal workings of the FLN. Finally it adopted Chadli as the (sole) candidate for a presidential election to be held on 22 December. In an 87 per cent turnout, 81 per cent voted for Chadli, the relatively high proportion of illegal abstentions reflecting both substantial public scepticism and the population's increasing confidence, whetted by a newly strident press.

Chadli began his third term of office by turning his attention to the reform of the constitution of 1976. His advisers drew up amendments which effectively abandoned Algeria's theoretical commitment to socialism and the one-party state, and replaced it with a commitment to multi-party democracy. Algeria was to remain a 'democratic and popular republic' but the word 'socialist' was dropped. A supervisory constitutional council was created and the presidential term was cut from seven to five years. This increased the power of the presidency in key areas such as defence and foreign affairs to the disadvantage of the army and the FLN. Chadli was particularly anxious to repair his credibility which had been severely dented in the October 1988 riots, and intended his role as 'father of the nation' to be that of a powerful arbiter between its various factions. However, the most important element of the new constitution was the legalisation of associations of a 'political character', though those based exclusively on religion, language, region, sex and race or which advocated violence or extremism were prohibited. The government justified its decision to legalise the Front Islamique de Salut (FIS) by interpreting the clause as allowing organisations 'inspired by Islamic values'. The constitution also sustained the interior ministry's right to suspend a party's activities if it was deemed to constitute a threat to public order, and prohibited parties from receiving funding from abroad. The new constitution also redefined the position of the army as the 'protector of national independence'. In March 1989 the army's political committee announced its retirement from public political life, a move which both Chadli and the FLN had encouraged. However, ultimate authority remained with the army, as was to be well illustrated by the military interventions of June 1991 and January 1992.

Although the reforms were ground-breaking, they did not represent a genuine commitment to democracy. Rather, the regime resorted to political pluralism in order to outflank its opponents; Chadli's eager acceptance of the subsequent proliferation of political parties reflected his desire to see the Islamists outmanoeuvred by subverting their appeal as the 'natural' opposition. Seventy-three per cent of voters approved the amendments in yet another referendum in February, though at 79 per cent the turnout was the lowest ever in an Algerian referendum or election and perhaps this was the most genuine reflection of Algerian public opinion at any time since independence. The relatively high 'no' vote and absention rate illustrated the genuine opposition to the new constitution among supporters of the Boumediennist old guard and the Islamist movement, itself split between moderates, who supported the amendments, and the hardliners of the newly-established FIS, which flatly rejected them.

The political class, however, reacted to the constitution with enthusiasm. Even before the law was passed in July there were twenty-eight political parties ready to apply for registration – in the event it was the tiny reformist Parti Social-Démocrate (PSD) which was the first to be legalised, on 5 September. The most significant of the new parties were the FIS, the FFS, the PAGS, Ben Bella's Mouvement pour la Démocratie en Algérie (MDA) and Said Saadi's Berber/intellectual Rassemblement pour la Culture et la Démocratie (RCD). The government agreed to fund the parties and pay the salaries of journalists working on newspapers that represented their political views. This comittment inevitably resulted in the establishment of numerous bogus political parties, while many parties, most notably the FFS, chose to decline the state subsidy. Although Aït Ahmed was the first of the three historic exiles to return to Algeria in a stage-managed welcome in December 1989, popular memory of its leader's abortive coup attempts in the 1960s and its very clear Kabyle support base limited the FFS's prospects from the outset. Ben Bella's MDA was legalised in March 1990. In the draft electoral law adopted by the Assembly on 20 July any party gaining more than half the vote would win all the seats in any single constituency, with the remainder being distributed proportionately among the other parties. Parties polling less than 10 per cent would be disqualified. The law was a blatant attempt to engineer the polls in favour of the FLN, the party to which all members of the Assembly belonged

Chadli exploited the popularity of the new constitution to dismiss Kasdi Merbah, with whom his relations had deteriorated during the summer of 1989, and replaced him with the relatively young and inexperienced Mouloud Hamrouche, a fresh wave of protests in Algiers and other cities against unemployment and economic problems providing the pretext. Hamrouche had served on the FLN central committee since 1979 and had been an influential member of Chadli's 'presidential circle' of advisors during the 1980s. The new prime minister announced an ambitious programme of economic, social and political reforms and appointed a cabinet of technocrats where, for the first time, young professionals outnumbered the FLN party cadres. Hamrouche's cabinet marked a further stage in the decline of the FLN's hold on government, though it proved ill-advised in that Algeria's politicians clearly lacked the experience to execute the ambitious reforms they planned.

Further changes affected the military and security apparatus. Chadli appointed the chief of staff, Major-General Khaled Nezzar, as defence minister, a post which since 1965 had been held by the head of state. Nezzar as the most powerful member of the 'presidential circle', had built up a reputation for 'moral rigour' and was a proponent of a less politicised army. Although his appointment marked a further strengthening of presidential power it also acknowleged the army's continuing key role in Algerian politics. In July 1989 the government disbanded the Délégation Générale à la Documentation et à la Sécurité (DGDS), the feared political police once headed by Kasdi Merbah, who, following in the footsteps of the respected *mudjahid* and parliamentary speaker Rabah Bitat, left the FLN to found a party of his own, the Mouvement Algérien pour la Justice et la Développement (MAJD) in October. This was yet another party which claimed to embody the 'genuine' ideals of the 'real' FLN.

Elections

The municipal and provincial elections of June 1990 were the first real test for both Chadli and the old guard. Chadli intended to outmanouevre the FIS and the genuine opposition by encouraging a highly suspect proliferation of mini-parties with almost identical ideologies; the old guard gambled on strong support for the FLN. When the campaign unofficially began in April it soon crystallised into a race between the FLN and the FIS, with the FFS taking up a position at the head of the other parties. Nevertheless, it was notable as the first occasion on which Algerian civil society had become apparent and for the

unprecedented freedom of expression allowed in the
media: it was the first time, too, that Algerians were able
to vote for political parties other than the FLN. After
repeated delays to allow the newly-established parties to
prepare, the government on 20 March adopted a system
of proportional representation, a clear attempt to protect
the in-built advantage enjoyed by the FLN. Moreover, the
FLN and the FIS were alone able to field candidates in all
1,541 municipal and 277 *wilaya* constituencies.

The results of the election were of enormous significance to Algeria as well as elsewhere in the Islamic world.
In a turnout of 65 per cent, 55 per cent voted for the FIS
and 31 per cent for the FLN. The FIS won 853 of 1,539
municipalities and took 32 of the 48 *wilayas*; the FLN won
487 municipalities and 14 *wilaya*s; independents won 106
municipalities and the *wilaya* of Tindouf; while the RCD,
benefitting from the FFS's decision to boycott the polls,
took 87 municipalities and the *wilaya* of Tizi Ouzou. The
FIS's most impressive performances – i.e. where it
assumed outright control – were in Algiers, Constantine,
Blida, Djidjel and Relizane although it won working
majorities in key towns such as Batna, Tlemcen, Skikda,
Annaba, Medea and even in the relatively liberal city of
Oran. The FLN's vote was centred on rural or semi-rural
communities such as Laghouat and Khenchela. The FIS's
clear victory was deeply unsettling for Chadli, the FLN
and the political élite alike. Abassi Madani, the leader of
the FIS, claimed the result as an unequivocal popular
rejection of the FLN and the Chadli regime and immediately called on the President to bring forward parliamentary elections, scheduled for 1992, and presidential
elections, due in 1993. The FIS leadership openly claimed
to be the legitimate rulers of Algeria and they now
attempted with some success to set the political agenda.

However, there were numerous factors which mitigated
the FIS's strong showing in the 1990 elections. First, the
turnout of 65 per cent was markedly low – probably the
result of a combination of voter apathy, confidence that
non-participation would go unpunished, suspicion that the
elections would be rigged, and a response to boycott calls
by parties such as the FFS and the MDA on the ground

that they had had insufficient time to prepare. Secondly, many of those who voted for the FIS did so as a protest against thirty years of FLN misgovernment and corruption, as an exercise of the right, so long denied, to criticise a hated regime. As in most Islamic societies with centralised and totalitarian regimes, Islamism is the most authentic and effective channel for the articulation of opposition, particularly after the discrediting of Western ideologies such as Marxism and socialism in the 1980s. Although the FIS is an authentic Islamist party in the sense that it takes Islamic law and custom as the source of its political programme, during the 1990 elections it was primarily a vehicle to express popular opposition to an unpopular regime. However, the numbers of Islamists who were genuinely attracted by the FIS's 'revolutionary' credentials and its impressive organisation and mosque-based welfare programmes should not be undersestimated. It was they, too, who inevitably benefited most from the FIS's electoral success in the subsequent months.

Despite incipient rifts within its leadership, the FIS in 1990-1 was Algeria's best-organised and fastest-growing political movement. Its newly-elected municipal officials ensured that the party retained a high public profile, imposing minor 'Islamicising' measures, such as banning the wearing of shorts on beaches and the outlawing of the use of French by FIS-run local councils. The Gulf crisis which erupted in August 1990 provided all political factions with a platform on which to display their Arabo-Muslim credentials, but it was the FIS which exploited it to the best effect. The party also made political capital by maintaining a barrage of criticism against the Hamrouche government, highlighting its controversial reforms, such as allowing foreign firms to sell goods on the local market for the first time since the 1970s. There also were sporadic protests in a number of northern towns directed against the worsening living standards, rising consumer price inflation and an unemployment rate of approximately 25 per cent.

Alarmed by the growing popularity of the FIS and the unpopularity of the government, the FLN determined to

ensure for itself the greatest possible advantage in the
forthcoming parliamentary elections. A new electoral law
passed by the Assembly in April 1991 established a
system of single-member constituencies in which the
candidate who gained an absolute majority took the seat.
If no candidate won such a majority in the first round, the
best-placed three candidates entered a second round of
voting three weeks later. The law banned election
campaigning in mosques and schools, and limited proxy
voting to those living abroad, members of the armed
forces and those too ill to vote in person. This was clearly
aimed to work to the disadvantage of the Islamist parties
because many Islamist men insisted on representing their
wives. After repeated delays Chadli set 27 June as the date
for the first round of the elections. Virtually all the
opposition parties objected to the electoral law, and in
particular to the allocation of a disproportionate number
of parliamentary seats to underpopulated rural areas in
the south and east, where the FLN considered itself
strongest. The FIS singled out a constituency in the far
south which contained only 2,000 voters; by contrast the
FIS stronghold of Bab el-Oued had 160,000.

Abassi called a strike for 25 May 1991 as a protest
against the controversial electoral law and early presidential elections, though his additional motive was to seize the
initiative from his more hardline rivals within the FIS's
ruling council (the *Madjlis ech-Choura*). Although the strike
caused widespread disruption in Algiers, the public
response was otherwise weak in most key economic
sectors elsewhere, mainly because most of the potential
participants had no jobs from which to strike. The poor
response provided fresh capital for Abassi's opponents
within the ruling council, which on 30 May issued a public
statement registering its opposition to his position and
ordering a return to work. This move enraged Abassi,
who countered by urging party militants to mount daily
demonstrations and marches in Algiers, hoping thus to
provoke a confrontation with the government which he
felt he could win. Abbasi's gamble paid off. On 4 June the
military forced the government into allowing it to remove
FIS militants camping out in Algiers's main square. In the

subsequent pitched battles between Islamists and the military in Algiers, Constantine and Oran perhaps as many as 50 people died. Major-General Khaled Nezzar then forced Chadli on 5 June to declare a state of siege, postpone the elections indefinitely and dismiss Hamrouche and his government. It is likely that hardliners within the FLN, who opposed Chadli and the reforming Hamrouche in equal measure, were enthusiastically encouraging Nezzar in his actions.

The events of June 1991 marked the return of the military to the centre of Algerian politics. Nezzar and the military establishment had become increasingly frustrated with what it perceived as the 'laxness', liberalism and political games played by Hamrouche and his supporters. The clampdown of June 1991 also signalled the military's decision to prevent the establishment of an Islamist government, and this was borne out when security forces arrested hundreds of FIS activists, including Abassi and his deputy, Ali Belhadj, on charges of conspiracy to overthrow the state. For the FLN, the downfall of Hamrouche deprived the refomers within the party of their standard-bearer, opening the way for the pragmatists of the middle ground to reassert themselves in the party.

Another reformist, Foreign Minister Sid Ahmed Ghozali, was chosen to replace Hamrouche as prime minister. Carrying out a pledge to appoint Algeria's first cabinet of 'independents', Ghozali kept only six of the twenty-nine ministers who had served in Hamrouche's government or who had played an active political role within the FLN. Ghozali persuaded the respected diplomat Lakhdar Brahimi to serve as foreign minister and brought back Nordine Aït Laoussine, a former colleague of Ghozali at Sonatrach in the 1970s and latterly an energy consultant in Geneva, as energy minister. The appointment of a leading member of the FFS, Professor Hocine Benissad, to the economics ministry, was intended to lend the government something of the air of a secular/social-democratic alliance. Ghozali's cabinet separated the FLN party structure from the formal mechanisms of the government for the first time since independence. A further historic separation of party from state occurred on 28 June when Chadli resigned as chairman of the FLN during a special emergency meeting of the central committee called to debate the wave of FIS-inspired violence.

Ghozali's principal task was to organise and oversee the legislative elections which had been postponed from late June. He wanted to obtain the widest possible consensus in the process of amending the electoral law, and publicly opposed the unneccessary arrests or repression of the FIS. However, it was becoming increasingly evident that although the Chadli-Ghozali government was respected by some elements of the secularist establishment, it carried little political weight elsewhere, including the majority of the population. The label of caretaker prime minister doomed Ghozali's genuine attempts to persuade the Algerian people that his government marked a genuinely radical departure from what he called the 'two negative stages since independence, hypocritical socialism and shameful liberalism'. In addition, by allowing the army a free hand in the June 1991 crisis, the government had abandoned control of internal security to the military and, as a consequence, found itself increasingly sidelined.

Ghozali's amendments to the electoral law were passed in October 1991 after weeks of excited debate. The final form of the new electoral law was essentially a compromise between the FLN-dominated Assembly desperate attempts to ensure its re-election and proposals drawn up by the government and the 'democratic' political parties at a national conference held in September. The law increased the number of constituencies to 430 and lowered the minimum voting age to 25. On 28 October the Constitutional Court reversed the Assembly's decision to allow a husband or wife to vote on behalf of each other by showing a marriage certificate. Despite the atmosphere of recrimination and uncertainty over whether the FIS would stand, Chadli set Thursday 26 December as the date of the first round of the elections. In late October Ghozali appointed Major-General Larbi Belkheir, one of the President's closest aides, as interior minister in his first cabinet reshuffle. He also dismissed Hocine Benissad, whose handling of the Assembly had prompted widespread criticism, and assumed personal responsibility for the economy. The FIS, although now headed by the more moderate Abdelkader Hachani, actively encouraged the atmosphere of tension throughout the election campaign by repeatedly threatening to boycott the vote. In the event Hachani joined the leaders of forty-eight other parties and more than 1,000 independent candidates in the polls in the belief that a boycott would undermine his own moderate leadership of the FIS and deliver the party into the hands of the extremists, whose predilections to violence had been illustrated by a series of attacks by extremists on border guards at Guemmar in late November.

The results of the election shocked the entire Algerian political élite. In an admittedly low turnout of 61 per cent, the FIS won 188 of the 231 seats decided outright in the first round, equivalent to 47 per cent of the vote. The FLN managed only 15, ten less than the FFS which won 25 seats in its heartland of Kabylia and a considerable vote in other areas. Three independents were also elected, but no other party managed to gain a single seat. The government and the FLN filed more than 400 complaints of electoral irregularities with the Constitutional Court, but even with the maximum allowance for reballots, the FIS needed to win only 28 seats of the 199 which were to be decided in the second round of voting scheduled for 16 January 1992 – almost a certainty.

The FIS began to act as a party preparing for power. It dismissed fears that the ruling élite would directly intervene in some way to prevent it forming a government and published its first-ever manifesto. In Algiers it opened an exhibition to expound its electoral programme and its pledges to establish an Islamic state. However, apart from declaring that Islam would be propagated by '*al-targhib*' (persuasion) or '*al-tarhib*' (terror), it remained vague on the precise methods it proposed to employ. The party's promises to introduce Islamic economics, ban married women from most workplaces, prohibit the production, sale and consumption of alcohol and restrict the activities of the press did nothing to allay the fears of the ruling élite and the modernisers, who had entered into

a state of panicked shock as the implications of the
election result sank in. Despite a series of anti-FIS 'pro-
democracy' marches, the democrats and the modernisers
seemed powerless to prevent the FIS from assuming
power.

To what extent were the results of the election a defeat
for the established order of the FLN rather than a
'genuine' victory for the FIS? As with the results of the
June 1990 elections there were numerous mitigating
circumstances. First, there was the remarkably low
turnout. Even allowing for the probable electoral fraud
and over-estimates of previous polls, only 61 per cent of
eligible voters cast their ballots on 26 December, 1.2
million and six percentage points less than in June 1990.
This can be explained by both voter apathy (the public
quarrels of politicians had alienated many voters) as well
as a protest by non-participation; many Algerians were
thoroughly disgusted by the behaviour of the state and its
political stooge, the FLN, during the 1980s, but were not
attracted by the FIS or any of the other opposition parties
and thus abstained. Others perceived the election as
merely a contest between the FLN and the FIS, considered it no choice at all, and abstained. Secondly, the
profusion and confusion of the self-styled democratic
parties served to split the third force in Algeria: non-
Islamist, anti-old guard FLN and broadly social-
democratic. This explained the FFS's position as the
second largest party with only twenty-five seats. Thirdly,
almost 900,000 eligible voters had not received their
polling cards by election day. All in all, the genuine
Islamists were probably outnumbered by those motivated by despair at high unemployment and dire housing
and living conditions – the so-called 'economic' Islamists
– and the protest voters, and in real terms the FIS vote
actually decreased between June 1990 and December
1991.

During the first two weeks of 1992 the Algerian political
and military élite became locked in fevered debate over
whether to allow the second round of the elections to
proceed, and thus cede control of the state to the FIS, or
to halt the experiment with political liberalisation. Chadli

favoured proceeding with the second round of the
elections in the hope that he, backed by the military,
would be able to control any extreme political initiative
which the FIS might try to execute. Those in favour of
cancelling the second round included Major-General
Nezzar and numerous other senior military officers,
Ghozali, Larbi Belkheir, several cabinet ministers and
much of the Westernised political and economic élite.
They believed that any parliament in which the FIS
enjoyed an absolute majority, and thus the right to amend
the constitution, would surely end in disaster and jeopardise the achievements the country had made over the
past thirty years. Of course, a FIS government also
threatened an end to their own privileges.

Those in favour of cancellation prevailed. During the
second week of January Nezzar presented Chadli with an
ultimatum to resign and thus create a constitutional crisis
which the military could use as a pretext to annul the
elections. On 11 January Chadli interrupted a live
television broadcast to announce his resignation, declaring that 'given the difficulty and gravity of the situation'
he considered his resignation 'necessary to protect the
unity of the people and the security of the country'. The
Constitutional Council ruled that the constitution's
provision for its chairman to serve as interim head of
state until new presidential elections could be held was
'invalid', and as the constitution was effectively suspended
an illegal committee assumed power. This committee, the
'Higher Security Council', consisted of Ghozali, the chief
of staff Abdelmalek Guenaïzia, and four senior government ministers. The Higher Security Council then
cancelled the polls on the ground that it would be
impossible for the second round of the elections to go
ahead in the present circumstances.

Chadli Bendjedid never publicly explained why he
apparently so readily complied with the military's
ultimatum. The President would have faced seemingly
insurmountable problems in dealing with a FIS-controlled
parliament and may even have welcomed a way out of
the crisis. Whatever the reasons, Chadli was the first
major victim of Algeria's ill-fated experiment with political

restructuring, principally because he had no clear conception of his goals. The lack of a clear direction in the first ten years of his administration had resulted in the reversal of many of his predecessor's policies and the emergence by the mid-1980s of an ideological vacuum which was filled by a precarious and ill-considered policy of democratisation, destroying the fragile consensus between rulers and ruled that had existed in the last years of Boumedienne's rule and preparing the ground for the post-1988 crisis. The ageing ruling élite and the FLN, whose legitimacy was based on its members' mythicised role in the war of independence, were increasingly alienated from the mass of the population, most of whom were *arabisant*, under thirty and resentful. For the majority of Algerians, the thirteen years of Chadli's rule were a disaster, a period in which the impressive gains of the Boumedienne years were thrown into jeopardy and the country's wealth was embezzled by its government.

4

THE ECONOMY IN CRISIS

The role of Algeria's economy in the post-Chadli crisis is often underestimated. Many commentators and academics focus on political factors in a country where the real balance of power is often concealed, and where there are only rare but tantalising glimpses of the Byzantine behind-the-scenes struggles for influence. But Algeria's economic crisis was a major – and, according to some some writers, the primary – cause of the post-Chadli crisis. This chapter will show how ideology shaped the economic objectives and policies of successive Algerian governments, particularly during the eras of Ben Bella and Boumedienne. As befitted a vibrantly nationalistic country which had experienced one of the most violent struggles for independence ever known, the ideologies selected were often revolutionary, visionary and, ultimately, over-ambitious and unrealistic. Attempts to correct the flaws inherent in the 'great leap forward' of the Boumedienne era dominated and complicated government economic policy under Chadli, though it was the collapse in the price of oil in 1986 that ultimately set in train the sequence of events leading to the constitutional coup of January 1992. Afterwards, the regime's concern to protect its own interests and its fear of exacerbating the political and social crisis combined to undermine any efforts towards implementing the economic reforms that Algeria so desperately needed.

The Economic Environment

There are enormous differences in economic activity between the north and the Saharan regions of Algeria. The north, which can be further sub-divided into a region of coastal hills and plains, the Atlas mountain system, the High Plateaux, and the Saharan Atlas ranges, is narrow but fertile and supports the bulk of the country's fast-growing population. Here are found the country's great cities, Algiers, the country's capital and largest settlement with an official population of more than three million but with an unofficial figure probably at least double that; the second city, Oran, with some 600,000 inhabitants; Constantine, with a population of around 440,000, and Annaba, with some 340,000 inhabitants. Also dotted along the Mediterranean coast are impressive testimonies to Boumedienne's grandiose industrialisation vision: the industrial complexes at Arzew (near Oran), Mostaganem, Algiers, Bejaia and Skikda.

To the south lies the Atlas mountain system, which extends south-west to north-east across the entire Maghreb. In Algeria the Atlas comprises three sub-regions: the Tellian Atlas, running parallel to the heavily populated narrow coastal plain, where peaks can attain a height of between 500 and 1,000m.; the Saharan Atlas, rising from 1,000 to 2,500m.; and separating these two, the High Plateaux of the Shotts, with an average altitude of 1,000m. The Tellian Atlas comprises a series of mountain chains separated by deep valleys and wide fertile plains. The Mitidja plain, to the south of Algiers, and the Bejaia plain, to the west of the Petite Kabylie, contain the most productive farmlands in the region while most other basins and plains tend to be arid.

The undulating expanses of the High Plateaux are themselves divided into western and eastern halves. The former, west of a line extending from the Hodna Depression, through Miliana to the Mediterranean, is character-ised by strings of small mountain ranges and, in the far west, rolling hills. Here, unpredictable and minimal rainfall has given rise to pastoralism. To the east, higher and more rugged mountain ranges frame the productive region known as the Plain of Constantine. Settled farming dominates in the valleys and plains and even in the terraced hillsides of Kabylia and the wild Aurès to the south. Historically, the population density of the eastern half of Algeria has been double that of the west. The Saharan Atlas is more broken than the Tellian ranges, comprising five chains: the Ksour, Amour, Ouled Naïl, Ziban and Aurès. The Aurès chain contains the most precipitous mountains in the country, which to the north-east join imperceptibly with the southern ranges of the Tellian Atlas.

Northern Algeria has two climatic zones. From the northernmost margins of the High Plateaux to the sea, the winters are warm and wet and the summers hot and dry, often described as of the Mediterranean type. Summer temperatures can reach a humid 40C, though 25C is an average, while winter temperatures rarely fall below 12C. However, the rainfall is generally uneven and many Tellian rivers dry up completely during the summer. A semi-arid, steppe-type climate takes over on the borders of the High Plateaux.

In antiquity northern Algeria supported vast tracts of forests but centuries of overcultivation have left only 4.4 million ha. of forest. Soils in the more accessible parts of the Tellian Atlas tend be thin, allowing only scrub plants and shrubs to survive, while the more remote slopes have thicker soils and support oak and pine. The High Plateaux are generally bare, with only bushes and esparto grass. Only the overcrowded coastal areas are suitable for arable farming, producing a wide variety of Mediterranean crops, while livestock rearing is also common. The populations of the other 90 per cent of the land area, in the Tellian Atlas, the High Plateaux, the Saharan Atlas and the Sahara itself, tend to engage in subsistence agriculture or the herding of sheep, goats or camels.

The Saharan regions, which constitute some 80 per cent of the country's total area, are a world apart from northern Algeria. Occasional areas of highland – the Eglab, Tademaït, Tassili-n-Ajjer – break up vast areas of gravel and massive sand accumulation, such as the Grands Ergs Occidental and Oriental. The financial backbone of Algeria's economy, the production and exploration districts of the oil and gas industry, are found on the northern and eastern fringes of the Sahara. French companies first began to produce crude oil in 1958 at Hassi Messaoud, then a small village on the strategic north-south routes near the Grand Erg Oriental, and in the Polignac Basin near the Libyan border. The French companies were joined later by other Western firms such as Shell and Phillips and, after independence, by the state oil company, Sonatrach. Hassi Messaoud has grown into Algeria's oil capital, with more than twenty foreign oil companies based there in 1996. From 1991 the area of exploration extended to the south-east, west and south of Hassi Messaoud; in 1995 the British company BP signed one of the largest-ever agreements with the Algerian government to extract gas in the remote central Saharan Salah district.

The far south of the Sahara is dominated by volcanic massifs, such as the Ahaggar, rising to almost 3,000m., and the Adrar. Here the climate is arid, with sparse rainfall. Temperatures hover around 32C but can pass 50C in the high summer. Vegetation is extremely sparse, though there are pockets of cultivation around oases. Otherwise the region supports a few thousand nomads engaged in temporary pastoralism in areas after rainfall, though tourism has on occasion contributed much to the economy of the far-south town of Tamanrasset.

For centuries before the French occupation two activities characterised Algeria's economy: traditional subsistence agriculture and handicrafts. During the colonial era there evolved a dual economy divided between the traditional and underdeveloped Muslim and the modern European sectors. The majority of Muslim Algerians were engaged in agriculture, raising barley, wheat, figs and olives on the least productive lands of the interior rejected by the *colons*. As the population grew, particularly in Kabylia, Muslims increasingly became a source of cheap labour for the European-run industries established in the northern towns and cities, though many urban migrants merely exchanged underemployment in the countryside for unemployment in the towns.

The French colonial authorities ensured that the *colons* enjoyed economic superiority over the Muslims. The authorities encouraged them to acquire most of the more fertile lands nearer the coast where they planted vines, soft wheat, olives, tobacco, citrus fruits and market garden produce for export to metropolitan France in return for capital goods and consumer durables. Unlike Muslim holdings, *colon* farms were mechanized and received considerable subsidies from the state. This modern sector accounted for around two-thirds of all agricultural output and virtually all agricultural exports. French banks financed and largely controlled the Algerian banking system and mining operations, and most of the profits were reabsorbed into the metropolitan French economy. However, although the *colons* constituted almost all of the administrative and professional classes, they did not construct a significant industrial sector, and manufacturing was limited to processing primary products.

Infrastructure and the foundations of an industrialisation programme were positive legacies from the colonial era. The French constructed an impressive network of road, railway and postal communications in Algeria as well as modern ports and airports and an efficient administration and education system. During the 1950s General de Gaulle's drew up the 'Plan de Constantine' which projected a massive industrialisation programme from the construction of an oil refinery at Algiers to a petrochemical complex at Arzew and an iron and steel works at Annaba. The authorities also intended to redistribute 250,000 hectares of state lands. It was hoped that the industrial elements of the programme would create 400,000 new jobs, and although the war prevented the plan from being realised, it played a key role in shaping industrialisation policy immediately after independence.

Given the pivotal role of France and the European *colons* in the economy of French Algeria, it was inevitable that the departure of most non-Muslims at independence would have a disastrous efffect on the economy. More than a million *pieds noirs* fled from independent Algeria rather than live in a state dominated by Muslims, rendering Algeria at independence almost devoid of engineers, teachers, managers, administrators or modern farmers. It has been estimated that in July 1962 the *haute bourgeoisie* numbered no more than 50,000 and the *petite bourgeoisie* about 180,000. Whole agricultural communities had been resettled in *regroupement* villages and countless farms and fields had been destroyed. In addition, there were the cumulative effects of years of civil war, under-investment and increasingly obsolete equipment. The government of independent Algeria inherited an economy that had been integrated with that of metropolitan France and with very few people qualified to manage it.

Under Ben Bella and Boumedienne

The Algerian economy remained in crisis throughout the three years of the Ben Bella regime. Thousands of Muslim Algerians left to find work in Europe and escape an unemployment rate of around 45 per cent. In 1964 workers' remittances totalled around $200 million. With the exception of the hydrocarbons sector, all areas of the economy recorded negative growth. As income only reached 60 per cent of the government's expenditure, the government was obliged to rely massively on aid donations from France, the Soviet Union and some Arab states. The Ben Bella regime failed properly to address the problem largely because of its own instability. Instead of taking concrete action the government became embroiled in a three-way debate over the ideological basis of the new state's economic policy.

The strongest ideological group were those in favour of worker self-management: *autogestion*. This had been anticipated soon after independence when thousands of workers spontaneously took control of farms and factories. Ben Bella's March Decrees of 1963 officially put self-management into practice and allowed the government to nationalise all estates or properties formerly owned by *colons* and assign them a government-appointed manager. The agricultural sector underwent the most upheaval, though workers in other sectors, such as industry and even hotels and cafés, were encouraged to follow suit. In Algeria the move was politically popular but led to widespread criticism that it had not gone far enough; internationally the policy attracted widespread attention and prompted the government to pour in finance and support. However, it neglected the underdeveloped traditional modes of production that still accounted for around 80 per cent of agricultural production.

Autogestion was effectively nationalisation by the back door. Despite the programme's collectivist rationale, government-appointed managers tended to take control of the management committees and the workers effectively became employees of the state, which to some extent had assumed the position of the pre-independence *colon.* The fact that the committees were entirely dependent on state institutions for finance and for marketing their produce supports this analysis.

State capitalism made some advances during the years of the Ben Bella regime, however. Pursuing some of the objectives of the Plan de Constantine the government began work on the el-Hadjar steelworks near Skikda and the construction of a third oil pipeline from the Saharan oilfields of Haoud el-Hamra to Arzew. It also took over the French government's shares in a number of industrial concerns, such as Sonatrach. The government established similar corporations to exploit the steel, petrochemical, construction and machinery sectors.

Under Boumedienne, rapid large-scale industrialisation, land redistribution and nationalisation were the three economic policy objectives. The President and his advisers believed that these three policies would allow the state to take control of the country's natural resources, steadily reduce Algeria's economic dependence on foreign – particularly French – aid and thus guarantee Algerian independence. The President handed the task of drawing up the outline strategy to Belaïd Abdessalam, a close confidant who served as minister of industry from 1966 to 1978, and who made an unexpected yet short-lived political comeback in 1992-3 as prime minister.

Abdessalam's strategy projected the establishment of a self-contained economy by 1990 that would satisfy Algeria's basic requirements for consumption as well as utilising to the full local raw material and manpower. Development was to be implemented in various stages: the first was the 'pre-plan' of 1967-9. This was followed by the first four-year plan of 1970-3 and the second of 1974-7. After a one-year plan in 1978, which reflected growing concern over the actual achievements of previous plans, the first five-year plan lasted from 1980 to 1984. As Richard Lawless has remarked, the strategy 'prioritised capital accumulation over consumption and industrialisation over agricultural development'. However, in addition to laying the foundations of a managerial bureaucracy the strategy encouraged centralisation which Boumedienne's critics labelled as 'Stalinist'.

Abdessalam and his associates eventually selected the theory of *industries industrialisantes* ('industrialising industries') as the basis for their industrialisation programme. Gérard Destanne de Bernis, a French economist at the University of Grenoble, formulated the theory by synthesising the works of other economists such as François Perroux, A.O. Hirschmann and E. Gannagé. However, the work of the rival 'structuralist' UN Economic Commission for Latin America (ECLA) also influenced the architects of Algeria's industrialisation programme. Destanne de Bernis believed that a newly independent state such as Algeria must focus on industrialisation to promote an internal 'dynamic of development' in order to overcome the extroversion and internal disintegration of an economy shaped by colonisation. The model gave priority to industries deemed to be the engine of further industrialisation, principally in the energy, metallurgical, chemical and heavy machinery sectors, which would produce raw materials and machinery for other industries while at the same time same time consuming locally produced raw materials and agricultural products. The theory privileged industry over agriculture on the ground that the increased productivity and efficiency of the *industries industrialisantes* would simultaneously encourage development in other sectors.

Destanne de Bernis's model also projected that the development of heavy industry would in the long term encourage light industries. In turn this would create the extra employment necessary to absorb the rural population surplus and thus satisfy the growing demand for consumer goods.

Abdessalam banked on hydrocarbons revenues, foreign loans and remittances from Algerians abroad to finance the regime's three-pronged programme. The contribution to foreign currency earnings of hydrocarbons revenues steadily increased from the mid-1960s, passing the 90 per cent mark in the 1970s. Borrowing from Arab, Western European, Japanese and American banks grew during the 1970s until President Chadli was obliged to set an annual limit on foreign borrowing in 1980. Remittances from Algerian migrant workers abroad were an additional, though declining, source of revenue.

The industrialisation process proper began during the first four-year plan of 1970-3. In the first three plans, the hydrocarbons sector consistently received more than its planned share of investment (see Table). The capital and intermediate goods sector received slightly less, while agricultural and infrastructural development fell consistently behind planned targets. This disparity reflected the growing problems experienced by the agricultural sector, particularly the increase in imports, combined with the limitations inherent in a centrally planned and bureaucratic system. The government concentrated industrial sector development along the Mediterranean coastline in four major investment areas: Algiers, Oran and Arzew, and the Skikda-Constantine-Annaba triangle. Nine special programmes were launched between 1966 and 1973 to redress the over-concentration on the coast. With a few exceptions these were largely unsuccessful and underfunded.

At independence, Algerian agriculture was in crisis. The sector faced the problems of low productivity, the overbearing interference of state bureaucracy, and a growing demand for food in the increasingly crowded cities of the north. Its biggest challenge, however, was how to adjust from its previous integration with France. Ben Bella's March decrees of 1963 had effectively upheld the two-tier system prevalent under the French: the self-managed sector inherited the bulk of the land farmed by the *colons* while small peasant farmers continued to work in the private sector accounting for 75 per cent of arable land. The self-managed sector underperformed due to lack of worker incentives and an overbearing bureaucracy, while the private sector failed due to under-investment, outmoded production methods and the poor nature of much of the soil. Low investment, archaic farming practices, the poor quality of much of the soil and ill-conceived government pricing policies all contributed to the problem.

PLANNED AND ACTUAL DEVELOPMENT, 1967-77

	1967-9		1970-3		1974-7	
	planned %	actual %	planned %	actual %	planned %	actual %
Hydrocarbons	41.9	50.9	36.9	47.1	40.6	48.6
Capital and intermediate goods	47.0	40.6	48.9	46.2	47.6	44.5
Consumer goods	11.1	8.5	14.2	6.7	11.8	6.9
Total industry	48.7	55.3	44.7	57.0	43.6	62.0
Agriculture	16.9	16.4	14.9	13.0	13.2	4.7
Infrastructure	34.4	28.3	40.4	30.0	43.2	33.3

Source: R. Lawless, p. 165

The government first recognised the need for radical reform of the agricultural sector as early as 1962 when the Ben Bella government promised to create an internal market for emerging state-owned industries among the newly organised peasants and thus slow the rate of rural-urban migration. Nothing, however, was actually done. The calls for reform had increased when Boumedienne took over in 1965, by which time Algeria was importing 30 per cent of its food. In the following six years the government drew up an ambitious programme to rectify the situation. Its objectives were to revitalise the private agricultural sector; to encourage the production of sufficient food and raw materials to feed a growing population and an expanding industrial sector; and to improve living standards among rural populations to enable them to buy the products produced by industry. This, it was hoped, would dissuade them from moving to the cities and thus halt the worrying drift towards urbanisation. In 1971 Boumedienne announced that the reforms – the 'agrarian revolution' – had begun.

There were three stages to the 'revolution'. The first, which ran from January 1972 to June 1973, involved the nationalisation and redistribution of public lands, property inherited from the French colonial administration, land owned by the communes, tribal lands, and *habous* lands. These lands were to be redistributed in 14-20 ha. plots to the *fellahin*, or poor peasants, though they remained the property of the state. Under the terms of the transfers the state granted the farmers permanent rights to work their newly acquired land on condition that they worked it themselves, did not sell it, and used all equipment in common with other members of agricultural production cooperatives, the Coopératives Agricoles de Production de la Révolution Agraire (CAPRAs). By 1975 between 700,000 and 800,000 ha. of land had been parcelled out, with about 75 per cent being suitable for agricultural purposes.

The second stage, which started in June 1973 and lasted until June 1975, involved the partial nationalisation and redistribution of lands and palm-groves owned by absentee and large-scale landlords. As a basis for the second stage the authorities used a census taken in 1972. This showed that 16,500 landowners (equivalent to only 3 per cent of all farmers) owned around 25 per cent of all cultivable land. The government also planned to build 1,000 model socialist agricultural villages that, in combination with the CAPRAs, were to consume the output of state industries. By 1981 the government had built 140 of these villages, started construction of a further 203, and established more than 6,000 agricultural co-operatives. The third stage of the reforms began in 1975 and entailed an initiative to nationalise public pasture lands used by herdsmen.

Theoretically the administration of the reform programme was entrusted to the Assemblées Populaires
Communales (APCs). In practice, however, they were
subject to constant supervision and scrutiny by the *wilaya*
authorities and the ministry of agriculture's Commission
Nationale de la Révolution Agraire (CRNA). Its members
comprised mainly the rural intelligentsia who often used
classical Arabic to speak to farmers who did not under-
stand it, or distributed written explanations of the reforms
to illiterate peasants.

Opposition from the landowners was one of the main
causes of the agrarian revolution's failure in its prime
objective to realise a large-scale transfer of ownership of
land towards those who worked it. Although the reforms
reorganised public lands and to some extent curbed the
power of small-scale absentee landlords, they did not
constitute a genuine revolution. There is much evidence
suggesting   collusion   between   the   middle-
ranking state officials who implemented the reforms and
the landowners, and there are many recorded instances of
landowners removing records of their holdings from the
registry to avoid their nationalisation. The subdivision of
land among family members, the destruction of citrus
groves and the slaughter of animals were also used to
sidestep expropriations.

Nationalisation was the third key component of
Boumedienne's economic strategy. The strategy, which at
the time was popular with most governments in the
developing world as well as in Western Europe, was a
logical component of the government's nationalistic
ideology. The first nationalisations took place immediately after independence but the rate of nationalisation
was highest during the years 1966-71 when the state
assumed control of foreign mining, manufacturing,
insurance and agricultural companies.

However, it was the nationalisation of the oil and gas
industry that attracted most international attention. A
nationalistic attitude towards the hydrocarbons sector
was first apparent during the war of independence when
the FLN singled out French oil companies operating in the
Sahara for particular opprobrium. The first nationalisa-

tions in the hydrocarbons sector occured in August 1967 when the state took over the local distribution networks of Esso and Mobil; the next year fourteen Algerian petrol product companies were nationalised. When the government nationalised the local interests of Shell, Philips and Elewrath in 1969, Sonatrach became the largest oil producer in Algeria. In February 1971 the state nationalised the last remaining French oil companies in Algeria, Elf and CFP-Total, as well as all pipeline networks and natural gas reserves. Soon after, Boumedienne prohibited all concession-type agreements and reformulated the conditions under which foreign oil companies could operate.

Although later governments began to reverse the oil and gas nationalisations of 1971, even in the mid-1990s there remained a strong feeling that Algeria alone should have control over its own resources. The sector has always occupied a special place in the perception of all Algerians. Foreign companies have continued to be suspected of being agents of foreign neo-colonialism and economic imperialism and even though the governments of the post-Chadli crisis have tried hard to welcome the companies, their presence has to a large extent been seen as a necessary evil.

Despite these ambitious reforms, Algeria's economy had improved little by Boumedienne's death in 1978, and in many respects was worse. While the government's concentration on *industries industrialisantes* did indeed lay the foundations of a semi-industrialised state, it was accompanied by low productivity, rising costs and a growing dependence on imported skills and goods. Likewise, the successive four- and five-year plans were only partially successful, mainly because of the disparities between sectoral investment, the speed of development and the gradual disintegration and incoherence of the plans themselves. Moreover, Abdessalam's strategies encouraged the emergence of two-tier economic structures, over-rapid urbanisation and, above all, a growing foreign debt needed in order to pay for the industrialisation programmes. Problems such as shortages of skilled managers and workers, spiralling investment costs and widespread delays in reaching targets prompted the government increasingly to turn to foreign companies after 1974. Although this shored up the industrialisation programme, it increased the overall costs, undermined national control over the planning process and compromised the central planning that underpinned the whole economic initiative. There was also a growth in industrial unrest: in 1969 there were 22 strikes; by 1977 the number had exceeded 500. This was largely caused by the lack of incentives to skilled workers who resented the proportionally higher wage increases awarded to unskilled workers. On the positive side, however, the average annual growth of the Algerian economy was 7.2 per cent, and the country's industrial production doubled between 1966 and 1978. Although employment growth was slow, there was a significant increase.

The Chadli Years: Towards Economic Crisis

Algerians often refer to the 1980s as the '*décennie noire*', the black decade. This is an indictment not only of the political failure of the Chadli regime, but also of the economic mismanagement and growing corruption that accompanied it. The economic crisis that Algeria suffered from 1986 (the so-called '*après-pétrole*' era) was the result of both external developments and Chadli's ill-conceived attempts to reform and repair the failed economic policies of the Boumedienne regime. Moreover, it was this economic crisis that laid the foundations for the massive social unrest of October 1988 and the rejection of the state at the elections of 1990 and 1991.

In marked contrast to the Boumedienne years, it was economic and political expediency rather than economic theorists that directed economic policy under Chadli. Belaïd Abdessalam and his protégé, the head of Sonatrach, Sid Ahmed Ghozali, had both been levered out of their power-bases by 1981, and from 1978 to 1986 those most closely involved in forming and implementing economic policy were Colonel Mohamed Abdelghani, Algeria's first prime minister, and Abdelhamid Brahimi, the minister of planning. By the mid-1980s President Chadli had also collected a small group of reformers to advise on economic policy, and it was this group which published a series of five studies, collectively entitled *Les Cahiers de la Réforme*, that set out to diagnose and cure Algeria's economic ills. There was a growing acknowledgement of the shortcomings of a central command economy and an acceptance that private enterprise must be co-opted to assist in the realisation of development objectives. The ideal of decentralisation also became increasingly popular during the Chadli administration.

Chadli's initial objective was to adopt a more flexible economic policy to address the problems and inconsistencies that had characterised the Boumedienne regime. At a special session of the FLN entitled 'Towards a Better Life' in 1980, the party drew up a five-year plan which, in sharp contrast to earlier plans, prioritised agriculture, light industry and social infrastructure. The plan cut investment in the hydrocarbons sector by 75 per cent and increased investment in agriculture from the actual figure of 4.7 per cent in the 1973-7 four-year plan, to 11.8 per cent. The government also set out to improve the productivity and capacity of existing industrial plants constructed during the previous decade, some of which were barely operational. It proposed to do this by restructuring state companies into new subsidiaries or autonomous regional entities with the aim of rendering them more profitable, more efficient and more market-oriented. The subdivision of Algeria's most important state-controlled organisation, Sonatrach, into thirteen component entities was the most important example of this. The plan also encouraged the private sector which had evolved largely as a result of the shortcomings of previous economic strategies and which, by the 1980s, had become an important economic actor.

The government also tried to reform the long-neglected agricultural sector. Most of the 70,000 farms nationalised in the 1970s were broken up into smaller units and distributed to private owners, and the prices paid to producers were allowed to rise. In a bid to improve productivity and the quality of management, the gov-

ernment in 1987 replaced most CAPRAs with co-
operatives run by two or three families. This was one
example of a successful reform: in spite of a drought,
supplies of fruit and vegetables increased, though a high
proportion of produce was prevented from reaching
urban retail outlets because of growing problems with
corruption, the black market and distribution.

However, by and large the plan failed to repair the
damage of the Boumedienne years. Buoyant with cash
from the rise in hydrocarbons revenues of the late 1970s
the government enthusiastically opened the doors to
consumer imports, and state organs dedicated to importation such as Enapal and Onalait evolved as new centres of
power. Positive results – such as the 9.5 per cent annual
growth rate recorded by the industrial sector betwen
1979 and 1984 – were mainly due to the final realisation
of many projects inuagurated in the 1970s, and the
average annual growth rates in other sectors were
generally poor. In drawing up a second five-year plan,
subtitled 'Work and Discipline to Guarantee the Future',
in 1984, the government under Prime Minister Abdelhamid Brahimi implicitly recognised that the earlier plan
had been premature and that a period of austerity was
required.

Meanwhile, the government was forced the grapple
with the problem of the country's growing foreign debt.
Its origins lay, as we have seen, in heavy foreign borrowing in the 1970s to finance Abdessalam's industrialisation
programme. Although Chadli had set an annual ceiling of
50 million dinars on borrowing in 1980, the constant
demand for imported food and consumer goods as a by-
product of liberalisation measures continued to soar. The
debt service ratio grew from 39.9 per cent in 1984 to 76.9
per cent in 1988. The principal reason for this sudden
increase was the removal of OPEC oil price restraints in
1985 which led to a fall in earnings from $13 billion in
1985 to $8 billion in 1987. The Chadli regime stubbornly
refused to reschedule the debt and instead chose to
refinance shorter-term debt with long-term arrangements.

By the late 1980s Algeria's economic problems and
rapid rate of demographic increase had combined to push

up unemployment and adversely affect living standards. After an employment boom in the 1970s (the official rate of unemployment fell from 22 per cent to 17 per cent in 1977), the figure had risen to 22 per cent by 1988. In the six years from 1985 to 1991 the rate of unemployment increased by an annual factor of 2.9. The under-25s were the worst affected section of the population: every year 180,000 well-educated youths entered a job market that grew by only 100,000. A sizeable number of these, popularly referred to as *hittistes* (or 'wall-leaners' - from a corruption of the Arabic word *heet*, wall) tried to escape the frustration and despair of long-term unemployment by participating in the *trabendo,* the black market in difficult-to-obtain goods. Inflation soared into double digits and consumption fell, as even the most basic cost of living increased enormously in a relatively short period.

The steadily worsening economic situation also encouraged corruption among the nomenklatura. Bribery was rife and a handful of corrupt individuals controlled the highly profitable food distribution system. Senior military officers and party officials gradually gained control of large amounts of land formerly owned by the state during the 1980s, often to construct luxurious villas and private factories or to sell it off at inflated prices. Such arrogant displays of wealth squared badly with the fact that Algeria was importing around two-thirds of its food needs by the late 1980s. Although the extent of the problem was well known, the government took no action to bring the perpetrators to justice.

As the crisis increasingly appeared unmanageable, the government, encouraged by the International Monetary Fund (IMF), accelerated the process of structural reform designed to lessen state control and move towards a market economy. In December 1987 the government introduced *autonomie de gestion* (management autonomy) in public-sector companies. This created large companies called *fonds de participation* which held interests in more than 200 companies known as *entreprises publiques économiques.* They were to be responsible for their own profitability and for finding their own supplies, sales and financing. By 1990 about 300 of the state's 450 enterprises had been made autonomous, though the government still imposed high quotas on hiring of employees. In 1988 the government replaced the ministry of planning with a National Planning Council responsible for the general direction of economic policy.

The government also attempted to address the problem of the increasing obsolescence of much of the equipment in the state sector resulting from years of underinvestment. In 1986 the Brahimi government attempted to pass a new law to attract increased foreign investment as a means of encouraging the transfer of modern technology and up-to-date equipment from foreign firms to Algerian enterprises. A secondary objective was to diversify the economy away from its overdependence on the hydro-carbons sector. The FLN, however, rejected the law and instead passed controversial legislation restricting foreign participation to 49 per cent.

After 1988

The general direction of Algerian economic policy remained more or less constant until the appointment in October 1989 of Mouloud Hamrouche as prime minister. Hamrouche's predecessor, Kasdi Merbah, had refused to reschedule the foreign debt and the economy deteriorated accordingly. The Hamrouche administration was more willing to address fundamental problems. Its economic policy, which was heavily influenced by economy minister Ghazi Hidouci, projected a full transition to a market economy by accelerating the pace of *autonomie de gestion*. In theory, newly independent and autonomous firms were to invest using the excess liquidity of the black market, thus improving the availability of badly-needed agricultural goods. In practice, however, a serious lack of spare parts and raw materials, enduring and unchanged bureaucratic attitudes, and continued government control of access to foreign exchange hampered the development of such 'transitional enterprises'.

Although Hamrouche's reforms were bold in conception they encountered strong opposition from the FLN and the trade unions. Various protracted debates within the Assembly obstructed the planned reforms, for instance over the competence of the Central Bank to review applications for concessions. Hamrouche also encountered strong opposition from the UGTA, which claimed with justification that the transition to a free market economy would inevitably lead to increased unemployment and social unrest. Food shortages, unemployment and price rises of 50-100 per cent caused by the sudden lifting of price restraints prompted a series of demonstrations during the spring of 1990, culminating in a two-day general strike organised by the UGTA in March 1990. The private sector put many workers on half pay and laid off many more.

In April 1990 Hamrouche introduced a new Money and Credit law that paved the way for foreign companies fully to enter the Algerian economy. The legislation also granted independence to the Central Bank. The bank – subsequently named the Banque d'Algérie – was also entrusted with managing investment strategy through the channel of a new Conseil de la Monnaie et du Crédit (CMC).

Hamrouche's successor Sid Ahmed Ghozali retained, elaborated upon and in some areas reversed the principal features of Hamrouche's economic policy. In October 1991 he assumed direct responsibility for the economy on the dismissal of Hidouci, and began to concentrate on attracting hitherto elusive foreign investment. The prime minister hoped to raise $7 billion by selling the government's stake in Algerian oilfields to foreign companies and thus increase oil production by 200 million tonnes a year. The idea had first surfaced in 1987 during discussions with two European oil companies over the possibility of increasing their share in fields being exploited by Sonatrach. The plan involved foreign firms being able to take up to 49 per cent of the shares in known and future Algerian oilfields in partnership with Sonatrach. Three possible formulae were mooted: production sharing; selling production rights on an existing oil field; or pre-selling oil to a production partner at a discounted price. The APN passed the legislation, which also allowed Algerian public sector firms to attract additional investment from private firms in the mining sector, in November 1991.

The government intended that the new legislation would be an improvement on the existing 1986 law which had been designed to utilise foreign expertise in identifying new fields and exploiting oilfields under-used since the nationalisations of 1971, which had effectively closed Algeria to foreign investors. For a country with such promising oil reserves, Algeria had achieved little in comparison to other large oil producers. From 1980 till 1991 Sonatrach had sunk an average of only twenty new wells a year, whereas the number required to maintain the level of reserves was estimated to be 100.

The legislation was revolutionary in the Algerian context and drew criticism from many political quarters, including the FLN and the FIS, on the ground that it compromised national sovereignty. In 1992 the FIS's exiled spokesman, Rabah Kebir, underlined his party's nationalist credentials by warning that a FIS administration would re-examine the 1991 law. Justifying his policies in July 1991, Ghozali remarked: 'I'm broke. I prefer to leave to future generations an economy that works and empty oil-fields rather than leaving full oil-fields and a broken down economy.' Algeria, he added, had undergone 'two negative stages since independence: hypocritical socialism and shameful liberalism, which have led to bureaucracy and parasitism'. In October Ghozali appointed as as energy minister Nordine Aït Laoussine, a former technocrat who had founded his own oil consultancy in Geneva, and a figure popular with the oil and gas sector.

The governments of the post-Chadli era by and large retained the economic policy objectives formulated by Hamrouche and Ghozali. The acceptance that the government must encourage and use private enterprise to assist the development of the public sector were articulated in the policies of prime ministers Ghozali, Redha Malek, Mokdad Sifi and Ahmed Ouyahia, though under

Belaïd Abdesslam the government temporarily revived the dominance of the state sector over private enterprise.

5

THE POST-CHADLI CRISIS

The military intervention of January 1992 plunged
Algeria deeper into the political and social crisis that had
been under way since 1988. The interruption to the
democratisation experiment begun in 1989 deprived the
regime of the new legitimacy that had begun to supersede
the old revolutionary and nationalist legitimacy in place
since 1962. By cancelling the elections, the military and its
clients within the political élite abandoned any possibility
of renewing the state's credibility by broadening participation in government.. Instead, the regime opted to take
refuge in its revolutionary past.

Four themes link the regimes of the post-Chadli crisis:
the unsuccessful attempts to regain the legitimacy lost in
January 1992; the failure to restore law and order in the
face of a systematic campaign of violence waged by
armed supporters of the FIS; repeated capitulation to
international pressure to reschedule Algeria's debts, thus
further eroding the regime's authority; and finally the
move towards political normalisation that led to the first
successful multi-party elections in Algeria, which were
held in June 1997.

The High State Committee

The military's first task was to set up structures to
function as a collective presidency until the expiry of
Chadli's presidential mandate in December 1993. It
established a Haut Comité de Sécurité (HCS) under the
chairman of the Constitutional Council Abdelmalek
Benhabyles, which immediately cancelled the second

round of the election and imposed a nationwide state of siege. On 14 January the HCS created the Haut Comité d'Etat (HCE), a five-member transitional body to act as a collective presidency. As such the HCE mirrored the Council of the Revolution that Boumedienne had established in 1965 to legitimise his military coup. It was also a good example of the Algerian tradition of rule by committee as articulated by the *djamaa* village and tribal councils and underlined the ruling élite's instinctive distrust of a Western-style, one-man presidency such as Chadli had ill-advisedly endeavoured to create during the latter half of the 1980s. In addition, the military intended the unconstitutional HCE to present to Algerians and the world a 'reasonable' face of the military coup that had just taken place. The HCE, however, did not live up to its mandate: during its two-year existence it failed to address any of Algeria's problems – its economic distress, the acute misgovernment, its constitutional identity or the role of religion in the state. Once again the modernists, exploiting fears that the 'obscurantists' were set to triumph, had prevailed.

The man selected to chair the HCE was Mohamed Boudiaf. Boudiaf had earned a reputation as one of the wartime FLN's most able and impressive political operators, but political disagreements with Ben Bella in 1963-4 forced him into exile, first to France and later to Morocco. In the context of Algeria's deepening political, economic and security crisis, Boudiaf seemed a suitable candidate. His authority and appeal were based not only on his war record but also on the very fact that he had been absent from Algeria during the various crises that beset the state between 1963 and 1992. General Khaled Nezzar, who remained in his post as defence minister, was the most powerful member of the HCE, illustrating once again the military's continued grip on power in Algeria. The three other men appointed to the committee were Tedjini Haddam, Ali Kafi and Mohamed Ali Haroun. Haddam had served as minister of religious affairs and later of health during the 1960s, and later ambassador to Tunis and Riyadh in the 1970s. Since 1989 he had held the post of rector of the Paris mosque, though he had maintained close contacts with the government in Algiers and particularly with Sid Ahmed Ghozali. Although his appointment was meant to appeal to the Islamist section of the population, he was a well-known opponent of the FIS, despite the fact that his nephew Anouar Haddam had been appointed as the organisation's US spokesman. Kafi, who was secretary-general of the Organisation Nationale des Moudjahidines (ONM), was perhaps the most influential member after Nezzar, while Ali Haroun had entered Ghozali's first government after a career as a lawyer defending political prisoners in the Boumedienne and Chadli eras. With the obvious exception of Boudiaf, all the members of the HCE enjoyed good relationships with Ghozali, though none of the five members of the committee were on good terms with the FLN.

Boudiaf had three main objectives. The first was to create a new umbrella political front, provisionally entitled the Rassemblement Patriotique Nationale (RPN), to fulfil the role originally intended for the FLN in the early 1960s. Secondly, Boudiaf was determined to end the high levels of corruption both in government and society that he believed – justifiably – to be one of the root causes of Algeria's predicament. Thirdly, he was prepared to use whatever methods were necessary to safeguard the secular-nationalist character of independent Algeria and to prevent religious parties, primarily the FIS, from coming to power. Boudiaf also vowed to end instability in Algeria and improve the country's economic performance. A desire to address the numerous political, economic and social problems resulting from what he saw as almost thirty years of misrule in the name of the FLN linked all Boudiaf's objectives.

In a keynote speech delivered in April 1992, 100 days after being appointed, Boudiaf broke with precedent to analyse what he believed to be the real crises facing Algeria:

What are the pains that this country is suffering from? In reality... Algeria is suffering from three crises: a moral crisis; a spiritual crisis; and an identity crisis. For thirty years our people have been torn between East and West, between the French and Arabic languages, between Arabism and Berber-

ism and between traditionalism and international values...
After long years during which a single party and the dictatorship of a single language prevailed, democratisation has
become a necessary stage... The exploitation of Islam for
political and partisan aims, and also the resorting to democracy and lies found, for a specific period, listening ears among
the deprived and marginalised sections of the population.

It is likely that Boudiaf was sincere in his intention to
steer Algeria back towards some measure of democratisation. He, as well as key officials such as Foreign Minister
Lakhdar Brahimi, made frequent promises to hold fresh
elections by the end of 1994, though always with the
proviso that 'security and stability' be restored first.
Although it is entirely possible that such pledges were
made in good faith, Boudiaf was well aware that, as ever,
ultimate authority resided with the military establishment
in Algeria, and a resumption of democratisation was
impossible without their consent.

In April 1992 Boudiaf established an interim advisory
body, the Conseil Consultatif National (CCN), to act as a
mini-parliament. The council comprised sixty men and
women who, like Boudiaf, had not been active in Algerian
politics since independence and who, ideally, were
untainted by allegations of corruption. Among the
members were former ministers and diplomats, such as
Redha Malek and Mohamed Mazouzi, and a wide
spectrum of economists, academics, journalists, traders
and businessmen ranging from Mohamed Djemaoun, the
chairman of the Association of Imams, to Abdelhak
Boumachra, the president of the Islamic Scout Movement. The feminist writer Khalida Messaoudi, the
president of the Association for the Triumph of Women's
Rights, was the prominent woman member. The council,
however, came under criticism from all sides for including
too many left-wing intellectuals (many of its members
were PAGS activists) and for being conceived as merely a
rubber-stamp body for the military establishment. Both
criticisms were to a large extent undeserved, but the
council soon showed itself unwilling and unable to
legislate as a replacement for the dissolved Assembly.
This prompted Boudiaf to accelerate his efforts to found

the Rassemblement Patriotique National (RPN), with which he planned to replace the three groupings of political parties – the Bloc of Seven, the Bloc of Thirteen and the Bloc of National Fundamentals – which had emerged in the June 1990 and December 1991 elections and which in part contributed to the unrepresentative success enjoyed by the FIS. Boudiaf also hoped that the RPN would be more relevant to Algeria's overwhelmingly youthful population. In May 1992 twelve secularist parties merged to form the Rassemblement Démocratique National (RDN), which was intended to form the nucleus of the RPN, and which was the forerunner of the RND that won the June 1997 parliamentary elections. Boudiaf apparently planned to stand as the candidate of both the HCE and the RPN in the presidential elections scheduled to be held at the end of the HCE's mandate in December 1993, but which never took place. Boudiaf and Ghozali both favoured a ban on the FLN and, perhaps rather simplisticly, publicly blamed the political crisis on the FLN's encouragement of the FIS as a counterweight to the growing power of the presidency under Chadli. The single-party status devised for the FLN by Ben Bella, and his subsequent exile in protest doubtless accounted for Boudiaf's antipathy towards the party.

From the outset the HCE and its military backers resorted to repression in its struggle against the FIS and its supporters. Thousands of FIS supporters were rounded up, and on 22 January General Nezzar ordered the arrest of Abdelkader Hachani on charges of inciting rebellion within the army. Later the authorities detained the party's external affairs spokesman, Rabah Kebir, and began to replace hundreds of pro-FIS imams, including Abdalkader Moghni of the Sunna mosque in Bab el-Oued, with pro-government figures. The authorities used laws under the 1989 constitution for the first time to ban political activities in mosques and supplemented them with regulations prohibiting FIS supporters gathering outside mosques. In almost every sizeable town in northern and eastern Algeria throughout January and February there were clashes between riot police and Islamists after Friday prayers. On 9 February the HCE declared a year-long state of emergency. This introduced press censorship and granted the army the right to detain 'suspects' and impose curfews. On 3 March the interior ministry began judicial moves towards the formal banning of the FIS. All these moves encouraged FIS supporters to turn towards the Islamic extremist fringe; less than twenty-four hours after the imposition of the state of emergency, 'Afghans', Algerian Islamic extremists who had fought alongside the *mujahideen* in Afghanistan, killed six policemen in the Algiers casbah, signalling the start of the terrorist campaign that was raging many years later. However, the FIS's semi-clandestine armed wing, the Mouvement Islamique Armé (MIA) was initially the more significant extremist organisation.

The regime was undeterred and systematically set about destroying the FIS and its party organisation. Boudiaf was determined that the FIS, and probably the other religious parties, be excluded from openly participating in a more broadly-based political environment, though he did appear to favour dialogue with the Islamists as a means of lending authenticity and legitimacy to his 'national dialogue'. In March the HCE ordered the dissolution of the 400 local and provincial councils that had been run by FIS supporters since June 1990 and replaced them with new 'executive delegations' of three to five members appointed by the government. The Supreme Court in late April rejected the FIS's appeal against its dissolution, and in June Abassi Madani and Ali Belhadj received twelve years each for conspiracy against the state (Abassi was released in July 1997 after serving five years of his sentence). The charges, which referred to the activities of seven senior FIS members in the strike of June 1991, were legally dubious, and there was widespread concern that the convictions were unsound.

As the intensity of Islamic extremist violence accelerated in the spring of 1992, Boudiaf appeared ever less tolerant and more prepared to use force to stamp out the FIS and the extremist groups. In June he stated that he would refuse dialogue not only with 'criminals and bandits' but also with those 'who damage Algeria's credibility and manoeuvre to destabilise the country'. By the time of his assassination at the end of June 1992, Boudiaf was popularly perceived as a figure once again pledging unrealisable reforms while being controlled by the military. However, he did display unease over the internment of up to 6,000 Islamist activists at remote camps in the Saharan towns of Ouargla, Reggane, In Salah and Adrar. Witnesses described conditions at these camps, deliberately located hundreds of miles from the FIS heartlands in the northern coastal cities, as insanitary and harsh, and there were a number of documented cases of inmates dying due to the bad conditions. The Algerian Human Rights League (LADH) and Amnesty International visited the camps and strongly criticised the security forces and conditions in the desert, though nothing was done. In March Boudiaf set up a human rights monitoring centre under his direct personal control, but his pledges to phase out the camps by the summer of 1992 came to nothing.

But it was Boudiaf's stand against government corruption rather than his opposition to the Islamists that cost him his life. In a speech delivered soon after his arrival from Morocco in January, he remarked: '...one has to act against these people [the 'mafia'] who have monopolised the possessions of the state... We will prosecute them and take all necessary measures to recover these goods for the state. This is one of my main goals because everybody expects such a thing; it was requested by many people, journalists and others.'[1] Boudiaf was not the first Algerian head of state to declare himself a 'white knight' against official corruption: Chadli Bendjedid had used similar charges against a number of his political foes, including figures such as Belaïd Abdessalam, to remove them in the early 1980s. However, the situation had become a major feature on the political agenda by the 1991 parliamentary elections when the former prime minister, Abdelhamid Brahimi, claimed that government officials had siphoned off 26 billion dollars, not coincidentally equivalent to the amount of Algeria's foreign debt. The problem of corruption had convinced Algerians that their country

---

[1] Summary of World Broadcasts, 20 January 1992.

had fallen prey to a gang of criminals and it was one of the prime reasons behind the FIS's electoral success. To win real credibility with the Algerian people, Boudiaf was almost obliged publicly to address the problem.

In a keynote speech on 22 April Boudiaf set out five guiding principles behind his anti-corruption campaign:

'First: nobody...can use me as a means of vengeance or for settling of accounts. Second: the dossier of property acquired through suspect methods will be dealt with within the framework of the law and by means of justice. Third: the people have a right to demand the shedding of light on the management of the state's monies and property. It also has the right to look into these issues. We promised to open this case and we will honour our promise. Fourth: in the future, all precautions will be taken and all necessary means will be adopted to put a final end to these practices that corrupt our country and tarnish its reputation. Fifth: I agree to the setting up of an investigatory commission to study some cases of corruption. It would be appropriate for this commission to be supervised by members of the National Consultative Council.'

One of Boudiaf's highest-profile targets was the former secretary-general at the defence ministry under Chadli, Major-General Moustepha Belloucif. Belloucif was accused of having redirected around six million US dollars to numbered bank accounts in Switzerland in the early 1980s to finance the furnishing of his private apartment in Paris and twelve villas in Algeria. The campaign also accused the former director of planning at the defence ministry Lt.-Col. Fekir Mohamed el-Hebri and the ex-director of administration at the presidency, Abdelkader Tidjeni.

The details of Boudiaf's assassination remain unclear. On 29 June members of the 'special intervention unit' (GIS) opened fire and killed Boudiaf as he gave a speech in the north-eastern city of Annaba. The murder was well planned and executed and had been preceded by two abortive attempts to kill Boudiaf in towns near Annaba. The authorities were determined to obscure the evidence and protect the culprits from the beginning, in much the same way as the assassinations of early FLN luminaries such as Mohamed Khider and Krim Belkacem were never satisfactorily explained. A four-man commission of enquiry presented its initial findings in July. It ruled out the possibility of a single-assassin theory but it offered no opinion on who might have been behind the killing. The actual killer of Boudiaf was identified as GIS Sub-Lt. Lembarek Boumaarafi, who allegedly had well-known sympathies with the Islamists and whose mission to kill Boudiaf had been greatly eased by the incompetence and inefficiency of the security services. For the first time, security arrangements had been handled by Boumaarafi's GIS instead of the presidential bodyguard. The investigating commission released a video of the assassination showing the actual moment of the killing and accompanied by a macabre 'confession' on the soundtrack by Boumaarafi himself taking full responsibility for the planning of the murder. Ten members of the presidential bodyguard and the GIS were arrested for criminal incompetence and neglect but later released without charge.

Although unproven, it is likely that senior elements within the same military establishment that had brought Boudiaf to power ordered his assassination. Nezzar and Ghozali had selected Boudiaf primarily to provide a façade of revolutionary credibility to their unconstitutional arrangements and to signal the regime's fissure with the FLN. However, Boudiaf exceeded his undeclared 'mandate' in important ways. First, he failed to consult the military élite in his efforts to establish the RPN. Second, and perhaps more crucially, the military and the political élite considered his campaign against official corruption a serious threat to their own privileged position, and possibly feared that the newly created RPN would gather sufficient momentum to win presidential elections to the disadvantage of their own candidates, jeopardising the military's automatic control of government. A third and probably less credible factor behind the assassination was Boudiaf's rumoured intention to begin talks with moderate members of the FIS, though there is no evidence to support this argument. Whoever was responsible, the assassination ensured Boudiaf's mythicisation in subsequent years. The political classes pointed to his commitment to political reform and frequently expressed the view that he had been the most honest head of state in Algeria's history.

Boudiaf's assassination necessitated more changes in the composition of the government. In order to sustain its supposed distance from the government, the military appointed a civilian, Ali Kafi, to succeed him as chairman of the HCE. Sid Ahmed Ghozali remained as prime minister for just one week of Kafi's presidency; his resignation had been widely expected given the impossibility of his position faced with an increasingly reactionary and authoritarian regime. The military then attempted to promote a qualified return to the economic 'successes' of the Boumedienne era by appointing as prime minister Belaïd Abdessalam, the architect of Boumedienne's economic strategy. After almost ten years in the political wilderness his reputation for decisiveness and vision and his continual criticism of reformists like Hamrouche had, since 1989, fuelled a slow political rehabilitation. The new prime minister tried to strengthen his appeal for legitimacy by characterising the Chadli period as an 'interval' in which 'the state was exposed to the game of personal interests, deviating from its basic tasks... [Algeria] lost its prestige and the ability to play its vital role. The national economy was subjected...to sabotage and the shaking of its foundations, and this has strongly affected our credibility abroad....'

In the event Abdessalam's period in office, from July 1992 to August 1993, was an almost unqualified disaster. He continued the precedent established by Ghozali and held both the economy and finance portfolios and appointed supporters to most key positions. In his policy programme, announced in September 1992, he showed just how little he had changed during more than ten years away from the centre of government with his continued belief in the primacy of the state over the private sector. Abdessalam advocated reverting to the interventionism of the 1970s instead of pressing ahead with the structural reform programme instituted by Hamrouche and Ghozali. The key elements of Abdessalam's 'war economy' were swingeing austerity measures; a refusal to implement essential structural reforms; and a refusal to come to an agreement with the IMF. His programme also confused potential foreign investors with unworkable compromises between nationalism and reformism and a drift towards recentralisation of the economy. He stubbornly refused to alter his aloof, dogmatic and authoritarian personal style, and this provoked hostility among virtually the entire population. The HCE finally yielded to pressure from its military backers, the international community and the public, and dismissed Abdessalam on 21 August 1993 after only thirteen months in office.

Although the next prime minister, Redha Malek, advocated a return to the reformist economic policies of Ghozali, he was as committed as his predecessor to eradicating the Islamist movement by force. Malek was practically the only leading secularist-nationalist figure to have risen rapidly through the ranks of the government since the January 1992 coup, and his last position had been as foreign minister. He articulated his staunch opposition to the Islamists in a book published shortly before his appointment, arguing that FIS participation in power would fundamentally undermine the principles on which the Algerian state was based. Malek justified his position by pointing to the increasing attacks on the security forces by the Mouvement Islamique Armé (MIA) in its campaign to persuade the military to readmit it to the constitutional process. The unofficial estimated death toll between February 1992 and November 1993 was more than 3,000, though the real figure could have been as high as 6,000. In August 1992 a bomb exploded in the departure hall of Algiers international airport, killing ten people and injuring more than 120. In early October national television broadcast videotaped confessions by four men who admitted planning the attack, among them Hocine Abderrahim, a former colleague of the Islamist *maquis* leader Moustafa Bouyali during the 1980s and a close aide of Abassi Madani, and a senior Air Algérie pilot.

The regime exploited the enormous effect of the Algiers airport attack on public consciousness to introduce more repressive anti-terrorist measures. The HCE established a special anti-terrorist unit at the defence ministry under Major-General Mohamed Lamari, a former commander of the land army who had been retired during the Ghozali era. It also created three mobile special courts presided over by a panel of unidentified civil and military judges to try those accused of offences deemed to be 'terrorist' . The courts usually handed out exemplary punishments, often death, and defendants had no right of appeal. The minimum age for a suspect to be tried was lowered from 18 to 16; the maximum permitted period of incommunicado detention was extended from 48 hours to 12 days; Algerians were banned from joining any 'foreign terrorist' group; and the possession of weapons and the distribution of 'subversive' literature were outlawed. In November 1992 the government dissolved the 'spider's web' of entities supporting the FIS: local and *wilaya* councils and charities, cultural groups and labour organisations controlled by the FIS or its supporters. In early December the government introduced a nightly 10.30 p.m.-5 a.m. curfew in Greater Algiers and the six adjoining provinces.

The re-emergence of torture was an inevitable corollary of the HCE's anti-terrorist campaign. The Ligue Algérienne de Défense des Droits de l'Homme (LADDH) in November 1992 lamented that 'torture, which had been considered eradicated since the riots of October 1988, is re-appearing in Algeria', charges repeatedly echoed by Amnesty International. By late 1993 there was mounting evidence of the existence of several clandestine 'death squads' in the Algiers region, operating under a variety of such names as the 'Organisation of Free Algerian Youth'. These groups were believed to have been cover organisations for vengeful security force personnel, seizing Islamist leaders and known criminals for summary execution, though it is entirely possible that members of the regime were also involved.

In the summer of 1993 the HCE began to call for dialogue with the opposition to promote a political resolution of the crisis. In May, Ali Kafi announced plans to hold a referendum on constitutional change by the end of 1993, as well as to establish a new transitional body to

oversee a resumption of the electoral process on the
expiry of the HCE's mandate in December 1993.
However the worsening security situation obliged the
HCE to extend its mandate to January 1994 and abandon
the plans for a referendum. In the last four months of
1993 there were continuous rounds of talks between the
regime and the opposition political parties, excluding, of
course, the FIS. Ostensibly the talks aimed for as broad as
possible an input into the choice of successor to the HCE
on the expiry of its mandate on 31 December 1993. The
real reason, however, was the desire on the part of the
HCE and its military backers to remain in power for as
long as possible by securing the tacit endorsement of the
three main political parties (the FLN, the FFS and the
FIS), which since the assassination of Boudiaf in June
1992 constituted the major repository of political
authority in Algeria.

The initiative failed over the regime's refusal to relegalise the FIS. The FLN and the FFS announced their
preparedness to participate but stuck to their one
principal condition - that the FIS be re-legalised and
invited to participate in the dialogue process. Although
the two parties were both genuinely commited to
democracy, their insistence on the FIS's involvement was
more based on a fear that to co-operate with the regime
and thus implicitly collude with it would jeopardise their
own authority within their constituencies and further
lessen the chances of a viable democracy developing in
Algeria. The regime responded by extending the invitation to take part in dialogue to a wide range of small
political parties that had received only a tiny proportion
of the vote in December 1991 and could thus be dismissed as marginal. When it became clear that the HCE
was unable to co-ordinate the 'dialogue process', Lamari
in October 1993 entrusted its organisation to an eight-
member Comité National de Dialogue (CND). Three of
its members were senior military officers.

In the last months of 1993 divisions deepened within
the military over which course the regime should adopt to
solve the crisis. The divisions are often neatly parcelled
into two major trends: the 'eradicators' and the

'conciliators'. The terms are English renderings of the French *éradicateurs* and *conciliateurs*, and as such reflect a particularly French analysis of the situation: we shall see later how there were in fact many more shades of opinion. 'Eradicators' referred to those who advocated the harsh repression of the Islamist movement and its supporters. Generally, they favoured the construction of a new Algeria in the image of a modern, secular France. Foremost among the eradicators were officers who had served in the French army before the war of independence and who had held high office since the beginning of the crisis in 1988: Major-General Mohamed Lamari, Kafi's interior minister Selim Saadi, Major-General Benabbas Ghezaiel, and Major-General Mohamed Mediene. Their political friends included Kafi and Redha Malek and much of the so-called *hizb Fransa* and its political allies, such as the RCD, the UGTA, the ONM and the former communists of the Ettahadi party. Despite their self-appointed role as guardians of the modern Algerian state, and the political support extended them by foreign governments such as France, these sections of society combined were a minority and enjoyed minimal support among the general population. The term 'conciliator' described those who believed that the state could only survive through a process of dialogue and compromise. The conciliator camp found considerably more support among Algerians. Led by the two main legal parties, the FLN and the FFS, the conciliators proposed that the state must accommodate the Islamist movement.

When the dialogue process failed to promote the faintest glimmer of consensus on a successor to the HCE, the military once again stepped in with their own candidate. The eradicators dominated the HCE and the CND and flatly refused to consider the political rehabilitation of the FIS. The HCE called a 'national consensus conference' in January 1994 to discuss its formula for a new transitional government and to choose a president, but only an unrepresentative collection of trade unions and minor interest groups attended the discussions after the FLN, FFS and other significant political parties refused to attend. The military convened a special meeting of the

HCS to select a head of state. In a development reminiscent of the army's choice of Chadli Bendjedid as successor to Boumedienne in 1979, the committee chose one of its own, the defence minister, Lamine Zeroual.

Lamine Zeroual

The military selected Zeroual for his career background and his distance from the post-1988 military establishment. Unlike Lamari and his associates, he had never been trained in the French army and had fought within the FLN from a young age. His distinguished military career had ended in 1989 when he resigned over plans formulated by Khaled Nezzar to modernise the armed forces on French models. He had not been involved in the army's moves against the FIS in June 1991 and January 1992, nor (reputedly) in the assassination of Boudiaf. His reputation for honesty and - perhaps most important - integrity were supplemented by impeccable Algerian nationalist credentials; he was perceived as having more psychological connection with the *arabisant* majority than the *francisant* ruling class. Even if he owed his elevation to the eradicators, he was a natural focus for the conciliators within the regime.

Zeroual, however, immediately precipitated a new conflict within the military and the ruling élite by opening direct talks with the FIS. In a speech soon after his inauguration, he announced his preference for a 'dialogue that excluded no one', interpreted by all as implying the inclusion of the FIS. After holding direct secret talks with Abassi and Belhadj, he ordered the release in February 1994 of two members of the FIS's collective leadership council, the *Madjlis ech-Choura*, Ali Dejddi and Abdelkader Boukhamkham. However, when this policy drew a barrage of criticism from the prime minister Redha Malek, the interior minister Selim Saadi, and the general staff, Zeroual was forced to halt his initiative, though in return for changing tack the general staff in April approved his request to dismiss Malek and Saadi. Zeroual replaced Malek with the technocrat Mokdad Sifi as prime minister though, in the spirit of balance, he appointed the general staff's candidate Abderrahmane Meziane Cherif as interior minister.

A second attempt at dialogue with the FIS in August also ended in failure. Zeroual opened the initiative by inviting eight parties for talks, though only five – the FLN, Ennahda, the MDA, Hamas and the PRA – accepted and all explicitly called on Zeroual to invite the FIS. At the same time the president entered into a series of secret discussions with Abassi and Belhadj in prison, and he was rewarded when the former explicitly accepted the principles of political pluralism and '*alternance*' (the idea that political parties leave office when electorally unsuccessful). Encouraged, Zeroual transferred Abassi and Belhadj from Blida jail to house arrest on 13 September; three other senior FIS leaders were freed unconditionally. However, the optimism engendered by these developments lost momentum as the level of violence increased. Abassi insisted that his own acceptance of political pluralism and *alternance* was invalid unless discussed and endorsed at a full meeting of the *chouyoukh* (leaders) of the *Madjlis ech-Choura*. – a demand particularly hard to swallow because many of its members had joined the armed movement, requiring the regime to allow figures branded as terrorists openly to meet Abassi and Belhadj in Algiers. This was clearly unacceptable to Lamari and his supporters, who forced Zeroual to abandon the negotiations. On 31 October the President officially announced the breakdown of the talks, laying the blame on the political parties and announcing his plans to hold presidential elections at some point in 1995.

It was the opposition parties and not the government which organised the next attempt at a political settlement. In November 1994 the Roman Catholic Sant' Egidio community in Rome invited all Algerian political parties and the government to attend a conference aimed at finding a solution to the country's political crisis. The FLN, the FFS, the FIS, the MDA and Ennahda resented Zeroual's largely unjustified criticism of them for being behind the failure of the latest talks and readily agreed, though the 'eradicator' RCD and Ettahadi parties and the

Algerian government refused. The preliminary session in November was inconclusive but after a second round of talks the FLN, the FFS, the FIS, the MDA, Ennahda and the small PT signed a final communiqué, entitled the 'National Contract', on 13 January 1995. The Algerian regime claimed that the non-Islamist parties had aligned themselves with the FIS on foreign soil and immediately rejected the document. However, this position was unjustified. The contract was a remarkable landmark document in Algerian political history, proving that the regime, rather than the political parties, was the cause of the crisis. For the first time the FIS as a party endorsed the principle of political pluralism and *alternance*. The wording of the document also clarified the FIS's position towards the use of violence against the state. Although the party leadership reaffirmed the right of its supporters (mainly the Armée Islamique du Salut, which had superseded the MIA in 1994) to attack interests of the state on the ground that the regime had excluded the FIS from the constitutional process, the party condemned the use of violence against civilians and foreigners and distanced itself from the tactics of the more hardline organisation, the Groupes Islamiques Armées (GIA). The Contract was also remarkable for being the first occasion where non-Berber political parties explicitly recognised Algeria's Berber character. It affirmed: 'The consituent elements of the Algerian personality are Islam, Arabism and Amazighism.' In the preamble to the document, the signatories affirmed the rights of all parties in the Algerian crisis to guarantees safeguarding their respective interests.

A third, and again unsuccessful, initiative took place from April to July 1995. In response to a letter from Abassi offering new negotiations, Zeroual obtained the endorsement of the general staff to open new talks with Abassi (who remained under house arrest) and proposed a three-stage plan. First, Abassi was to call on all Islamists to renounce violence and give up the armed struggle, after which the government would release all FIS detainees who agreed to the proposals. In the second stage, the government would pardon all members of the armed groups who surrendered and laid down their arms during a pre-determined period. At the third stage, depending on the success of the second, the government would allow the FIS to re-form under a new name, on condition that the party agreed to the 'republican' principles of the 1989 constitution. Once again, Abassi personally agreed to the President's proposals, but on this occasion he was allowed to confer with six other *chouyoukh*, including Belhadj, Hachani, Abdelkader Boukhamkham and Ali Djeddi. They refused to accept the plan unless the regime first released all FIS prisoners unconditionally. The presidency's publicity machine deliberately led the Algerian and international press to expect a breakthrough to be announced on 5 July, the thirty-third anniversary of independence. Instead, Zeroual on 11 July formally reported the failure of the talks, explicitly blaming divisions within the FIS.

The following two years saw Zeroual consolidate his authority and steer events towards a stabilisation of the political situation, if not of the country's security, social or economic crises. During 1996 he developed a project to alter the constitution that would guarantee the military's privileged position while permitting what proved to be a surprising degree of political pluralism. Zeroual's project was a three-stage process: presidential elections; a referendum on changes to the constitution (one banning political parties that explicitly, if not implicitly, based their electoral platforms on religion or ethnicity, and which introduced an electoral system that would guard against 'destabilising' results); and multi-party parliamentary and, later, local elections. The new rules clearly favoured those political institutions that were prepared to play by the rules, whether nationalist, Islamist or Berberist. Those that refused were liable to be dissolved, and this happened to several of them.

On 16 November 1995 Lamine Zeroual won Algeria's first free presidential election. Never before had the Algerian people chosen their own head of state in an election remarkable for the apparent lack of interference or fraud by the state or any of its constituents. Zeroual won 61.34 per cent of the vote, while his nearest challenger, the moderate Islamist Sheikh Mahfoudh Nahnah,

attracted a respectable 25.38 per cent. The secularist Said
Saadi won only 9.9 per cent and the Islamic liberal
Nourredine Boukrouh a tiny 3.78 per cent. Even allowing
for some degree of electoral irregularity, the turnout of
74.92 per cent represented a major success for Zeroual's
programme to resolve Algeria's multiple crises – first to
elect a president and then move downwards through the
political system by organising parliamentary elections
and, finally, elections to provincial and municipal assemblies. This was the direct opposite of President Chadli
Bendjedid's plan that went so awry in 1992.

All political players interpreted the election results in
their own image. The moderate majority claimed Zeroual's victory as proof that the Algerian people had
rejected both the Islamist and secularist extremes that
bedevilled the country's politics. The secularists, for their
part, claimed the polls showed that Algerians had turned
their backs on the militant Islamist message expounded
by the FIS in the campaign for the annulled parliamentary
elections of 1991. This analysis was to a large extent
borne out by the very respectable share of the vote
obtained by Nahnah. Although an Islamist, his position
fell way short of the radical programme expounded by
the FIS. As with most things in Algeria, the truth is to be
found somewhere amidst all these interpretations.

The elections marked an important change in the
country's perception of itself and of its government. For
the first time, the head of state enjoyed a measure of
popular legitimacy, in many ways more than that claimed
by the Ben Bella and Boumedienne regimes. This was to a
large extent what the military establishment (*'le pouvoir'*)
had planned.

Despite the indications to the contrary, the military
conclave remained as powerful as ever. The principal
change wrought by the elections lay in the military's
willingness to exploit the constitutional process rather
than resist or, as in 1992, overturn it. The military
decided to support Zeroual as their candidate, even
though the former prime minister Redha Malek, who had
also announced his candidacy, more exactly represented
the interests of its senior members. As such, the military's

decision, which by all accounts was reached by consultation among senior officers, marked an important stage in that institution's conversion to democracy.

Two years later the situation had further evolved in favour of Zeroual and his advisers. On 5 June 1997 Algeria organised its first-ever multi-party parliamentary elections, the first occasion that the country had completed a full electoral process, and only the third Arab country to do so (after Jordan and Yemen). As expected, the pro-government Rassemblement National Démocratique (RND), which had been hastily formed only four months previously as a new vehicle for the various nationalist forces, won the largest share of the vote (33 per cent). The two next largest parties were the Mouvement pour la Société de la Paix (MSP, the new name for Hamas[2] required under the constitutional changes of 1996) and the FLN. Later that month Zeroual's prime minister, his long-term advisor Ahmed Ouyahis, announced the formation of a coalition government made up of his own RND, the MSP and the FLN.

Even though the new government was restricted by constitutional constraints, it was in a position to play a constructive role, albeit on Zeroual's terms. The seven cabinet seats allocated to the MSP and the FLN were all minor, and included several that were clearly 'poisoned chalices'. The FLN controlled housing: Algeria's chronic housing shortage is one of the main causes of the country's social and political crises.

The élite's commitment to democracy was of course suspicious. There was almost certainly some degree of fraud, largely in the form of the military stuffing ballot boxes with RND papers or 'losing' full ballot boxes in areas where the RND was likely to lose. Many observers were surprised by the implausibly low votes recorded for the MSP, Ennahda, the FSS and RCD, though the FLN may also have suffered. But despite the instances of fraud, there is no doubt that the RND genuinely won the largest

---

[2] A moderate Algerian party unconnected with the hardline Palestinian organisation of the same name.

number of votes. For whatever reason the party's pro-government, anti-Islamist stance struck a chord with the majority of Algerians, in both the relatively sophisticated capital, Algiers, and in rural areas. The RND's successful usurpation of the FLN as the main 'nationalist' party goes some way to explain its success in small towns and rural areas beyond Berber-dominated Kabylia.

RESULTS OF THE PARLIAMENTARY ELECTION JUNE 1997

Party	Seats	Share of vote %
PRO-REGIME PARTIES		
National Democratic Rally (RND)	155	33
National Liberation Front (FLN)	64	14
Independents	11	4
Others	3	5
ISLAMIST PARTIES		
Movement for a Peaceful Society (MSP)	69	14
Ennahda	34	8
BERBERIST PARTIES		
Socialist Forces Front (FFS)	19	5
Rally for Culture and Democracy (RCD)	19	4
TURNOUT	65%	

Across the country it was clear that the marginalised sections of society – primarily the young and the unemployed – abstained, as no party appealed to them. Such people seemed highly disillusioned with the regime, the state and the social order, all of which were oiled by patronage and nepotism. It was the rejection of this system that largely explains the success of the FIS in 1991, rather than the widespread genuine popularity of Islamic fundamentalism. Changes in the political landscape since then diverted much of this protest vote to the MSP and Ennahda, though it was by no means clear that the FIS would have attracted anything near the same level of support in 1997 as it did in 1991.

6

THE POLITICAL LANDSCAPE

From 1962 until 1988 the Algerian state rested on three separate yet interdependent elements: the army, the party and the state. Heads of state and the three elements all derived their legitimacy from their involvement in the Algerian war of independence and few Algerians questioned the right of the former *mudjahidine* to rule. The nationwide uprising of October 1988 drastically altered this situation. The interplay between President Chadli Bendjedid, the newly enfranchised political parties and the army shaped political life until June 1991, when the army returned to the front of the political stage. The elections of December 1991 for the first time transferred legitimacy from the army and the state to the political parties. Chadli's resignation in January 1992 established a new disorder that pitted the army, the government and its tiny band of political supporters against the now democratically legitimised parties, both the Islamists and the so-called 'democrats'.

The turmoil set in motion by the events of October 1988 highlighted the factionalism and clientelism that had underlain Algerian history since independence. These processes were played out on a bewildering number of levels – geographical, experiential, institutional, ethnic, historical, linguistic and familial, though the Algerian landscape was not static and the characteristics and composition of these factions were subject to constant change. The differences between the various factions and groupings were by no means purely ideological, though the identity of the Algerian state has remained a defining ideological issue throughout the history of independent

Algeria. The impact of this on Algerian political life cannot be underestimated: every regime was obliged to seek and establish a consensus between the various factions, or at least with the most powerful at the time, in order to carry through any important policy decision and claim legitimacy. The key importance of consensus in Algerian politics underlines the primacy of collectivism in the system, and the two leaders who attempted to ignore this reality – Ben Bella and Chadli Bendjedid – owed their downfall to it. Similarly, the governments of the post-Chadli crisis were unable to end the Islamic extremist insurgency due to their failure to obtain consensus from the various political entities that had won most votes in the December 1991 polls. The Algerian experience is all the more unique for the relative lack of class structure and tensions. The 'nation' was born out of the experience of 132 years of French colonisation and eight years of civil war. Although pre-existing élites had survived, their social importance was massively diluted and a vigorous egalitarianism took its place, though this became increasingly tarnished over the thirty years following independence.

Clans and factions are often formed among figures sharing a common geographical origin. The inhabitants of Algeria's various Berber regions retain more or less separate linguistic and cultural characteristics that distinguish them from the Arabised majority, and this has clearly created closely-knit Kabyle, Chaouia or M'zabite clans within, among other areas, politics, commerce and the media, though of course there are numerous instances of Kabyles integrating themselves into the majority. Traditionally, the majority of notables in political life have originated from the famous TBS (Tébessa-Batna-Skikda) Triangle in north-east Algeria. Louis Blin demonstrates that in 1991 36 per cent of political leaders and 32 per cent of leaders of parties other than the FLN originated from the TBS Triangle. The second most important area, in proportion to its population, was Kabylia, with the south and High Plateaux region third. It is interesting to note that those individuals who have come into greatest conflict with the dominant authority have tended to be

'outsiders': Ben Bella was a native of Tlemcen, Chadli
Bendjedid was born in Annaba, and Ali Belhadj was born
in Tunisia into a southern Algerian family. Regionalism in
the formation of the élites also reflects regional rivalries
and differences that emerged in the war of independence
and persisted into the 1990s: easterners and Kabyles, who
inhabit rugged upland areas, traditionally accuse the
originally agrarian westerners of not pulling their weight
during the war against the French. Indeed, FLN regimes
always regarded Algiers, as the prime centre of European
colonisation, with suspicion.

However, the importance of egalitarianism has tempered the significance of geographical origin in Algerian
society. The massive displacement caused by the French
occupation and the subsequent eight-year war of independence meant that Algeria in 1962 was in many
respects a new country. Although pre-existing regional
and tribal divisions remained vigorous, the Algerian
Muslim population was by and large equal. Despite the
privileges afforded to the various élites, the educational,
social, housing and welfare opportunities open to the vast
majority of the population were, at least in the 1970s,
considerably better in Algeria than in many other
comparable developing countries. Thus, attempts to
undermine, subvert or devalue this achievement – for
example the handing out of privileges to army officers
and FLN party cadres in the 1980s – were bound to incur
bitter resentment from the masses. This was one of the
principal factors behind the October 1988 riots. Until the
late 1980s membership of the FLN, albeit merely nominal
in many cases, or a military background were the two
essentials for entry into the ruling class. From the mid-
1960s onwards this first category increasingly included
well-educated technocrats, often relatively young men,
appointed to run government departments and public
sector corporations such as Sonatrach.

Government in Algeria tends to be collectivist: the
uncontested authoritarian rule of one man has been the
exception rather than the norm. Boumedienne was
obliged to rule through a Revolutionary Command
Council and relied initially upon the Oujda clan; Chadli

depended on the support of his presidential circle; and the military leaders of the post-Chadli period established the collective HCE to rule for them. One influence that explains this phenomenon is the traditional Kabyle *djamaa*, or village council. Although such councils have been an important component of most villages and small towns throughout the uplands inhabited by the Arabised tribes (*al-qbail*), it is among the settled hill people of Kabylia that the system retains most of its traditional vigour and relevance to daily life. The essential function of the *djamaa* is to legitimise the decision of the collective leadership, whether that of a village, a tribe, a clan, an interest group, a town or even a nation-state. In Algeria, there are *djamaa'at* at all levels and in all sections of society: in the former monolithic structure of the FLN; in the FIS; in the armed forces; and in the government. The HCE was the most striking example of a functioning *djamaa* in the post-Chadli era as its express purpose was to legitimise the military-backed regimes that assumed power to replace Chadli Bendjedid.

Houari Boumedienne was the most successful of all Algerian heads in navigating among Algerian factions. Even though he repeated and elaborated on many of the mistakes of his predecessor Ben Bella, particularly in the area of state control over freedom of expression he benefited by manipulating their interaction, skilfully strengthening his own position and authority while allowing himself to depend on no one. Factions within the armed forces were usually formed by common regional origin or loyalty to a particular patron-commander, the best example being the Oujda clan on whom Boumedienne depended from 1963 to the early 1970s. He established strong patron-client relations with key officers who saw in him the best protector of their own interests and this allowed him to establish his own personal control of the armed forces while at the same time neutralising possible opposition among senior officers who could have been tempted to imitate his own coup d'état in 1965. After Mahmoud Guennez, the leader of Ben Bella's Militia Populaire, attempted a coup in December 1967, Boumedienne abolished the general staff and created the Sécurité

Militaire under a Kabyle clique headed by Kasdi Merbah to intimidate ambitious officers as well as civilians.

The collectivist structure of the Boumedienne regime absorbed many of the ideological and factional disputes played out away from the public eye and resulted in a high degree of apparent unanimity in decision-making. During the first phase of his rule, from 1965 to 1971, Boumedienne appointed members of the Oujda clan to key positions within the government: Ahmed Kaid oversaw the development of the FLN and the disciplining of the powerful UGTA and student union; Cherif Belkacem was appointed minister without portfolio; and Mohamed Tayebi Larbi was appointed minister of agriculture. However, during the second phase of the Boumedienne era, in 1971-8, an informal alliance of the Oujda clan and a new generation of well-educated young technocrats who had been only marginally involved in the war of independence, such as Sid Ahmed Ghozali, shaped government policy and direction. It was during this time that Boumedienne adopted a more circumspect attitude towards the clan and gradually marginalised and removed them one by one.

Chadli Bendjedid relied upon factions as much as Boumedienne but was markedly less successful in achieving consensus. By the middle of the 1980s rapid demographic and social change was hastening the demise of the uneasy balance between army, party and state. By 1985 the groupings of the Algerian political landscape were becoming clearer: reformists, centred around Chadli's presidential circle; the 'old guard' of conservative military officers and FLN figures; the Islamists present in the mosques and universities; and Berber activists who had resumed their campaign in the Tizi Ouzou Spring of 1980.

The war of independence no longer conferred sufficient legitimacy on the army, party and state by the time of the riots of October 1988. From that moment, the three elements could no longer derive their nationalist legitimacy from their involvement in the war of independence or their conservative religious legitimacy from their strategic alliance with the religious establishment, away from whom they had already begun to drift in the late 1970s. The cleavage between the state and the Berber minority, a group effectively neutralised by Boumedienne, had also widened following the development of Berber activism after 1980. Chadli's decision to opt for political pluralism as a means of restoring the regime's legitimacy resulted in the formation of almost sixty political parties between 1989 and 1992. The regulations governing the formation of parties encouraged a plethora of organisations appealing to similar or identical constituencies, and many parties had but a handful of supporters. Many parties were bogus, established by shadowy elements within the regime or its organs and with no civilian support. Others were merely political pressure groups designed to further the interests of a very small clan or faction.

There were at least six principal political categories or groupings in the Algerian political order after Chadli: the state, comprising the army and the state apparatus; the illegal Islamist tendency, the FIS and the GIA; the legal Islamist parties, the AIS, the MSP (ex-Hamas) and Ennahda; the long-established nationalist institutions, the FLN, the UGTA and the ONM; the Berberist elements, the FFS and the RCD; and the inconsequential Marxist tendency, the former communist Ettahadi and the minute PT. The establishment in 1997 of a new force, the Rassemblement National Démocratique (RND), at the instigation of Zeroual and his supporters, cut into the support of the FLN and other nationalist forces, as demonstrated by its victory in the June 1997 parliamentary elections. We have seen how conflicting conceptions of Algeria's identity – Arab, Berber, Islamic, modern – had dominated the country's politics since before independence. Under Ben Bella, Boumedienne and Chadli the state designated itself Arab and Islamic while it borrowed heavily on foreign models, both European and Arab, for economic, political, social and cultural development. This compromise ignored the aspirations of the vast majority of Algerians who felt as alienated from the westernised culture of the *francisants* as from the unfamiliar fundamentalism of the Islamists. It also overlooked the particularities of the Berber minority. Thus the central ideological issue underlying Algerian politics throughout the years of the post-Chadli crisis remained unchanged, while the issue of the re-legalisation of the FIS and its readmission into the constitutional process provided the immediate question at issue, at least until the elections of 1997.

The Army

Ultimate authority and real power in Algeria have resided in the armed forces since the departure of the French in 1962. Notwithstanding a weakening of its influence during the Ben Bella era, the army has more or less directed the government ever since. The armed forces obtain their legitimacy from the systematically mythologised role of the ALN during the liberation war and perceive themselves as the true guarantor of the principles and aspirations of the Algerian 'revolution' and statehood, vigorously promoting the idea among the population at large. This process of mythologisation continued with the short frontier war with Morocco in 1963, in which the army 'proved' its ability to defend Algeria's borders against an historic foe, and was sustained through Boumedienne's coup of 1965 and the 'great leaps forward' between 1965 and 1978. The army reaffirmed this myth during the early years of Chadli's presidency but by 1991 very few Algerians subscribed to it.

The senior officer ranks of the armed forces generally adhered to the broad developmental principles that found their greatest expression during the Boumedienne era: Arab unity and the resurrection or reimposition of Algerian Arabo-Islamic culture ('Algerianisation'). Where in the 1970s this also implied broad support for the government's étatist and socialist policies, at least some elements of the officer class began to recognise the need for some degree of a free market economy in the 1980s. Moreover, the officer class saw no contradition in its adherence to the Arabo-Islamic elements of Algerianisation and its tendency to reject the radical Islamist policies of the FIS. The military has sat at the apex of Algerian political culture since 1965, and Islamists represent an explicit challenge to this situation.

The army is the largest and most coherent organisation in Algeria. The Armée Nationale Populaire (ANP) in the mid-1990s was the largest in the Maghreb and one of the most powerful in the Arab world. In 1995 it comprised 138,000 men, of whom 70,000 were conscripts on eighteen-month service, including 5,500 in the navy, 12,000 in the air force, and 23,000 gendarmes. Although its original primary task was the defence of the republic – 'to participate in the development of the country and the building of socialism' – its members have frequently been called upon to restore order and take part in public sector construction work. In addition, in 1995 the interior ministry controlled a gendarmerie force 23,000 strong, which used mainly French equipment. The regular army of 120,000 men was divided into twenty brigades; two units of around 15,000 men specialised in the mainte-nance of public order. Despite the existence of informal internal sub-groupings, the ANP is one of the few institu-tions in Algeria –perhaps the only one – that transcends regional, ethnic and factional differences. Together with the FLN of 1962-89 the ANP considers itself as the embodiment of the Algerian state. Even in the 1990s, the status of having been a *moudjahid* conferred social as well as political kudos, particularly among the older genera-tion, though it also makes the holder a target for assassi-nation.

The ANP's officer class is well trained and enjoys a privileged lifestyle closed to most Algerians. Initially, army officers were drawn entirely from the wartime ALN but by the late 1970s a younger, technocratic officer class was taking their place. Many of them were trained in France, the Soviet Union and even the United States. There are also a number of military academies inside Algeria, the most prestigious of which is in a former French officer school at Cherchell. Here cadets undergo rigorous training regimes in an environment of privilege and relative comfort. In particular, there are impressive sports facilities unmatched in civilian educational institutions such as universities. Since the mid 1960s this training process created a coherent officer class which felt itself removed from the masses it professed loyally to defend. Officers benefit from subsidised housing, schooling and welfare provision, and from the late 1960s its senior members have been placed in every major political and administrative entity in the country. Under Chadli the government created the 'anti-poverty programmes' (*programmes anti-pénuries*, PAP) that channelled desirable real estate to army officers at very low prices, while luxury villas were granted to senior officers. Clientelism was rife among army officers, with *wilaya* commanders wielding a disproportionate amount of power, and officer cliques clustering around figures such as Nezzar, Lamari and Zeroual. For the rank and file, conditions were not so favourable. Training in even basic soldiering was poor; living conditions – particularly in the desert – were often deplorable; and the vast majority of conscripts looked on their experience in the army as one to forget. This situation worsened immeasurably amid the terrorism of the post-Chadli crisis: most superior officers, while they took refuge in 'bunkers', left lower-ranking officers exposed to terrorist attack.

After independence the ANP developed first into a modern professional army and then, encouraged by Boumedienne, became increasingly involved in politics. Its transformation from an informal liberation militia into a powerful political force had almost been completed by the early 1970s, as Boumedienne undermined the disproportionate influence of the wartime *wilaya* commanders and increased central control over the armed forces. Both Ben Bella and Boumediene turned to Egypt and the Soviet Union for assistance, loans and equipment, though France continued to provide military advisers and retained use of the strategic Mers el-Kebir naval base. However, at least 90 per cent of the Algerian army had been equipped from Soviet sources by 1972. The process of rationalisation of the ANP continued through the 1970s, as the younger generation of officers, who had been trained in the Soviet Union or other communist states, became increasingly involved in the government's political and legislative processes. As Hugh Roberts remarks, the ANP's newspaper, *el-Djeich*, controlled by these leftist younger officers, serves as a useful barometer of government thinking throughout the period.[1] The climate for the longer-established military commanders, however, was less favourable: although all were nationalists, few entertained genuine leftist leanings. This led to upheavals within the inner military élite in 1974, after which Boumedienne accelerated the gradual process of replacing conservative commanders with younger officers. This culminated in the marginalisation and removal of most of the Oujda clan who remained at the time of Boumedienne's death in 1978.

Despite the military's role in his own political career, Chadli tried to depoliticise the ANP during his thirteen years in power. Early in his presidency he confounded those who considered him to be no threat to the privileges of the military élite when he reshuffled the commanders of the five military regions and re-established the general staff. These moves were later interpreted as evidence of the Chadli regime's essential conservatism since it was the most politically active officers who suffered most in the reshuffle. Instead, Chadli encouraged and promoted the less overtly political generation of younger officers who had been trained in France or the Soviet Union, and who, unlike the left-leaning generation of the early 1970s, favoured the concept of an army loyal to the institutions of a republic. Among these young officers were the senior figures who were directly involved in the coups of June 1991 and January 1992: Khaled Nezzar, Abdelmalek Guenaïzia, Lamine Zeroual, Mohamed Lamari, M'Hamed Touati and Mohamed 'Tawfik' Mediène.

The riots of October 1988 destroyed popular respect for the army and led to its temporary withdrawal from the centre of government. When Chadli called in the troops to 'avoid a catastrophe' – no less than the survival

---

[1] See H. Roberts, 'The Politics of Algerian Socialism' in R. Lawless and A. Findlay (eds), *North Africa: Contemporary Politics and Economic Development*, New York: St Martin's Press, 1984.

of the régime – the army took the full force of years of the population's pent-up anger and frustration aimed at the state, the FLN and the ruling élite. Confronted with soldiers firing on unarmed protesters and against a background of widespread torture of detainees, the symbiosis between senior ANP members and the state made the two indistinguishable in the eyes of ordinary Algerians. The regime had used the army to suppress a popular revolt for the first time in the history of independent Algeria, and in the process some 500 people had been killed. This irredeemably sullied the myth of the ANP as the heir to the glorious wartime ALN in the minds of Algerians and set in train a series of events that culminated in the withdrawal of senior army officers from the FLN's central committee in the rapid democratisation of 1989. According to the new constitution of that year the army's mission was to 'safeguard national independence and sovereignty...and to defend the unity and integrity of the country'. In following months the army remained silent as the government organised the municipal and provincial elections of 1990 and began to prepare for parliamentary polls. In June 1990 Chadli appointed the reform-minded chief of staff Khaled Nezzar as minister of defence, an office that had been held by the president since 1965. This was intended to underline the separation of the armed forces from the state.

However, the army did not remain separate from politics for long. Nezzar and his supporters among the military élite considered the legalisation of an Islamist party to be a grave error. When the government called in the army to restore order in June 1991, Nezzar took the opportunity to reinforce its self-appointed role as the last defence against the Islamist threat and to protest against what he perceived as the 'laxity, liberalism and political games' of the Hamrouche government by ordering Chadli to declare a state of siege, dismiss Hamrouche and arrest Abassi and Belhadj. June 1991 marked the beginning of the rupture between Chadli and Nezzar, and relations worsened throughout the remainder of that year. In late December senior officers panicked over the

likelihood of a FIS majority in Parliament and the
prospect of Chadli being obliged to strike deals with a FIS
government over constitutional changes or the army's
privileged position. During January 1992 the army forced
Chadli to resign, established an unconstitutional junta in
his place, overturned the democratically-expressed
wishes of the Algerian people and ensured its control of a
puppet 'collective presidency', the HCE. Using Article 11
of the state of siege, the army interned thousands of FIS
activists and reasserted state control over democratically-
elected FIS-run local authorities by dismissing the party's
elected officials. The only move not entirely to its own
advantage was the choice of Mohamed Boudiaf to chair
the HCE, a figure who, unfortunately for the army,
proved far too ambitious in his plans for Algeria, making
the involvement of senior army officers in his assassination highly probable. The army, after all, had intended the
intervention to be an unequivocal and public statement of
its opposition to the FIS and its ideology.

The failure of Chadli's experiment with democratisation
led to the return of the military's direct influence over and
participation in government. Nezzar retained the office of
minister of defence as well as a seat on the HCE and
pursued a policy of 'divide and rule' over the disoriented
political establishment, the state apparatus and the
marginalised Islamist tendency. The HCE in August 1992
passed legislation allowing the army latitude to deal with
'insurgents' and 'terrorists'; the balaclava-helmet-wearing
Ninjas (special interior ministry forces) first appearing in
the autumn of that year. In October 1992 Nezzar
appointed a group of relatively young 'eradicator'
generals to spearhead the anti-terrorist operations, most
notable among whom was the commander of the land
forces, Mohamed Lamari. There were further reorganisations within the top echelons of the military
establishment in the spring and summer of 1993. General
Nezzar, who had suffered from multiple illness since at
least 1990, resigned from his post as defence minister in
July 1993 but retained his position on the HCE; Lamari
supplanted Major-General Guenaïzia as chief of staff. It is

ironic that Chadli's attempts to reverse a central feature of the Boumedienne regime, the military's involvement in government, led to its wholesale revival.

Lamine Zeroual's appointment to the defence ministry was an attempt to balance the strengths of the two main clienteles at the top of the armed forces, the older, more Europeanised officers and their younger, more 'Algerianised' counterparts. The older generation, clustered around generals such as Khaled Nezzar and Mohamed Lamari, conceived of an Algeria forged from a contradictory mixture of Boumediennism, European liberalism, socialism and Arab nationalism. Most had spent long periods training in France, the Soviet Union or other Arab countries; some had come to the ALN late in the war from the French army. Many had earned reputations for corruption and sanctioning brutality and torture. Zeroual, on the other hand, was chosen precisely because he was untainted by any of these charges, at least in the eyes of the public. He had joined the FLN as a young man and resigned from Chadli's general staff in protest at plans to remodernise the armed forces along French lines, and thus his *arabisant* credentials were impeccable. Although the decision to appoint him to the presidency in January 1994 appears to have been unplanned and a stop-gap measure, it was a clear compromise to the 'conciliators' on the part of Lamari and the 'eradicators'.

The post-Chadli crisis signalled the end of the myth of the army as the vessel of popular sovereignty in Algeria. From 1962 until 1989 the army derived its legitimacy from its organic link to the single ruling political institution, the FLN, but the separation of the ALN from the FLN in 1989 cut the army adrift from the state and the source of that legitimacy. At the same time the senior generation of army officers had ceased to be focused on a core of former *mudjahidine*, with a new professionally-trained élite taking their place. Many of this new generation – President Zeroual, for instance – were less politically dogmatic than their predecessors and more in tune with the middle echelon of the armed forces which adopted a middle ground between the two extremes of the hardline Islamists and the hardline secularists. In addition, the war of independence had ceased to have any real meaning for the youthful majority of the population. The crisis also highlighted the inefficiency and overbearing bureaucracy within the army. Poorly trained, equipped and commanded, the rank and file suffered a high casualty rate that must in part be attributed to bad command and strategy. Company commanders were obliged to refer all strategic decisions to the military hierarchy who vaguely spoke of *tout sécuritaire* policies (hardline security, regardless of the political consequences) without elaborating on strategic details.

Mention must be made of the more covert aspects of this *tout sécuritaire* policy. Trained by Algeria's former friends in Eastern Europe, organs such as the Sécurité Militaire (SM) earned a justified reputation under Boumedienne and Chadli as a ruthlessly efficient military intelligence agency identifying and pursuing dissidents inside and outside the regime. Even allowing for the Algerian's predilection for rumour and conspiracy-theorising, the SM is very likely to have been involved in covert activities in the early and mid-1990s, including the infiltration of its own or other agents into the various terrorist groups, notably the GIA, with the objective of providing valuable information on the their respective capabilities. Many believe, moreover, that the SM actually organised the formation of certain GIA *katibat* (cells) and helped carry out some of the more spectacular terrorist incidents, the aim being to generate public revulsion against the GIA, and by extension the entire illegal Islamist movement, and thus rally popular support for the state.

Although it is impossible to prove such allegations, the history of covert infiltration by *agents provocateurs* during the war of independence and the subsequent factionalism within the military establishment lend them credence. Moreover, the state's tight control of all reporting of terrorism against the security forces led many Algerians to look upon apparent claims of responsibility from the GIA or, more rarely, the AIS with suspicion, speculating instead who, or which faction, stood to benefit from the reaction to a particular terrorist incident. As might be expected, the enemies of the *Hizb Fransa* would routinely accuse France – its government, presidency or intelligence agencies – of covertly assisting its allies within the Algerian military, pointing out that the GIA's 'communiqués' always appeared to be issued in France. This speculation also extended to the dismissals, retirements and deaths of senior army officers as signalling the balance of power between the various clans and groups within the military heirarchy.

There was, however, a qualified change in the popular perception of the military after the presidential elections of November 1995. For three years the principal thrust of the military's strategy had been perceived as the the eradication of the 'terrorist threat', thus involving the torture of thousands and the summary execution of hundreds suspected of assisting it, earning the army, gendarmerie and associated organs a reputation more brutal than the Islamists. However, Zeroual's primary objective in November 1995 was for the state to regain much of the legitimacy that it had lost in the previous ten years. The plain fact of the organic connection between the state and the military meant that this regained legitimacy inevitably attached itself to the military. Whether Zeroual had worked with or without the explicit endorsement of the Lamari clan, the military and the government pointed to the elections as vindication of their *tout sécuritaire* policies and proof of the public's rallying to the nationalist and qualified secularist traditions of the state and its rejection of the radical Islamist movement. Furthermore, the war against insurgency derived continuing legitimacy from the security situation: although numerically superior, the security forces could never completely eradicate the AIS *maquis* groups who exploited the remote terrain of the Atlas mountains in the same way as the FLN had operated against the French in the war of independence.

However, the elections did not, of course, constitute any real change in the relationship between the military, the state and the governed. The senior echelons of the military remained determined to preserve their ideological vision of the Algerian republic and to protect the considerable economic privileges enjoyed by themselves and their families and associates. This was facilitated by the person of Zeroual, who although retired from the military, remained fully aware of the limitations placed upon his freedom of manoeuvre and of the approach required to prevent its hostility. Essentially this meant that the military would only countenance constitutional changes designed to guarantee its role as ultimate power and to divide rather than empower the opposition.

The FLN

Until 1991 the FLN was never a political party in the sense understood in the West or the former communist world. It was an institution intended to function as the source of political legitimacy for a military-based regime, a springboard for the ambitious, and a form of social security for those out of favour. Successive Algerian regimes used the FLN for different purposes: Ben Bella intended it as a rubber-stamp institution to underpin his personal power at the expense of his opponents; Boumedienne saw it as an engine for national politicisation; and Chadli attempted to neuter it and transform it into just one of many political parties, but one on which his own presidential legitimacy would rest. The FLN of the post-Chadli crisis bore little relation to its predecessors, which to many Algerians continued to embody the spirit, dreams and achievements of an independent Algeria. The party's decisive defeats in June 1990 and December 1991 unequivocally signalled the end of that special position.

Ben Bella wanted the FLN to serve his personal interests rather than those of Algeria; his primary objective was to create a cohesive political party to accommodate the many political and military factions that had emerged during the war and, perhaps more important, to inhibit the development of an active opposition. The rigours of war had reduced the FLN to the twin pillars of the Political Bureau and the ANP, and its alliance with the ALN was unstable. The strengthening of the FLN's party

structure, however, remained very much subordinate to
the establishment of Ben Bella's personal authority. As
Henry Jackson remarks, 'Instead of building the party
from the base upwards, he decided to organise it from the
top down.'[2]

While the party's first secretary-general after 1962,
Mohamed Khider, favoured a multi-party system, his
alliance with the powerful UGTA in November 1962
illustrated his intention that the FLN should be the
supreme political organ in the state and thus undermine
the personal power of Ben Bella. However, after Ben Bella
assumed Khider's post in April 1993, the president was
able to promulgate a constitution that granted sweeping
powers to himself and designated the president of the
assembly number-two in the state. Although several
articles of the constitution defined the FLN as the sole
permitted party, in practice its policy-making powers
were minimal compared to those of the executive,
particularly the president. Furthermore, the membership
of the party had contracted to former wartime FLN
mudjahidine who were unwilling to accept or deemed
unsuitable for powerful appointments within the expanding administration.

The Boumedienne regime initially used the FLN as a
source of political legitimacy and a nursery for bureaucrats. From 1965 to 1977 the regime concentrated on the
process of building, expanding and strengthening the state
and mobilising the masses, and the secondary attention
paid to the FLN as a political organisation left the party
weak and of no direct consequence. The FLN provided a
vehicle for career advancement that the young and
ambitious were expected to join, and its members rarely
paid more than lip-service to its professed socialist
orientation. While the party acted as the symbol of
Algerian nationhood and the self-styled source of the
regime's legitimacy, political debate and decision-making
were in reality confined to the ranks of the bureaucracy
and the military. As Clement Henry Moore has re-

[2] Henry Jackson, *The FLN in Algeria: Party and Development in a
Revolutionary Society,* Westport, CTO Greenwood Press, 1977.

marked: 'Sociologically, the FLN resembled a political club more than a Leninist party; politically, however, it was supposed to exercise a Leninist hegemony over state and society.' Far from being a homogeneous political party, the FLN brought together numerous interest groups whose interaction constituted its internal activity. This state of affairs served the regime's purposes, and its half-hearted efforts to relaunch the party were almost bound to fail: the 'Year of the Party' (in 1968) and internal reorganisations in the early 1970s amounted to very little. No party congress was held in 1963-78; its organisational structures remained illogical and without real power. From 1967 to 1977 the FLN's function was largely confined to nominating candidates for communal, *wilaya* and Assembly elections and electing the President. In 1977 it was exceptionally allowed to nominate three candidates for each Assembly constituency.

However, Boumedienne did make genuine attempts to transform the FLN into a more effective arena for political mobilisation in the mid-1970s. The reasons for this were closely linked to the regime's commitment to its agrarian reform programme launched in 1971. Boumedienne wanted the FLN to function as the 'natural' engine for the propagation, organisation and execution of the plan, though its unsuitability for the task obliged him at first to turn to other mass organisations such as the UGTA, the Union Nationale des Femmes Algériennes (UNFA) and student associations as the vanguard of the agrarian reform programme and bring in the FLN later. As Hugh Roberts remarks, Boumedienne hoped that 'the struggle to secure [the programme's] implementation itself would lead to the emergence of a new generation of committed socialists from whom the cadres of a reformed party could eventually be recruited.'[3] However, Boumedienne did not feel able to initiate preparations for the FLN's first party congress until 1977, a full six years after the launch of the programme. The congress was to be the climax to a co-ordinated campaign to institutionalise Boumedienne's revolution and the conclusion of a series

[3] H. Roberts, 'The Politics of Algerian Socialism'.

of congresses of lesser organisations such as the UGTA. Boumedienne planned a new role for the FLN as a genuine socialist party active at the centre of political life and government, an engine for mobilisation of the masses and control of the bureaucracy. To direct this transformation Boumedienne in October 1977 appointed as party co-ordinator a senior military officer, Mohamed Salah Yahiaoui, to replace Ahmed Kaid who had been eased out of the post in 1972. However, Boumedienne's death in 1978 prevented his ambitions from being realised: in the event the party congress, which eventually took place in early 1979, was the stage for the struggle for the presidency played out between Yahiaoui and Bouteflika and ultimately won by the army's candidate, Chadli Bendjedid.

After Boumedienne's death the FLN developed as the principal stage for the articulation of opposition to Chadli's efforts to consolidate his position and to introduce economic reform. Chadli attempted to prevent this through the systematic isolation and removal of potentially troublesome opponents from within the ranks of the party, and he engineered his own election to the newly revived post of party secretary-general to subvert Yahiaoui's influence. Many former ministers, including the arch-Boumediennist Belaïd Abdessalam, were appointed to minor party posts, underlining the secondary importance of the FLN. In 1980 Chadli further increased his control over the party by creating a new post of head of the central committee's permanent secretariat to replace the position of party co-ordinator. Mohamed Cherif Messadia was the first incumbent. Henceforth, the central committee functioned as a kind of national *djamaa*, providing an arena for debate but without the mandate of extending the FLN's party control over the bureaucracy as had been envisaged by Boumedienne. The number of members of the Political Bureau was cut from between 17 to 21 to between 7 and 11 and the frequency of meetings was reduced from every week to every month. Chadli also granted himself the right to appoint the Bureau's members instead of merely proposing them. In December 1983 the fifth FLN party

congress obediently re-elected Chadli as party secretary-
general.

After purging the executive and party of troublesome
elements, Chadli set about strenghtening the FLN as the
sole legal political organisation in Algeria. This required
the ending of the tolerance hitherto extended to the
PAGS but also to the Berberists and Islamic activists who
had recently stepped up their activities in a number of
towns and cities. Henceforth all officers of mass organisations such as the UGTA (some of whom had more or less
openly been members of the PAGS) were obliged to be
members of the FLN.

There was a steady decline in the party's influence in
virtually all areas except economic policy between 1980
and 1988. The political classes valued the FLN more for
what it represented than what it was able to deliver, and
this mythicised identity largely accounted for the party's
candidates winning more than 87 per cent of the vote in
Assembly elections in February 1987. However, the
government's decision in July 1987 to permit the formation of local organisations without the express consent of
the authorities (though bodies deemed to threaten
'national security' or the revised National Charter
remained banned) excited substantial opposition among
FLN 'hardline' conservatives within the Assembly on the
ground that it would encourage the establishment of
opposition political organisations. The enmity between
the FLN and Chadli deepened at the sixth party congress
in February 1988, with the result that some leading
members of the party, possibly in tandem with the PAGS,
prepared themselves to argue against the party's endorsement of Chadli's candidacy in the forthcoming
presidential elections scheduled for December 1988.
However, the October riots ended the FLN's growing
confidence, and one of the effects of the subsequent
political upheavals was to allow Chadli to increase his hold
over the party and purge it of some troublesome hardliners. The violence directed against FLN premises and
figures deeply disturbed the party and permanently
altered its perception of itself. The most notable features
of the sixth congress were the appointment of Abdel-

hamid Mehri as party secretary-general and the return to the political stage of a handful of political figures marginalised by Chadli in the early 1980s, principally Belaïd Abdessalam who went on to serve as prime minister in the HCE regime of 1992-3.

The FLN was officially stripped of its privileged constitutional status as the sole legal party in February 1989. Henceforth, it fought a rearguard battle against opponents who blamed it, often unfairly, for the decades of misrule conducted in its name by bureaucrats and army officers. Over the subsequent stormy months leading up to the events of January 1992 the FLN never succeeded in its aim of ensuring a genuine separation of itself from the state in the minds of the public, despite the series of resignations of government figures from the central commitee. Public frustration and anger at the perceived misdoings of the Chadli regime and the adverse effects of its economic policies were the two main factors behind the party's very poor performance in the June 1990 and December 1991 elections. However, the FLN did not go into terminal decline during the first years of the post Chadli crisis. Its double electoral disappointment represented the masses' rejection and repudiation of the FLN as the *de facto* state itself, but not necessarily as a party and the political traditions and myths that it represented and tried to embody. The party derived a significant degree of legitimacy from the fact that it received more than 23 per cent of the votes cast in December 1991 and repeatedly and robustly spoke out in defence of the 1989 democratic constitution. Moreover, it adopted 'reasonable' positions on the main questions of the crisis years: it repeatedly called for the re-legalisation of the FIS as a key condition for the relaunch of the democratisation process. It also adopted a middle position on the question of the religious content of the constitution, supporting neither an Islamic nor a secular republic.

In January 1995 the FLN was among the five signatories of the National Contract. In it the FLN for the first time explicitly recognised the separate existence of Berber culture and the need for the Algerian constitution to acknowledge Tamazigh as an official national language alongside Arabic, formally abandoning thirty years of dogged adherence to Arabism. This marked an important stage in the development of political pluralism in Algeria and the FLN's coming-of-age as a genuine political party, one that culminated in its entering a coalition with the RND and MSP in July 1997. At the time of writing the three broad strands of Algerian politics are represented by the RND and the FLN of the nationalists; the FIS of the Arabists; and the FFS and RCD of the Berbers.

7

ISLAMISM AND THE GROWTH
OF THE F.I.S.

The relationship between Islam and the state in Algeria is highly complex, and is crucial to an understanding of the country's political and social identities. Since its arrival in the seventh century, Islam has bound together the delicate mix of indigenous Berbers and the Arabised population. Islam was also a central element in the political crisis of the post-Chadli years. Although this appears to be an armed struggle between the religious and the secular, it is more a confrontation arising from conflicting interpretations of the position of Islam in the Algerian state and more particularly in the constitution. Most Algerians genuinely believe that Islam should be the main source of law, though not the only one. Those who believe that Islam should be the sole source of law are in a minority, as are those who favour a French-style secular state.

Islamism and Nationalism

The inhabitants of what is now Algeria have developed their own particular brand of Islam. In the Middle Ages local Berber dynasties adopted Shia Islam as a means of asserting their independence from the Arab east, while in the Ottoman period it was Islam that bound together the various local and immigrant groups. In the nineteenth and early twentieth centuries the French colonial authorities deliberately set out to undermine Islamic civilisation in Algeria and replace it with 'superior' French culture. The French converted many mosques into churches or cathedrals and confiscated millions of acres of *habous* lands. The resentment this caused contributed significantly to the evolution of nationalism and the ultimate expulsion of the colonisers. Although the French designated the majority of Muslim Algerians as second-class citizens, the strong Islamic base of Algerian society remained intact and even the small Europeanised Muslim community retained at least a nominal adherence to Islam. Even in Kabylia, where the colonial authorities established Christian schools, the traditional position of Islam remained unchanged. As during the preceding centuries, Islam was the strongest binding force in a highly heterogeneous country plagued by constant tribal and family feuding; under foreign, non-Muslim influence this became even more prevalent. In Algeria, as in most other states in the Arab world, Islam was the most important stimulus behind the growth of Arab nationalism, a process animated by the idea of *jihad* – holy war – to which the nationalist leaders of the wartime FLN frequently exhorted their followers.

The emergence of Arab nationalism coincided with the Islamic revival in the eastern Arab world at the end of the nineteenth century. At the vanguard of this revival were the Egyptians Jamal al-Din al-Afghani, Mohammed Abdouh, Rashid Rida and Sayyid Qutb. Al-Afghani in particular is credited with founding the Salafiyya (also known as the Salafi or Salafite) movement which exhorts a return to the 'pure' Islam of the first four caliphs following the death of the Prophet Mohamed in early seventh-century Arabia. Salafis believe that Muslims should take from Western civilisation only what conforms to the word of Allah as revealed in the Koran. Although contemporary Maghrebi Islamists generally admit that much of their thinking had been based on Salafi teaching, some, such as the Tunisian Rachid Ghannouchi, accuse them of making unacceptable concessions to Western concepts and thought. Other contemporary Islamists also feel that the Salafis are inherently opposed to Islamism, or political Islam.

A further explanation for the growth of Islamism in Algeria, as in other Muslim countries, is a theory articulated by François Burgat, who argues that the emergence and development of Islamist tendencies corresponds to a 'third stage' in decolonisation. Burgat's first stage is political independence and his second stage economic independence. Islamism, which he decribes as 'the rocket of the third stage', reflects the desire of a formerly colonised people to regain its cultural and ideological past that has been disastrously disrupted by foreign occupation. This is clearly true of Algeria which since the 1980s has been undergoing the transition from the second to the third stage. Political organisations such as the FLN and the FFS employed political and ideological vocabularies imported from the West, specifically France, whereas the Islamists articulated their policies in a more 'traditional' and 'authentic' terminology. In Algeria, where the question of identity is crucial, the Islamists considered themselves as the purveyors of national authenticity articulated in an indigenous vocabulary. They believe that this develops, rather than refutes, the nationalism of the wartime FLN. As is often said, '*le FIS est le fils du FLN*', 'FIS is the son of the FLN'.

The roots of modern Algerian Islamism can be traced to the activities of a group of reformist religious scholars in the first half of the twentieth century. The leader of the scholars (Arabic: *ulema*) was Sheikh Abdelhamid Ben Badis, who was born in 1889 into a leading pro-French family in Constantine and educated at the respected Zitouna University in Tunis. In 1924 Ben Badis founded the moderate nationalist journal *al-Mountaqid* (The Critic) along with a group of likeminded Muslim reformist scholars that included Sheikh Tayeb al-Oqbi, Mubarak al-Mili and Bachir al-Ibrahimi. Ben Badis founded a second periodical, *al-Shihab* (The Meteor), when the French authorities closed the first in 1926. In 1931 Ben Badis and his friends founded the Association of Reformist Ulema (ARU) in Constantine. The ARU's message was simple: it stressed the Muslim nature of Algeria and rejected the arguments put forward by some moderate Muslim nationalists that Muslim rights would be best safeguarded under continued but reformed French rule. The ARU also preached a return to the basic values of early Islam, condemning alcohol, tobacco and popular entertainment. The first government of independent Algeria ultimately adopted the ARU's famous creed, 'Islam is my religion, Arabic my language, and Algeria my country', as its motto. The association also vigorously attacked the marabouts and the *tariqat* for promoting superstition and obscurantism, and criticised the religious establishment for collaboration with the French authorities and promotion of traditional regional and religious rivalries. The reformists also established their own schools to teach classical Arabic and to disseminate the concepts of pan-Arabism and the idea of the independent 'nation' of Algeria. By 1954 the ARU claimed to have more than 10,000 members.

Although the ARU prepared the ground for the nationalists, initially it played little direct part in the independence struggle. The association's campaign against the tribal-based marabout system assisted in the development of the idea of a Muslim Algerian state that would transcend tribal and regional differences. In 1926 Ben Badis wrote in *al-Shihab*, 'We ...have searched in history and in the present, and we have discovered that the Algerian nation does exist...The Algerian nation is not France, cannot be France, does not want to be France.' However, although the organisation made a central contribution to the growth of the nationalist movement, it also delayed the religious revival in Algeria. In re-emphasising the classical Arabic language of the Koran, it promoted the influence of educated urban intellectuals over the illiterate rural population who turned instead towards the more secular-minded and vernacular nationalists. Although Islam remained a central rallying point during the war of independence and immediately after, reformist Islam was largely subordinate to Arab nationalism until the 1960s. The ARU did not ally itself to the FLN until the relatively late date of 1956. As Hugh Roberts remarks: 'In making the Islam of the Reformers its own, the FLN subordinated it to, and implicated it in, the construction of the Algerian nation state.'[1] Furthermore, it would be misleading to label the reformist *ulema* as Islamists in the sense understood in the 1990s. To them the purification of Islam and the raising of pan-Arab consciousness in Algeria far outweighed the temptation of becoming involved in mere politics.

The first governments of independent Algeria suppressed the reformist Islamic trend in favour of the left. Marabouts enjoyed a limited resurgence in some rural areas, but the regime curbed intellectuals and political activists who favoured recourse to Arabo-Islamic tradition as the basis of 'Algerian socialism'. The authorities also discouraged the teaching of Muslim studies at universities. A a prominent member of the FIS, Rachid Benaissa, recalls:

> We simply asked for a certificate of Islamic civilisation, not theology.... In 1964 I was threatened with a revolver for that. Another day, a motion was carried by a General Assembly of students which demanded that social sciences and exact sciences be studied 'in conformity to the Charter of Algiers and the recommendation of the secretary-general of the party, Ahmed Ben Bella'. I rose up and asked whether Ahmed Ben Bella understood the law of gravity... I left the room covered with blood. [1]

Instead, the regimes of Ben Bella and Boumedienne sought to create a compromise between Islam and socialism: 'Islamic socialism'. This owed little to either, and failed at both. Many writers have concluded that while the state and much of the population used traditional Islam as a common reference point during the first two decades of Algerian independence, the regime employed the Western ideology of socialism as the engine for rapid development. The secular left dominated policy-making until the early 1980s and this directly contributed to the development of radical Islamism in the 1980s.

---

[1] In 'Radical Islamism and the dilemma of Algerian nationalism: the embattled Arians of Algiers', *Third World Quarterly*, 10, no. 2 (April 1988).

[2] Quoted in F. Burgat, *L'islamisme au Maghreb*, Paris: Karthala, 1988.

However, Islamists were already organising in the early 1960s. Immediately after independence, some of their number decided to forge an independent path outside the emerging political centre. In 1964 al-Hachemi Tijani, Mohammed Khider and Malek Bennabi created an Islamic cultural association entitled *al-Qiyam* (Values) with the objective of proclaiming the supremacy of Islamic values over 'national-populism'. It also sought to respond to 'colonialism and decadence' and to call on the government to impose *sharia* (Islamic law). It was the first real manifestation of political Islam in post-independence Algeria. Tijani declared that his ideology had been shaped by study of the writings of the Salafis and of various contemporary and near-contemporary Islamist thinkers, such as the Lebanese Chakib Arslan, the Egyptians Hassan al-Banna (founder of the Muslim Brotherhood), Sayyid Qutb and Mohammed al-Ghazali, as well as the Pakistani Abu Ala Mawdudi. However, the members of *al-Qiyam* emphasised their exposure to French cultural and political traditions and vocabularies on the premise that those who have studied and digested non-Islamic thought are better qualified to criticise it than those who simply ignore it, such as the *ulema*. Bennabi, for instance, spent much time in France and wrote mainly in French. Ironically, strong connection with French culture tended to convince Bennabi's disciples that his works had a superior perspicacity that set them above his contemporaries. This phenomenon remained relevant in the post-Chadli crisis – many members of the FIS leadership had been educated in Western thought and science.

Al-Qiyam came into conflict with Ben Bella when it developed as an early channel for the articulation of public opposition to the authoritarian nature of his regime. The organisation promulgated the ideas of the Egyptian Islamists and called for the state to enforce Islamic customs, such as the closure of shops during the hours of prayer. Its supporters also occasionally mounted campaigns against 'immodestly dressed' women. More worrying to the regime, however, was its explicit denunciation as 'illegal and dangerous' of all non-Islamic political parties, regimes and leaders. Growing popular opposition to Ben Bella's orientation towards the 'atheistic' communist states, and the widely-held view among both the middle class and the religious establishment that the President paid inadequate attention to Islam, increased *al-Qiyam's* popularity. Ben Bella was unable to suppress the organisation and instead tried to undermine its support by adopting elements of its agenda, such as the introduction of religious education in schools. The President also perceived the *ulema* as an important threat and placed *ulema*-run *medresat* (Islamic colleges) under the control of the ministry of education. It is also very probable that Ben Bella would have moved to suppress *al-Qiyam* altogether had he not been removed by Boumedienne in June 1965.

The Islamists enjoyed something of a revival during the first phase of the Boumedienne regime. One of the Oujda clan's stated aims was to reduce the influence of the Marxists and redress the balance in favour of the Arabo-Islamic nationalists. With the removal of Ben Bella, the leading *ulema* hoped that the new regime's orientation would allow them to exert a greater influence over policy-making in the areas of religious affairs, education and the family. Boumedienne, who wished to derive some degree of religious legitimacy from the Islamists and who believed he could control them if he allowed them some leeway, to some extent encouraged this hope by appointing Ahmed Taleb Ibrahimi as minister of education and later of culture and information. Ibrahimi was the son of the former ARU president Sheikh Bachir Ibrahimi who had been placed under house arrest in 1963 for criticising Ben Bella's reliance of Western ideologies. In 1969 the regime began action to limit the activities of remaining Christian missionaries in Algeria and embarked upon a large-scale programme of mosque-building.

However, by the summer of 1966 an awareness of the potential threat posed by the Islamists such as *al-Qiyam* began to outweigh Boumedienne's keen advocacy of the restoration of the Algerian Muslim heritage. In September the authorities suppressed the association in the *wilaya* of Algiers, ostensibly for sending a protest to President Nasser over the hanging of the Muslim Brothers' leader,

Sayyed Qutb. The association was formally banned
nationally on 17 March 1970. A similar association,
Djounouds ('Soldiers of Allah'), was also suppressed.

The fissure between the Islamist movement and the
Boumedienne regime widened during its second phase
between 1971 and 1978. Although it would be misleading
to assert that the rise of Islamism in the 1980s was a
direct reaction to Boumedienne's socialist reforms, it was
during this period that the idea of an Arabo-Islamic, or
Islamist, alternative began to gain currency among the
regime's principal opponents, the disposessed landowners. In subsequent years, this alliance grew to encompass
many of those who felt the government had failed them
or who opposed the authoritarianism of the regime. Many
Algerians considered the *ulema* as the rightful defenders of
the traditional Islamic concept of the inviolability of
private property, and the agrarian revolution consequently increased support for them. As the state gradually
nationalised large estates owned by Muslims and replaced
them with collective farms, the *ulema* made an informal
alliance with the victims of the government's actions. The
opposition to the agrarian revolution consciously
employed a vocabulary that appealed to the religious
consciousness of the population; there were even
rumours circulating that prayers made on nationalised
land were not valid. The *ulema* became the unofficial
leaders of the non-political opposition as private donations for mosque-building and for religious associations
mounted. The Islamists also made capital out of the
regime's reorientation towards the left, which it criticised
as atheistic and alien to Algerian culture and tradition.

Ironically, Boumedienne's mobilisation of students
after October 1972 also contibuted to the rise of Islamism. In response to proposals from the students
themselves, Boumedienne in 1972 designated the
Volontariat des Étudiants pour la Révolution Agraire
(VERA) as the leader of the promotion of the agrarian
revolution. In the short term this new politicisation of
students strengthened the regime, but it also sowed the
seeds of a critical awareness among students that later
directly assisted the rise of radical Islam. In order to

convince sceptical peasants many students claimed that
the reforms were entirely consistent with the Islamic
tradition that forbids the 'unjust possession of another's
goods'. The advancement of the agrarian reforms
encouraged students critically to examine existing
structures, including the key institutions of the state itself.
Meanwhile, the politicisation encouraged conservative
students in their campaign for an acceleration of Arabisation; subsequent events amply demonstrated the short
step from Arabisation to Islamisation. However, some
observers have overstated the importance of *arabisant*
students in this movement. The enduring superiority of a
Francophone education meant that many ambitious
Francophones, whose careers were thwarted by lack of
opportunity, formed the embryo of the radical Islamic
tendency that evolved into the Islamist parties of the
1980s. Ironically, in the late 1960s and early 1970s,
francisants were more active Islamists than the *arabisants*.

In December 1974 tracts appeared on the streets of
Algiers calling for a constituent assembly and *shoura*
(consultative council). These had been written by
Islamists who were opposed to the development of
Boumedienne's personal power. In the same year the
most redoubtable of the surviving reformist *ulema*,
Abdellatif Soltani, published a book in Morocco entitled
Le Socialisme c'est le Mazdakisme. The work, which remains
banned in Algeria in the 1990s, is widely considered as a
key ideological source of modern Algerian Islamism.
Soltani likened the Boumedienne regime to that of the
Mazdaks in Persia in the fifth century BC and denounced
it for allowing foreign customs introduced during the
French colonial era to persist, such as the consumption of
alcohol, the liberalisation of relations between the sexes
and even the commercial promotion of Roman ruins as
tourist sites. He also criticised its toleration of 'impious'
authors, such as Kateb Yacine and the feminist Fadila
Mrabet, and advocated a radical Islamist solution as the
sole path for the salvation of the Algerian people. Concerned by the growing popularity of his illegally distributed book and copies of his fiery sermons, the authorities
placed Soltani under house arrest. Ironically, a govern-

ment campaign organised in 1970 by the education minister, Mouloud Kassim Nait Belkacem, had focused on identical themes to Soltani's: 'the shameful behaviour of husbands; cosmopolitanism; alcoholism – one of the principal causes of divorce; [and] snobbery, which encourages people to follow the West and imitate its customs and to adopt semi-nakedness simply because it comes from the West.'

Although the regime came down decisively against the religious option in the National Charter of 1976, the document did include several important concessions to the Islamists. Although the Charter reaffirmed Algeria's commitment to the path of socialism as the most effective way forward for the Muslim world, it designated Islam as the state religion and reconvened the National Assembly – a response to the demands for a *shoura*. The government outlawed gambling in March 1976 and adopted the Muslim weekend the following August. However, the reorganisation of the ministry of religious affairs as a subordinate department of the presidency effectively cancelled out even these small concessions, though the Islamists were more dismayed by the regime's refusal to consider Islam as *the*, rather than *a*, source of the constitution. The Islamists' opposition to the Charter prompted the first real incident of Islamist violence directed against the FLN régime when Mahfoudh Nahnah imitated the wartime *mudjahidine* by sabotaging an electricity pylon near Blida. He received a fifteen-year prison sentence for this act, though he was released in 1981 and went on to found the Hamas party in 1990.

The enormous movement of people from the country-side to the cities in the 1960s and 1970s and the social change that resulted was another factor that contributed to the growth of Islamism in Algeria. By the early 1970s the majority of the population of cities such as Algiers and Oran were of rural origin. These immigrants brought to the cities a much more conservative and traditional outlook on life: patriarchal structures and Islam had survived the French occupation in the rural environment far more intact than in urban areas. The mixture of Arabo-Islamic socialism preached by the regime was largely irrelevant to them, and this created a deep gulf betwee them and the government, mirroring wider conflict between traditionalists and modernists in Algeria. First- and second- generation rural immigrants to the city were to form the natural constituency for the Islamists in the 1980s.

The Islamist movement had grown rapidly by the time of Boumedienne's sudden death in 1978, but as yet it was by no means the major force that it would become in the 1980s. By encouraging the politicisation of a large proportion of the population as a means of mobilising popular support for his socialist policies, Boumedienne had prepared the ground for the undoing of these policies. Ultimately, he fuelled the growth of socialism's implacable enemy, Islamism. Newly politicised Algerians did not share their president's vision of a homogeneous nation state based on socialism that would incorporate and thus neutralise all the regional and ethnic diversities of Algeria, and it was this dissent that the Islamists would exploit. In 1978 the Islamist movement was about to explode into life.

Islamism under Chadli Bendjedid, 1978-92

The accession of Chadli Bendjedid occasioned a radical change in Algerian politics. The new regime's systematic unravelling of the socialist institutions constructed by Boumedienne created a policy vacuum of which the Islamists took full advantage. The regime's own rejection and criticism of Boumediennism, and its attempt to co-opt the *arabisant* lobby as a counterweight to the leftists who had supported the former president, further fuelled the drift towards fundamentalism, which, in the absence of any viable alternative, became the fastest-growing and most dynamic political movement in Algeria in the early 1980s. By this time, almost twenty years after the departure of the French, new divisions had appeared in an already heterogeneous and faction-ridden society. The younger generation had begun to resent the government and its imported ideologies for its failure adequately to deliver its ambitious promises of the preceding two decades. Despite Algeria's huge oil wealth, there were high rates of unemployment and large sections of the population spent long days of idleness in public sector employment, often in positions for which they were over-qualified. While the older generation continued to look back proudly on its part in the war of independence – and often reaped the rewards with privileges such as subsidised housing and guaranteed public sector jobs – the better-educated and Arabic-speaking younger generation had become increasingly alienated. Furthermore, the regime's reliance on a corrupt and inefficient bureaucracy contributed to the contempt in which it was held. As all channels of opposition were co-opted, restricted and then closed, the mosques, with their attractive notions of justice and equality, represented an attractive and open alternative, one which had the inestimable advantage of legitimacy born of tradition, particularly among the urban poor who originated from conservative rural areas.

The Iranian revolution of 1979-80 was a turning-point in the growth of Algerian Islamism. Disregarding the important dogmatic differences between Shia and Sunni Islam, Algerian Islamists saw Ayatollah Khomeini as an inspiring Muslim ideologue who proved for the first time that Islam could triumph over political systems copied from the West. Khomeini bestowed an historic legitimacy upon the 'Islamic solution'. Algerian Islamists also drew parallels between the removal of a dictator supported by the Western powers with the Algerian war of independence which remained as much a key reference point for Algerian Islamists as it did for the FLN. This was closely connected with Algerians' perception of themsleves and of their country as the products of a revolution. However, the influence of 'Khomeinism' on Islamism in Algeria and the wider Maghreb can be overstated. Khomeini himself was a Shia figure, whose political outlook was specific to the traditions of the imam within Shia Islam. The Iranian experience served as a broad inspiration to Islamists of the Maghreb rather than as a direct model.

Algeria's Islamists in the early 1980s were in any case in no position to emulate the Iranian revolution. The movement was disorganised, unstructured and without a coherent and unified national leadership, notwithstanding the activities of such prominent mosque-based agitators as Sheikhs Soltani and Abassi Madani. There is no established clerical class in Sunni as in Shia Islam that can constitute a natural spearhead and organiser of any popular Islamist agitation. Although Islamists tended to refer to themselves as *Ahl el-Da'wa* – the People of the Call – there was no official name to designate the movement as a whole. *Ahl el-Da'wa* inevitably implies a mission connected to the concept of *jihad*, holy war, though the interpretation of the word varies between extremists, who resort to terrorism, and those who advocate peaceful means. This argument illustrates the differences between what is often termed 'Islamic fundamentalism' and its Christian counterpart. The modern interpretation of *jihad* implies the use of violence, something almost always eschewed by Christian fundamentalists. Islamic fundamentalists who employ violence typically cite the Koranic injunction to every Muslim to 'command that which is proper and forbid that which is reprehensible'. However, the majority of Algerian Muslims, fundamentalists as well as moderates, reject social terrorism in all its forms.

In the early 1980s the Algerian Islamist movement had yet to make the important transition from a loose network of locally organised groups to a national radical political movement, a process which had already occurred to varying degrees in neighbouring Tunisia and Morocco. In Tunisia in the late 1970s Rachid Ghannouchi and Abdelfatah Mourou had created the Mouvement de la Tendance Islamique, and more than twenty Islamist political associations had been established in Morocco by the beginning of the 1980s. Algerian Islamists, meanwhile, faced a challenge from their former detractor Ahmed Ben Bella, who founded his own Islamist force, the Mouvement pour la Démocratie en Algérie (MDA) in 1982. Ben Bella conveniently abandoned his historic commitment to socialism when he correctly assessed the Arabo-Islamist tendency as the most credible engine of opposition to the ideological confusion that beset the Chadli regime. Ironically, the MDA, headed by the one-time persecutor of *al-Qiyam* and the Association of Reformist Ulema (ARU), was the leading Algerian Islamist movement in exile between 1980 and 1985. It reprinted anti-regime tracts written by a shadowy organisation calling itself *Nidha al-Islam* ('Call of Islam') and widely suspected to have been the ARU's invention, and sent some to Western embassies in Algiers and news organisations.

The Battle for the Mosques

For the Islamist movement, mosques represented an incalculable and in-built advantage over the state and over non-religious opposition parties. He who enjoyed control of a mosque in the person of its imam enjoyed a perfect platform for political agitation and even election-eering. In common with many other Muslim countries, colonial suppression of mosque-building had resulted in a relatively small number of mosques at independence. Immediately after independence the regime prioritised the construction of new mosques and the conversion into mosques of synagogues and churches and independent religious foundations. Between 1962 and 1972 the authorities inaugurated 4,474 mosques, including 183 converted from churches.

There were three types of mosques constructed during this period. 'People's mosques', those built hastily in shanty towns or improvised in the remains of existing buildings or on building sites, were illegal, often run by religious associations, and frequently attracted the attention of the authorities. Although the constitution declared that the state must authorise all religious activity, 'people's mosques' constituted an element of resistance to the interference of the state bureaucracy. However, although later exploited by the Islamists, they were not initially explicity constructed by and for them. 'Free mosques' were established as the domain of the Islamists. These were usually mosques that Islamists had started to build but left unfinished: this circumvented the regulation that imposed official control on all working mosques – i.e. those completed and inaugurated. This was particularly true in the case of mosques in areas that were to become the heartlands of the FIS such as the Algiers suburbs of Bab el-Oued, Belcourt, Kouba and Bachdjarrah. 'Private mosques' were constructed and funded by local notables, some of whom supported the Islamists. A fourth type, the 'state mosques', were those that had been constructed before the coming of the French in 1830.

Politics entered the mosque in 1978 when discussion on wider issues facing the Algerian nation as a whole began to supplant the normal forms of preaching. This had traditionally taken the form of commentaries on the Koran and sermons on the issues of daily life. Preachers such as Abdellatif Soltani, Ahmed Sahnoun and Abassi Madani travelled an informal circuit between Algiers, Constantine, Laghouat, Oran, Blida and Medea, exchanging ideas and preaching the basic concepts of an Islamist movement. The tendency, which remained disorganised and without central direction, grew stronger with the slight easing in the attitude of the newly-installed Chadli regime and in reaction to influences from abroad. The main targets of these Islamist preachers at the time were the Boumediennists and the leftists, particularly the PAGS, whose influence had endured despite the change in regime in 1979. Chadli and the regime itself were secondary targets. It was not until 1980 that the various Islamist tendencies and groupings coalesced into something approaching an organised movement under the collective leadership of Soltani, Sahnoun, Abassi and other preachers.

The Islamists also made extensive use of the state education system and the media to propagate their message. Islamist sympathisers employed in *lycées* and Institutes of Arabic Language and Law would often spend their free time acting as imams in 'free mosques', which provided them with a valuable opportunity to impose their views on students. There was also a proliferation of Islamist publications issued in the early and mid-1980s. Most, such as *Dawa*, *al-Hadith* and *al-Iqtisad al-Islami* were produced abroad and distributed more or less openly via the network of 'free mosques'. Foreign-produced Islamist books dominated the scene until 1986 when a growing number of independent or even officially-funded Islamic publishing houses began to appear in Constantine and Algiers, turning out original works as well as new commentaries and reprints. The Islamists also made extensive use of sermons recorded on cassette tapes. Although inhibited, at least in the early 1980s, by the continuing state monopoly on the production and distribution of cassette tapes, several Islamist organisations circulated copies of taped sermons made by Egyptian, Lebanese, Saudi Arabian and other Arab *khatibs* (orators) as well as Algerians. The focus of the sermons echoed the targets of the imams in the 'free mosques': the pernicious influence of the West; the growing sinfulness of society; and the irreligiosity of socialism. As Bruno Etienne has commented, 'Cassettes were to the Islamists what the printing press was to the Calvinists: the channel for ideological difusion.'[3]

The Egyptian preacher Sheikh Mohammed al-Ghazali proved very influential in the 1980s. Ghazali had formerly held high religious appointments in Egypt, Mecca and Qatar, and in 1982 the Chadli regime appointed him director of the Scientific Council at the Faculty of Islamic Sciences at the Emir Abdelkader University in Constantine. The appointment represented one of the first moves by the Chadli regime to pacify and outflank the Islamists and had an enormous and unintended influence on Algerian society. The media and the growing number of quasi-independent publishing houses almost immediately sought out Ghazali to give his learned opinion on all manner of religious issues. These were all-encompassing as he rejected capitalism as much as communism and stressed Islam as the only reliable source of economic, political and social values. In common with the situation prevailing in Egypt in the late 1980s, Ghazali's weekly televised sermons inspired hundreds of thousands of young Algerians. Ghazali was an important propagandist

---

[3] Bruno Etienne, *L'Islamisme radicale*, Paris: Hachette, 1992.

for the Islamists without explicitly encouraging his audience to ally with them. However, Ghazali had fallen out of favour with both the regime and the nascent FIS by 1988-9 and he left Algeria in May 1989. He continued to play a key role in the radical Islamist movement in Egypt in the early 1990s.

The emergence of an extremist fringe is often a corollary of the development of Islamism wherever it occurs and this was graphically illustrated by the Algerian experience of the early 1980s. Islamist zealots began to stage small-scale attacks against those considered to be the enemies of Islamism with increasing frequency in 1979-80, leading to an inevitable collision with politicised leftist and Berberist students. In the aftermath of the Tizi Ouzou Spring, Islamist students in May 1981 disrupted a meeting of the official and leftist-dominated Union Nationale de la Jeunesse Algérienne (UNJA) at Algiers University, and in the following months student clashes spread to Oran and Annaba. An attack in March 1981 against a shop selling alcohol in el-Oued was followed by the death of a policeman during an Islamist demonstration the following September in Laghouat. This unrest had erupted when Islamists 'annexed' a mosque and tried to install one of their own men; three days of rioting ensued when their leader was arrested. In the report of the incident in the state-controlled media – the first admission by the government of the conflict between the state and the Islamists – the state insisted that it alone was qualified to defend the 'original purity' of Islam.

The Chadli regime first attempted to clamp down on the Islamist movement in response to growing agitation on university campuses. In November 1982, 400 Islamist students were arrested following the murder of a leftist student, Kamel Amzal, by an Islamist student, Fethallah Lassouli, on the Ben Aknoun campus of Algiers University. Soltani, Sahnoun and Abassi convened a massive prayer meeting and rally, which some reports claim more than 100,000 attended. They demanded the immediate application of Islamic law, the ending of secondary and higher education for women, and the prohibition of the consumption and sale of alcohol. Such overt and audacious opposition to the government and its policies was unprecedented. The authorities placed Soltani and Sahnoun under house arrest and imprisoned Abassi along with another Islamist imam, Mohamed Said. The authorities banned a march in protest against the arrests and detained its organisers. Among them was Sheikh Ali Belhadj, a young charismatic preacher who was gaining a large following in Algiers. In early December Chadli warned that he would take any measure necessary to defend the country and the unity of the nation. A few days later the first news broke of an armed Islamist group led by a veteran *mudjahid*, Moustapha Bouyali.

In 1984 Chadli began to adopt elements of the Islamists' agenda in an effort to outflank them. The government published a new family code shaped by conservative and fundamentalist thinking and founded Islamic cultural centres throughout the country. In April 1984 it was so concerned by the popularity of the Islamists that it considered it wise to send official representatives to the funeral of Sheikh Abdellatif Soltani in the Algiers district of Kouba, the most significant public manifestation of Islamist strength before 1988. Soon afterwards, the government released Abassi, Sahnoun and twenty-one other detainees. Later in the year, the ambitious Emir Abdelkader University of Islamic Sciences, one of the largest in the Islamic world, opened in Constantine. This institution has subsequently played a central role in the development of the Islamist movement in Algeria.

Although there in no evidence showing that the Islamists actually started the riots of October 1988, the unrest provided the Islamists with their first real opportunity to influence the actions of the FLN government. It is not clear exactly when the incoherent and disparate revolt against the excesses of successive FLN régimes began to rally behind the Islamists, but those wearing beards, white caps and *goundouras* were skilfully projecting themselves as the unofficial leaders of the uprising in its last days. Ali Belhadj emerged as the central rallying point for the protesters in Algiers after being involved in the massacre in the Place 1 Mai on 10 October. Along with

Nahnah and Sahnoun, he met President Chadli in an unprecedented meeting aimed at defusing tensions. The scene was now set for the emergence of the first legally-sanctioned mass Islamist movement in Algeria.

The FIS

On 21 February 1989 twenty-eight Islamist preachers met at the Sunna Mosque in Bab el-Oued in Algiers to establish the Front Islamique du Salut (FIS). Most senior among them were Abassi Madani, Ali Belhadj, Mohamed Said, Mahfoudh Nahnah, Benazzouz Zebda, Abdelbaki Sahraoui and Hachemi Sahnouni. The Front appointed Abassi Madani as its spokesman and chairman of its collective leadership council, the *Madjlis ech-Choura*. This made Abassi the party's *de facto* leader, though no such position ever officially existed. The Madjlis consisted of thirty-eight members and was the supreme deci-sion-making body of the FIS. The term had first been used by the Prophet Mohamed in the seventh century, and the founders of the FIS selected it for its religious connotations. Like the early Arabian Madjlis the council operated by debate and consensus, though this some-times meant that debates on key issues could last for days and lead to the issuing of contradictory public policy statements, as occured following the arrests of Abassi and Belhadj in June 1991. A twelve-member executive bureau directed the day-to-day running of the FIS and was supported by a number of departments, such as propa-ganda, political affairs and foreign relations, and even the production of sermonising cassettes. On a local level, the party organised its activities in small urban or rural units known in Arabic as *ousra*, or family cells. The use of the term *ousra* was a further conscious attempt to seek legitimacy for the FIS by adopting the sacred vocabulary of Islam.

The FIS focused on the formula 'Islam is the solution' and eschewed detailed expansion of its political pro-gramme. The party's principal objectives were the foundation of an Islamic republic and the reinforcement of the religious aspects of the Algerian state that had always existed but which had become obscured by the hegemony of the small secularist minority. Despite its claim to be a socialist state, Algeria had never been secular, and we have seen how religious conservatism had survived the Boumedienne regime and revived rapidly in the 1980s. Indeed the FIS represents far less of a divergence from the political traditions of the state founded by the FLN than is at first apparent. It rejected committing its programme to print until the period following its victory in the December 1991 polls, preferring instead to disseminate its message through the mosques and the media. For many Algerians, the FIS was the harbinger of hope, prosperity and justice and the bestower of dignity; for others, it represented tyranny and obscurantism.

As a broad front of Islamists, the FIS was from the beginning dogged by division and disagreement. The two principal factions within the party were the 'Algerianists' (the Djeza'ara, successors of the *Khouandjis*) and the Salafis. The Djeza'ara, an Arabic acronym for the Islamic Association for the Edification of Civilisation, attracted the more moderate, Arabo-Islamic-nationalist tendency of the Islamist movement. They favoured the 'Algerian' solution of organising a revolution among the Algerian population itself, an approach which owed much to the spirit, if not the precise vocabulary and ideology, of the nationalism developed by the wartime FLN. This was popular among the more highly-educated of the FIS's supporters. Although Abassi never openly declared his allegiance to any faction within the FIS, he is usually considered to have supported the Djeza'ara. The Salafis' supporters were usually found among fundamentalist imams such as Ali Belhadj. The radical and obscurantist nature of the Salafis inevitably allied them with the Islamic extremist tendency, first the former partisans of Mustafa Bouyali and later armed groups such as the so-called 'Afghans' and the GIA.

The divisions within the FIS first surfaced in the run-up to the constitutional referendum in February 1990. Abassi and the Djeza'ara moderates were prepared to make real concessions to the democratic framework constructed by Chadli and favoured endorsement of the proposals as they stood. However, Belhadj's Salafi wing rejected democracy except as a means of gaining power. For them, Islam was the only solution: all laws, customs and practices were codified in the Koran, Sunna and Hadith, and ideas like political pluralism had no place there. Belhadj argued that Muslims could not support a pluralistic system that was 'in conflict with the ideology [of the FIS] and that contradicts the beliefs of our people' and called for a boycott. In the event, however, the boycott failed and Algerians overwhelmingly approved the constitution.

The FIS attracted massive popular support through its ambitious social welfare programme. Enormous demographic pressures and falling government maintenance budgets in the 1980s had placed an intolerable strain on health care provisions constructed during the Boumedienne era, and Islamist activists moved in to fill the gap by offering financial aid for hospital treatment or to buy medicines (the government had introduced charges in 1985). FIS members even attended neglected patients in understaffed hospitals during Ramadan. Activists offered to assist families of the deceased at funerals, and in the underprivileged Algiers suburb of Belcourt there were instances of FIS supporters handing out clothes to the families of school pupils at the beginning of the school year. The FIS's organisation of aid to the stricken area of Tipaza following the earthquake there in October 1989 was a key propaganda coup, especially as the authorities were slow to mobilise. Supporters even dispensed marriage guidance and distributed veils to female supporters who could not afford to buy them. The Front also intervened in labour disputes: mediation between FIS officials and striking workers on more than one occasion led to a return to work. These activities were financed from a variety of sources – originally from official and private donors in Saudi Arabia, which opposed the Marxist leanings of the FLN, and later from Iran. Collections made by FIS activists and donations from wealthy merchant Algerians, either out of genuine Islamist convictions or from simple resentment against the FLN, provided further sources of revenue. Through these actions the FIS tried to recreate social cohesion in a society that had become fragmented due to progressively intensifying economic and demographic pressures.

It is important to grasp that the FIS is a radical nationalist party that articulated its policies in the context of Islamism rather than as a purely fundamentalist organisation, such as the Muslim Brotherhood of Egypt. Indeed, the Front's weak credentials as a fundamentalist or Islamist organisation were a major contributory factor in its success. Lahouari Addi has remarked:

The masses did not vote for the FIS to win paradise in the next world, but rather to see Algeria's successful development and modernisation, and the restoration of morality in its government. In that respect, the FIS is secular. It is not really a religious movement but a political one which has sought legitimacy in religion.[4]

Although its discourse was undeniably 'Islamic' and its leaders unequivocally 'fundamentalists', the FIS was largely a product of the Algerian experience. In many respects it was an attempt to remodel and correct the FLN, which the FIS consciously or unconciously imitated.

The popular perception of the FIS as a revolutionary and corrective movement was its greatest strength. Many Algerians blamed the FLN for the mismanagement and corruption of the Chadli regime and the ruling élite for Algeria's social and economic problems. The FIS exploited this dissatisfaction and resentment of the ruling classes by claiming for itself the revolutionary legitimacy that the FLN had enjoyed until the 1980s. These themes shaped the FIS's campaign for the provincial and municipal elections of June 1990. In order to bring 'justice, morality and retribution' the FIS demanded the dissolution of the Assembly and a free election to choose a replacement. It also called for effective measures to curb inflation and unemployment and the establishment of an anti-corruption police force. The Islamists masked their own lack of any substantial political programme by

---

[4] *International Herald Tribune*, 18 January 1992.

gambling correctly that the FIS would be unable to respond. The mismanagement of the FLN regime provided Abassi and Belhadj with an easy target throughout the campaign and explained the party's easy victory: it won outright control of five provinces and majority control of nineteen others.

However, not everyone who voted for the FIS in June 1990 did so out of genuine Islamist conviction. The results reflected the disgust and frustration of the Algerian people with the profligacy and corruption of the state that until 1989 had been governed in the name of the FLN. It was this, combined with a remarkably low turnout, that accounted for the humiliatingly low vote for the government party. Ironically, the self-styled 'democratic' parties' tactically foolish policy of boycotting the election – prompted by their implacable opposition to the government – also indirectly assisted the FIS. It is impossible to quantify the percentage of 'real' voters for the FIS, that is those who genuinely voted for its brand of Islamism, though a figure of around 20-25 per cent is plausible. Moreover, there was little investigation into numerous reported irregularities at the polls, clashes between supporters of rival parties throughout the country and voter intimidation by FIS activists. The government admitted that irregularities had taken place, but did nothing for fear of further fuelling tensions.

After its election victory, the FIS embarked on a controversial policy of cleaning up the morals and standards of the provinces and municipalities under its control, claiming that it was pursuing a popular mandate to implement the *sharia*. The FIS-controlled council in the beach resort of Tipaza, west of Algiers, in July 1990 introduced a ban on shorts and swimwear in the streets, though the *wali* (provincial governor) subsequently annulled it. Later in the same summer FIS councils banned a concert of *raï* music[5] in Oran and prohibited the sale of alcohol and mixed sex education in Constantine. The FIS-controlled council in Setif banned alcohol while

---

[5] *Raï* music is a fusion of Algerian, Arab and European music traditions which often articulates the sexual frustrations of Algerian youth.

the town council in Djidjel ordered that all correspon-
dence with it was henceforth to be in Arabic. Although
FIS activists stopped visiting wine merchants to 'remind'
them of the Islamic injunction against alcohol, they began
instead to force FIS-run local councils to withdraw
licences from the merchants. Meanwhile the Islamic
extremist groups were encouraged by the FIS's moral
campaign to resume their strategy of violence. By the
turn of the year extremists had murdered or kidnapped
several of their opponents in and around Algiers and
Blida.

The FIS's victory of June 1990 encouraged Abassi
Madani to behave as the leader of the opposition and
Algeria's prime minister-in-waiting. This was particularly
the case after July 1990 when President Chadli pledged to
hold parliamentary elections in the first quarter of 1991.
But although Abassi gave numerous news conferences
and frequently criticised the regime, he expounded little
on the details of the FIS programme. His policy statements made no mention of plans for the economy;
instead he conceived grand schemes such as the construction of a new Algerian capital city in the exact centre of
the country. Abassi also tried hard, though without much
success, to allay fears that a FIS government would mean
a repressive Khomeini-style regime. He even hinted that
the FIS would enter a coalition with any 'honest' party.

The Gulf crisis of 1990-1 improved the FIS's domestic
standing by apparently underlining the pan-Arabist
credentials of Abassi and Belhadj. The two leaders
responded to the FLN's denunciation of the West's
military build-up against Iraq with a a well-publicised
series of 'mediation' visits to Saudi Arabia and Iraq in
August and September 1990. Although fruitless, the visits
marked the FIS's first relatively successful foray into
inter-Arab relations, though the crisis revealed publicly
the disagreement over policy between the two leaders.
Belhadj called for the FIS to establish camps to train
volunteers to fight for Iraq against the Western infidel,
while Abassi adopted a more cautious approach. These
disagreements over policy and worsening relations
between the Djeza'ara and Salafi factions began to lose the

FIS support by the end of 1990. Overshadowed by the impending war in the Gulf, the divisions became public when several FIS municipal councillors resigned in early January 1991. Although the men in question usually cited family problems, it was evident that operating difficulties within FIS-run authorities were discouraging many of its officials from continuing in their posts. Furthermore, many of those who resigned had misunderstood the real aims of the FIS at the outset but had been welcomed by a party eager to swell its numbers. The ruptures within the Madjlis widened in February 1991 when Belhadj gave a controversial speech elevating the Iraqi President, Saddam Hussein, to the status of 'defender of Islam'.

Abassi faced constant challenges to his personal authority over the FIS in the Madjlis, even at the zenith of the Front's popularity in 1991. He criticised the government's electoral law passed in March 1991 as 'an injustice and a fraud' and the Front mounted a vociferous campaign against the law during the run-up to the first round of the election. However, by the time Abassi called a general strike to press Chadli to bring forward presidential elections and to make alterations to the electoral law in late May, the divisions within the FIS had begun to undermine his personal authority. The relatively weak response to the strike call heightened tensions within the Madjlis, which publicly rebuked Abassi for his dictatorial style and passed motions demanding that the strike be cancelled. Opposition to Abassi and Belhadj, principally from the Djeza'ara faction, increased when the strike triggered off violence. On 26 June three Madjlis members, Sheikh Hachemi Sahnouni (considered to have been the number-three of the FIS), Ahmed Marrani (president of the FIS's social affairs commission) and Bachir Fkih, appeared on television on 26 June denouncing Abassi as a 'danger to Islam, Muslims and the nation' and called for direct talks with the incoming government of Sid Ahmed Ghozali. However, Abassi ignored his opponents and on 28 June threatened to launch a *jihad* against the regime unless the army withdrew from districts run by FIS councillors. This prompted another Madjlis member, Sheikh Mohamed Iman, to join in the criticism of Abassi.

On 30 June the authorities arrested Abassi and Belhadj for allegedly having 'fomented, organised, launched and led an armed conspiracy against the security of the state'. Six other members of the Madjlis were arrested two days later.

In late July the FIS convened an emergency two-day meeting in Batna to choose a provisional leadership after the arrests of Abassi and Belhadj. The remaining Madjlis confirmed the two men in their posts, dismissing a challenge from Said Guechi, a moderate who favoured negotiation with the government. The meeting dismissed five members of the Madjlis, including Sahnouni and Benazzouz Zebda, who had opposed Abassi's policy of resolute, occasionally violent, opposition to the authorities and appointed twelve new members, including the leading Abassi loyalist Mohamed Said. Most of the new members supported the Djeza'ara faction, though the events of June 1991 had temporarily blurred the differences between the two factions. The meeting appointed a petrochemical engineer, Abdelkader Hachani, to head a provisional executive committee. Meanwhile, although the arrests of Abassi and Belhadj had removed them from the centre stage of Algerian politics, they could control the FIS from prison by smuggling out communiqués and statements.

The question of whether to participate in the elections of December 1991 dominated the internal politics of the FIS in the four months leading up to the polls. The leadership repeatedly threatened to boycott the vote if the government refused to release the FIS detainees. Abbasi and Belhadj staged periodic hunger-strikes to underline their demands. But after protracted discussion in the Madjlis and in response to the wishes of Abassi, the party finally announced its decision to participate on 14 December. Conflict between the pro- and anti-Abassi factions within the Madjlis prevented the leadership from reaching a decision, and there is no evidence to suggest that the FIS was deliberately trying to frustrate Chadli and Ghozali. The disagreements were between the pragmatist Djeza'ara, who believed that democracy was the easiest route to power, and the Salafis, who considered participation in the elections as an implicit recognition of the 'un-Islamic' notion of democracy. The two factions also disagreed over the nomination of candidates to stand for the FIS; in particular, the Salafis criticised Hachani for promoting the nomination of candidates from similar backgrounds to his own. However, Hachani managed to convince the Madjlis to participate in the elections after a series of attacks in late November by 'Afghans' on police posts near Guemmar, on the Tunisian border, which the secular press exploited as 'proof' of the 'Islamist threat'. Hachani and his Djeza'ara supporters argued that to boycott the elections would further radicalise the party's supporters who would turn towards Belhadj and the Salafis to the detriment of the Djeza'ara.

Despite the disagreements within the Madjlis, the FIS mounted a well-organised and effective election campaign. Hachani and Abdelkader Moghni, an imam of the Sunna mosque in Bab el-Oued, acted as the two principal spokesmen. The Djeza'ara was organising the nomination of FIS candidates in all 430 constituencies even while the threat of boycott persisted. The Front's spokesmen propagated their simple message, 'Islam is the solution', through Algeria's enthusiastic and relatively free newspapers. Mindful of the bad publicity generated by the attacks at Guemmar, the Front's took care to prevent rallies from turning violent. In the event, the FIS attracted a spectacular 47 per cent of the vote in the first round of the elections on 26 December.

But the FIS failed to capitalise on its first round victory; the Front attempted without success to explain the benefits of an Islamist government to the Algerian people and did little to reassure the military that it would respect the constitution. Hachani called for early presidential elections as the president alone had the power to amend the constitution to allow the formal establishment of an Islamic republic, and this apparent respect for the constitution revealed the influence of the Djeza'ara, who not only favoured a gradualist approach to creating an Islamic state but were also anxious to prevent an intervention by the army. In Algiers the FIS opened an information centre to present its policies to the electorate

where voters were able to buy pamphlets on subjects
such as 'Islam and women' and 'Islam and human rights'.
This was its first effort at elaborating policy beyond the
simple message 'Islam is the solution'. The centre also
contained a crude model of a projected Islamic city, with
sports centres (a shrewd move as Algerians are fanatical
sportsmen but strangely deprived of public sports
facilities), cinemas, libraries and, of course, mosques.
Women would be obliged to wear the *hedjab* (headscarf)
and forced to stay at home on the grounds that they were
under perpetual attack from pernicious Westernisation
and that their role was above all as mother, sister, wife or
daughter. However, the Front is intended to allow
exceptions for certain reserved professions and for
women who were orphaned, divorced or widowed. The
FIS also planned to segregate the sexes in schools and in
higher education, and to ban alcohol. People's tribunals
would try 'traitors', presumably members of the former
government, and the non-Islamist press and other media
would be banned. But the party made no attempt to
reassure those who feared for the future of Algeria's
fragile democracy, and many FIS imams made public
statements hinting that all non-Islamist political parties
would almost certainly be suppressed.

The FIS's economic policy was crude and unspecific.
The Front reiterated its opposition to both capitalism and
socialism and proposed instead to create an 'Islamic
economy' in which moneylending and interest would play
no part. Yet the party emphasised its belief in the central
role of the marketplace in the Algerian economy. According to the FIS, increased exploitation of the country's
hydrocarbons reserves, particularly in co-operation with
international oil firms, would alleviate the ill-effects of the
transition to a genuine market economy. But, paradoxically, the FIS revealed the strong nationalist element
within its ideology in rejecting Prime Minister Ghozali's
proposals for greater foreign participation in the oil
industry.

The military intervention of January 1992 halted the
FIS's plans for government. It was clear that the unconstitutional regime that removed Chadli was determined to

crush the FIS and suspend the democratisation process. It was equally clear that the regime fully expected Hachani to call on the party's supporters to defy the coup and thus present it with a convenient pretext to suppress the FIS by force. Hachani duly complied on 12 January when he urged 'all veteran fighters, thinkers, religious leaders, senior army officers and soldiers, and sons of martyrs, social organisations and all who love Algeria to take a stand against this giant of power', though in subsequent statements he entreated restraint on the party's supporters to avoid any provocation that could serve as the pretext for official repression. Possibly Hachani's statements and the confusion among FIS officials helped forestall the immediate eruption of widespread anti-government violence by party supporters.

By the time the regime began to suppress the FIS in the third week of January, Hachani and the moderates were no longer in control. When extremist elements, possibly with Salafi backing, began to stage attacks against symbols of authority in Algiers in mid-January, the regime was given the pretext for which it had been waiting. On 22 January Hachani was arrested for allegedly urging 'desertion from the army'. The authorities then effectively outlawed all political activity by the FIS by banning all public gatherings around mosques and any political discussion inside them, and in the following weeks rounded up most of the remaining members of the Madjlis and hundreds of party activists. Many were summarily detained in remote Saharan prison camps. The government then appointed loyalists to replace imams in the 8,000 or so mosques controlled by the FIS. Abderrazak Redjam was the last effective leader of the FIS before the government finally outlawed it on 4 March. On 13 February Rejdam made a desperate appeal for a 'serious dialogue' with the regime before he himself went underground.

A two-week-long show trial in July 1992 marked the final act of the repression against the FIS. Abassi, Belhadj, Kemal Guemazi, Ali Djeddi, Abdelkader Boukhamkham, Nureddin Chigara and Abdelkader Omar all faced charges of conspiracy to overthrow the state relating to their actions during the events of June 1991. Abassi and Belhadj each received twelve years; Guemazi was jailed for five years; and Djeddi, Boukhamkham, Chigara and Omar each received four-year sentences.

There was international criticism of the trial as politically-motivated and widespread concern over its legality. The court itself appeared to disbelieve the regime's version of the events of June 1991. According to the FIS's defence, the prime minister, Sid Ahmed Ghozali, had made a secret agreement with the FIS for a peaceful end to the demonstrations in the main squares of Algiers, pledging to reinstate the dismissed workers and bring forward presidential and parliamentary elections. Although Ghozali and a number of his former colleagues refuted the defendants' testimony, some witnesses implied that Chadli had taken the decision to send in the army to break the strikes. This sufficiently impressed the military prosecutor to ask for prison terms rather than the death sentences, on the ground that the defendants did not bear sole responsibility for the violence. The court also acquitted the seven on a parallel charge of plotting armed insurrection.

The 'Ex-FIS'

The question of whether to lift the ban on the FIS, henceforth designated the 'ex-FIS', dominated Algerian political life in the years of the post-Chadli crisis at least until the political changes of 1996-7. When the military intervened in January 1992 to cancel the democratic project that would almost certainly have resulted in the formation of a FIS administration, the state was obliged to justify both its own existence and the marginalisation of the FIS by demonising the FIS as a threat to the 'secular' and 'modern' nature of the Algerian state. This position was a false one. The state established by the FLN had never been genuinely secular in the French sense of the word, the sense which continued to have the greatest resonance among the Algerian intelligentsia; the Algerian regime had always comprised religious as well as secular elements. Indeed, the principal point of divergence between the traditions best represented by the FLN and the FIS was that while the former argued for a greater emphasis on the secular aspects of the Algerian state, the latter favoured the reinforcement of its religious aspects. All the main Algerian political parties (the post-1989 FLN, the FFS and the FIS) were to a large extent heirs of the FLN before 1962. The FIS was the heir of the religious and conservative trend within the pre-1962 FLN; the post-1989 FLN inherited the centrist/nationalist strand, and the FFS was the successor of the Kabyle militants. This was well illustrated by the increasing convergence of interests between the three parties in 1993-4, culminating in the signing of the National Contract in January 1995.

Indeed, only a minority of Algerians adopted a staunch anti-FIS position during the post-Chadli crisis. Seven political groupings favoured lifting the ban on the FIS: the FLN, the FFS, the PT, the moderate Islamist Ennahda and Hamas parties and Ben Bella's MDA. Prominent politicians who publicly called for the relegalisation of the FIS included the former prime minister Kasdi Merbah and the former foreign minister Ahmed Taleb Ibrahimi. In contrast, only the communist Ettahadi and Berberist RCD (both with miniscule support), along with the veterans' organisation ONM and the UGTA trade union, were against. Mohamed Boudiaf also was strongly opposed to the FIS's re-entry into the democratisation process. Their argument was predicated on two tenets that were unjustified and facile: the belief that Islamism *per se* rejects democracy and that the FIS was determined to seize power by whatever means The FIS was itself divided over its own response to the state's ban and underwent further fracture when many members of the Madjlis were forced into exile to avoid arrest, resulting in a polarisation between 'externals' (that is, exiles) and 'internals'. Belhadj frequently publicised his support for the activities and policies of the GIA, an organisation which rejected negotiations with the regime until the ban on the FIS was lifted. Abassi adopted a more conciliatory tone. The FIS tried to address the problem in September 1993 when it reorganised its leadership under the chairmanship of its official spokesman, Rabah Kebir, who formed a new 'executive committee' to unify the opposition inside the country, and to 'prevent infiltration by the ruling clique's supporters'. The other principal members of the committee were Kamaruddin Khurban, Abdallah Anas and the party's Washington spokesman, Anouar Haddam.

In January 1995 Haddam and Kebir signed the National Contract in Rome. Among the key points of the contract's programme were undertakings by the FIS to accept the democratic principles of 'political pluralism' and alternance. This was the first occasion on which the FIS had, without being pressured, publicly adhered to democratic principles in the presence of other Algerian politicians. The fact that the document was signed by a Salafi such as Haddam bestowed upon the declaration maximum authenticity and gravity. The move was a clear sign that the FIS, along with the other two heirs of the pre-1962 FLN, was not responsible for the collapse of the three rounds of negotiations with the presidency in April and October 1994, and again in July 1995. Indeed, the failure of the regime to resolve the political crisis was largely the fault of one small group of people, and that was the coalition between the 'eradicators' in the military and their supporters in the political élite.

By the elections of June 1997 the FIS had become largely marginalised. The regime's policy of promoting the MSP and Ennahda to fragment the FIS's support and divide its vote had been successful to such an extent that the authorities felt confident enough to release Abbasi and Hachani from jail in July. There was no longer any question of the FIS being re-admitted into the political process.

8

TOWARDS A HOLY WAR

Attempts to overthrow the state by violence have punctuated Algerian history from the Donatist schism among rival Christians of the third and fourth centuries AD to the brutality and betrayals on all sides during the war of independence. The FLN used terrorist tactics to intimidate much of the population and ensure its domination of the nationalist movement, while *pied noir* groups such as the OAS staged a series of cold-blooded terrorist atrocities in the early 1960s. It is remarkable how wartime French-Algerian newspapers condemned the FLN for its terrorist outrages in almost identical terms to those used by the regimes and secularist press of the post-Chadli crisis; indeed, the Islamic extremists of the 1990s used strategies and tactics identical to those of the wartime *mudjahidine.* Just as it can be argued that the FIS was the son of the FLN, similar linear connections can be discerned between the Armée Islamique du Salut (AIS) and the wartime ALN, and between the more hardline Groupes Islamiques Armées (GIA) and the partisans of Mustafa Bouyali. In the 1960s Ben Bella and Boumedienne both faced rebellions by rival military commanders and in the 1980s the Chadli regime was faced with the Bouyali uprising. The period 1968-80 was the only time in which the authority of the state was relatively unchallenged by violent rebellion.

Muslim activists often turn to violence out of desperation as so-called modernist regimes seek to suffocate the evolution of political Islam to protect the interests of the ruling élite. Sometimes the regimes themselves create and protect activist groups in order to besmirch the reputation of more mainstream Islamists whom they perceive as representing a greater threat. The Algerian experience was a mixture of the two. Following the clampdown against the FIS in January 1992, Salafi hardliners within the FIS turned to the organisation's clandestine wing, the MIA, primarily to force the regime to lift the ban on the FIS and allow its re-entry into the constitutional process. The MIA's violent campaign gathered momentum throughout 1992 and 1993 and might well have forced the regime to reach an accommodation with the FIS had not a second and more hardline entity, the GIA, emerged in the summer of 1993.

There were around sixty Islamic extremist groups active in Algeria in the mid and late 1990s. They ranged from tiny cells operating in cities to militias boasting as many as 50-60 armed guerrillas active in remote mountainous areas. The Algerian regime was anxious to present the groups as posing a serious though not terminal threat, and thus the Algerian media often distorted reporting on their activities and composition. Such distortion also characterised the greater part of contemporary foreign, and particularly Western, reporting on Islamic extremism in Algeria. By July 1997 at least 100,000 people had died in terrorist violence over the previous three and a half years, though the real figure may have been as high as as 120,000. The inclusion in this figure of at least 115 expatriates killed during this period rendered Algeria statistically the most dangerous place in the world for foreigners, most of whom were murdered by the GIA or its allies. However, the blood feud and the vendetta have traditionally played a major role in Algerian society and a considerable proportion of murders and other attacks ascribed to terrorists in fact represented the settling of scores originating in times of greater security and stability. For example, the assassination in August 1993 of Kasdi Merbah, former prime minister and chief of the Sécurité Militaire, was probably the work not of Islamic extremists but his former enemies within the state apparatus. There were even reports of former landowners hiring militias to raid villages and regain their land under cover of extremist attacks in the Mitidja in 1996 and 1997.

The phenomenon of Islamic extremism in Algeria should be considered against the wider background of the Muslim world and the non-Muslim world's perception of it. Violent Muslim groups stepped up activities in several Islamic states in the early 1980s as the Iranian revolution and the Lebanese civil war increased the non-Muslim world's awareness of the growing importance of political Islam. Indeed, Western observers have found it difficult to distinguish extreme Islamism from its merely political or fundamentalist manifestations. As in other Muslim countries, the vast majority of Islamists in Algeria vigorously reject the use of violence to achieve their aims. A comparative study of countries where Islamic extremism has developed would produce a number of common factors. In Algeria, as in Egypt and Tunisia, extremism grew in an environment where the regime simultaneously rejected radical Islamism on one level while adopting parts of its agenda on another. At times these regimes appointed Islamist figures to government posts as a means of opposing leftist influence, particularly among students. In all cases, such policies contributed to the rise of Islamist political organisations and the emergence of extremist groups. Only in the case of Tunisia, where the regime in 1991 dismantled the En-Nahda organisation, was this situation reversed, and probably only temporarily.

Various internal and external factors influenced the methodology, and shaped the structure, of Algeria's Islamic extremist groups. First, the mythicised experience of the war of independence and of the *mudjahidine* who fought in it played a disproportionately large part in the psychology of Algerians in the 1980s and 1990s. Algerians had been taught from birth to believe that armed struggle is the most honourable route to achieving justice. Such ideas are also central to Islam, and there are countless historical examples of righteous Muslims engaging in holy war, or *jihad*. Second, the experience of extremists outside Algeria had a profound effect. In Egypt, for example, Islamists resorted to the gun in the 1930s and again in the 1970s, when the three principal groups Jihad, al-Jamaat al-Islamia and al-Takfir wal-Hijra emerged out of the dissatisfaction with the moderate Muslim Brotherhood in the city of Asyut in 1973. As with the Muslim Brotherhood, these groups also thought of themselves as a family (*ousra*). They originally campaigned among students in the Asyut area, obliging young women to wear the veil and segregating classrooms. Frustrated with the ponderous approach to Islamisation followed by the Muslim Brotherhood, Jihad and Jamaat militants began to single out Coptic Christians, the security forces and low-ranking officials for assassination. A high command of Islamic Groups, as they became known, emerged in October 1981 in the form of a *Madjlis ech-Chaab* composed of thirty or more radical sheikhs. The Egyptian Islamic extremists scored their greatest triumph in October 1991, when a junior officer, a supporter of Jihad, assassinated President Anwar Sadat on the anniversary of Egypt's 'victory' in the 1973 war against Israel. A new wave of terrorist violence in the Jamaat's traditional heartland in Middle Egypt began in March 1992 and claimed the lives of more than 700 people in the following three years.There are, however, critical differences between the situations in Algeria and Egypt. The state tradition was weak and still under construction in Algeria in the 1990s. Egypt is in many respects a nation-state where violent Islam will arguably always remain marginalised. The GIA's policy of deliberately targeting foreign nationals was one of the most important aspects of the Algerian terrorist insurgency which distinguished it from similar situations elswhere in the world (in the Egyptian case foreigners were attacked in order to damage the tourist industry, one of the country's biggest foreign exchange earners). While insurgent groups had occasionally singled out foreigners as convenient bargaining chips in previous struggles across the world, the Algerian experience was unprecedented.

Origins: Mustafa Bouyali and the 'Afghans'

Broadly there are two strands of Islamic extremists in Algeria: religious zealots and frustrated Islamists. Both have periodically allied themselves with criminals. In the context of the post-Chadli crisis, the GIA and the AIS respectively have represented these two strands, and are heirs to long traditions, although there is a considerable degree of overlap between them. Religious zealots were active in the 1960s but only rarely in the 1970s, and the first significant attacks did not begin until political Islamism was gaining momentum in the early 1980s. Armed zealots attacked a hotel, stocks of alcohol and prostitutes in the conservative towns of el Oued, Batna and Biskra in 1980. There was a sudden rise in Islamic extremist activity in 1982, when a shop selling alcohol, again in el-Oued, was desroyed and an armed group captured the Saharan rim town of Laghouat. For several days the raiders demanded that women be forbidden to work outside the home and that everyone consume dates and milk and walk barefoot.

A group of zealots led by Mustafa Bouyali anticipated the activities of the AIS and GIA in the 1990s. In 1981 Bouyali, a distinguished *mudjahid*, founded the Group for Defence against the Illicit, which later adopted the names of the MIA, the Algerian Islamic Movement and Islamic Jihad. The group was the first specifically violent Islamic organisation which aimed to overthrow the state by force, though Bouyali relied heavily on criminal elements and staged numerous armed raids and other criminal acts to raise funds. In April 1981 Bouyali's followers carried out an attack in Oran, and in July it emerged that the group had planned to attack the luxury Aurassi Hotel in central Algiers and the city's international airport. Bouyali's supporters attacked women whom they deemed to be immodestly dressed in various parts of the country and in July 1981 it emerged that the group had planned to attack the headquarters of the Union Nationale des Femmes Algériennes (UNFA) in Algiers. In August 1981 Bouyali's guerrillas hijacked the payroll from a factory near Algiers and shortly after attacked the police school at Souma, killing a cadet and seizing arms and ammunition. In 1983, however, Bouyali was forced to flee to the mountains around Larba to avoid a clampdown against arms smuggling. The remoteness of the region and its tradition-

ally recalcitrant population made it ideal territory for
Bouyali's *maquisards*, but the group began to disintegrate
when the regime despatched a force into the Larba region
in September 1983. Bouyali managed to elude capture
and stage occasional armed raids along with a large
number of followers until he was betrayed by a local and
killed during a showdown with the security forces on 1
March 1987. In the largest-ever trial of Islamists in
Algeria, involving forty-nine defence lawyers, 198 of
Bouyali's followers went on trial in June 1987. Four
defendants were sentenced to death and five received life
sentences, though the majority received sentences of
between one and twenty years, and fifteen were acquitted.

The Bouyali episode illustrates the parallels between the
wartime FLN, the nascent Islamist movement of the
1980s and the Islamic extremist insurgents of the early
1990s. Like Bouyali the FLN had used the rugged terrain
of the Larba region to launch attacks against the French
colonial forces during the war of independence. Similarly,
Bouyali's involvement in criminal activities anticipated
the crimes committed by the AIS and the GIA in the
1990s. His activities also encouraged armed extremists
after 1992 to tap into the *maquis* traditions of the mountains which provided an almost impregnable base.

The Algerian 'Afghans' also played an important role in
the formation of the Islamic extremist groups of the post-
Chadli crisis. While Mustafa Bouyali was waging his
campaign near Algiers, the conflict between the Soviet-
backed government and the Islamic-nationalist guerrillas
in Afghanistan was drawing to its conclusion in 1990. To
fight the Soviet-backed regime in Kabul the American
Central Intelligence Agency (CIA) and Saudi Arabia
provided enormous financial and military assistance to
the Afghan anti-communist guerrillas, the Mujahideen, at
their main base in Peshawar in northern Pakistan. It is
estimated that the total number of Muslims from Islamic
countries (Algeria, Egypt, Tunisia, Sudan, Saudi Arabia,
Syria, Jordan, the Occupied Territories, Iraq and Iran)
who fought with them exceeded 5,000, though the figure
could be much higher. The Pakistani embassy in Algiers
alone issued 2,800 visas to Algerian volunteers during the

mid-1980s. After mustering in Saudi Arabia, the volunteers underwent training in arms and guerrilla warfare in Pakistan. Saudi Arabia financed the operation, while Pakistan provided arms and military training. The CIA was also closely involved in the operation by providing finance and political support to the volunteers through its client Pakistan. Fighters in this Peshawar-based Muslim 'international brigade' received the relatively high salary of around $1,500 per month while fighting with the *Mujahideen.*

Most of the fighters were loyal to the ultra-conservative Islamist Hezb-i Islami party of Gulbuddin Hekmatyar, whereas the more moderate traditions of the Muslim west and centre was transformed into the Islamic extremism of groups such as Takfir wal-Hijra. As well as giving the fighters valuable guerrilla training and combat experience, the Afghan war exerted a critical psychological influence. Their participation in the victory of the Afghan Mujahideen over the Soviet-backed government in 1991 convinced thousands of young Algerians that a guerrilla campaign could indeed triumph over the might of the Soviet Union. There was an additional resonance for Algerians who had been inculcated with the almost mythical role of guerrillas in their country's own war of independence against the French: the Algerian volunteers left Afghanistan with a firm belief that Allah was on the side of the Islamists. One of the most important leaders of the Algerian 'Afghans' was Kamerredin Kherbane, who later went on to serve on the FIS's executive council in exile.

On their return to Algeria the 'Afghans' were often unable to find employment and soon drifted towards the extreme wing of the Islamist movement. Adopting Afghan-style robes, tunics and beards, they found a natural home in the groups of activists who in 1989-90 were beginning to attack 'immodestly' dressed women in the streets of Algiers and elsewhere. The problem intensified with the end of the Afghan war in 1991 when most of the 'Afghans' returned home. In November of that year at least sixty followers of 'Tayeb the Afghan' attacked a border post at Guemmar near the Tunisian border, resulting in the deaths of three border guards. The security forces pursued and killed thirteen of Tayeb's followers. The incident is usually considered to mark the beginning of the political violence of the post-Chadli crisis, and secularists pointed to the raid during and after the parliamentary election campaign as revealing the Islamists' true intentions. The 'Afghans' later coalesced with former followers of Bouyali and various disaffected elements of the FIS to form the nucleus of the GIA.

The MIA, the GIA and the AIS

The MIA, later to become the AIS, was the largest and most broadly-based Islamic extremist organisation of the post-Chadli crisis. Despite its radical discourse, the MIA was representative of, and connected to, the political traditions of the Algerian nationalist movement, with which it shared some common objectives. Because the majority of its members had been associated with the FIS, they tended to support its constitutionalist project: neither the MIA nor the AIS ever attempted to mobilise popular support on a massive scale or to provoke a collapse of the state by assassinating senior members of the regime. The organisation's strategy was to use violence with the aim of encouraging the state to abrogate its ban on the FIS and relegalise the party. To achieve its objectives the organisation mainly carried out a medium- and long-term strategy of attacking the security forces and junior civil servants. The AIS repeatedly demonstrated its links to the FIS by publicly supporting that organisation and its policies, specifically the National Contract of January 1995.

The GIA was the complement of the MIA and AIS. Most of its members had never been part of the FIS and most of them rejected the front's strategy of considering negotiation with the Algerian state to achieve power. The organisation totally rejected any dialogue or compromise with the state and, unlike the MIA and AIS, favoured short-term, spectacular terrorist attacks. Furthermore, the AIS was more akin to a traditional guerrilla group and exhibited the *maquis* traditions of the FLN. While the GIA was primarily an urban organisation (albeit with important footholds in the countryside around Tlemcen, Medea, and the hinterland of Djidjel), the AIS enjoyed a strong presence in rural areas.

The development of the MIA can be traced to the early years of the FIS. Like the war-time FLN, the FIS was conceived as an umbrella for all shades of Islamist opinion. Whether with or without the knowledge and sanction of the leadership (which was itself divided). there were extremist elements within the FIS from the very beginning. Some of these had established terrorist groups even before the military intervention of January 1992, though the exact date of the MIA's establishment is a matter of conjecture. Salafi hardliners believed that that an Islamic state could only be achieved through the use of force and thus tacitly encouraged these groups. Said Mekhloufi, a former army officer who had fought alongside Bouyali in the mid-1980s and who later became director of the FIS journal *El Mounqid*, was an important figure among the 'respectable' FIS hardliners who later went on to play a large part in the extremist movement. By the end of 1992 Mekhloufi had secured the title of the first ackowledged supreme leader of the MIA.

The distinctions between the FIS and the extremist fringe became increasingly blurred as the violence worsened throughout 1992 and 1993. Even allowing for the regime's readiness to ascribe almost every act of violence in Algeria to Islamic extremists, many party members and officials within and without Algeria were directly or indirectly involved in extremist activities. In the first six months of 1992 the organisation grew rapidly as thousands of frustrated FIS supporters went underground in the weeks after the cancellation of the elections. The sight of relatives and friends rounded up and transported to the Saharan internment camps was a major incentive for many to join the MIA. Official reports of 'terrorist' trials frequently mentioned the alleged perpetrator's former – or in some cases – current membership of the FIS. A notable example of this was Hocine Abderrahim, a former companion of Bouyali and

aide to Abassi who, together with three other FIS members, was sentenced in December 1992 for involvement
in the August 1992 bombing of Algiers international
airport. The regime claimed that the close links between
the FIS and the MIA proved that the FIS had planned to
use violence from the beginning.

The MIA was organised on the triangle system developed by FLN guerrillas during the war of independence.
Under this system each member of the cell knows only
two other members of the network, though not their rank
or status within the organisation as a whole. If detained
and tortured an activist's objective is to remain silent for
at least twenty-four hours to allow the other members of
the cell to go to ground and inform the network. This
allowed the network to continue functioning effectively
even when the presumed leadership of the organisation
had been arrested or temporarily incapacitated. The
network was highly decentralised: cells were based on
apartment blocks or *quartiers* and no activist ever came
into direct contact with the leadership. Although there is
strong evidence to suggest that the leadership took policy
decisions on strategy and targeting, the cell commanders
themselves made the day-to-day decisions. Little else is
known of the internal workings of the MIA and AIS.

A fundamental change in the situation during 1993 and
early 1994 led to the transformation of the MIA into the
AIS in 1994. Fierce clampdowns by the security forces
during the winter of 1993/4 and a series of attacks by the
GIA had created this changed environment. In many
areas the MIA was forced to withdraw from its strongholds in the main towns and cities into the interior, where
it immediately encountered a new challenge with the
arrival of guerrillas owing allegiance to the GIA, who had
themselves been ejected from urban areas by government offensives. In the spring of 1994 the MIA founded a
new network of armed Islamic groups under the new title
of the AIS. The objective was to correct the growing
perception of the MIA as a 'moderate' organisation whose
emirs lacked the determination and brutality of the feared
GIA. The veteran *maquisard* Abdelkader Chebouti was
appointed 'supreme leader' of the AIS but his chronic

illness meant that Mekhloufi was entrusted with the day-to-day running of the organisation. On the ground the AIS was divided into two 'military wings': the East (under '*emir*' Cheikh Madani Merzak, also known as Abou el-Haithem) and the West (under '*emir*' Cheikh Ahmed Ben Aicha, also known as Abou Salah).

The FIS leadership enthusiastically welcomed the formation of the AIS. Abassi and Belhadj approved the plan as means to reimpose their authority over the extremist tendency, to erase the MIA's failures in 1992-3 and to counter the increasing influence of the GIA, which was now operating without reference to the FIS leadership. Abbasi and Belhadj also saw the AIS as a means of conferring upon them the popular 'legitimacy' and authority derived from being commanders of an armed organisation, a position they had lost to some extent in the first round of talks with President Zeroual in April 1994.

The GIA was formed by a coalition of former followers of Mustafa Bouali, the 'Afghans' and hardline dissidents from the MIA and the FIS. Until 1993 the authorities tended to attribute occasional attacks on women, journalists and intellectuals to the 'Afghans'; and although the followers of a leading 'Afghan' extremist Abdelhak Layada used the term GIA, it did not appear, it did not appear in the Algerian press until September 1993. During the summer of 1993 the 'Afghans' began to form more closely organised groups in response to intensified security force offensives in and around Algiers. The army and gendarmerie would often round up hundreds of suspects after a terrorist attack, and on occasion summarily and illegally executed detainees as a warning to others. The survivors were more likely to join the radical GIA than the more moderate AIS. This, however, was both a strength and a weakness for the GIA, as it allowed Sécurité Militaire agents to infiltrate the organisation. Indeed, it is entirely plausible that elements of the regime were responsible for the transformation of the loose coalition of 'Afghan' groups within the GIA. There is much anecdotal evidence suggesting that undercover SM agents linked to the regime's 'eradicator' trend directed

GIA cells, on occasion selecting high-profile targets for assassination. Their objective would have been to carry out terrorist atrocities to reclaim public opinion for the regime.

The leadership of the GIA was frequently subject to dispute, and the average period for an incumbent was a few months. Leaders, who were known by the Arabic word for prince, *emir*, were either former 'Afghans' or known criminals, and very few played any substantial role in the FIS during its legal phase. Abdelhak Layada was the first leader of the GIA but he was succeeded by Mourad Si Ahmed, also known as Djafar al-Afghan, when he was captured in October 1992. When Si Ahmed was killed in an encounter near Algiers in February 1994, there developed a struggle among at least four GIA commanders. Eventually, Cherif Gousmi, the former radical preacher at a mosque in Birkhadem and FIS official, who used the *nom de guerre* Ahmed Abu Abdallah, took over, until he too was killed in a gun battle in September 1994. After taking control of the GIA, Gousmi established his own special cell formed entirely of 'Afghans' and known as the Death Battalion. The battalion carried out a series of terrorist atrocities throughout the winter of 1993-4 in and around Algiers, and was suspected of being responsible for the murders of foreigners there. In August 1994 Gousmi declared himself 'caliph' of Algeria and the former provisional leader of the FIS Mohamed Said designated himself 'prime minister'. Reports also spoke of a GIA 'government' complete with a 'political commission' and 'external relations department.'

The relationship between the AIS and the GIA fluctuated from outright hostility to cooperation and even an attempt at merger. The two networks operated in parallel until 1993, when the first reports emerged of clashes between rival *emirs*. In March 1994 the GIA 'liquidated' seventy MIA fighters whom it suspected of cooperation with the regime, while in August the AIS was reported to have killed a local GIA *emir* and members of his family in a particularly savage clash in the Blida Atlas. However, certain figures within the exiled leadership of FIS, most notably Anouar Haddam, from time to time made speeches that appeared to support the GIA. In May 1994 the AIS and GIA announced a merger, though this collapsed in April 1995 when Abassi entered into a third round of talks with President Zeroual. By the time the talks failed in July 1995, the GIA had officially expelled Abassi and Belhadj from its collective leadership and sentenced them to death.

A third force among the extremist groups operated under the title '*al-Takfir wal-Hijra*' (Redemption and Exile), which had originally been a local branch of a radical Egyptian group formed in 1974. It first came to public attention with a series of minor attacks against unveiled women and liquor shops during Ramadan in 1989, though its leaders, Mansour Meliani and Abdel-kader Cherati, appear to have thrown in their lot with the MIA during 1992. Many of its leadership fled Algeria in the spring of 1992 for exile in France, Canada and the United States, and by the end of the year the security forces claimed to have neutralised the group. Part of the GIA's strategy was to claim attacks in different names to confuse the authorities, and the use of *Takfir* may have been one such instance.

There is no reliable data on the numerical strength of the Islamic extremist groups. The authorities in April 1993 claimed that there were no more than 175 active guerillas (most of whom were members of the MIA) with a network of 925 supporters. These figures were almost certainly gross underestimates, and the true number of active guerrillas was more likely to be as high as 10,000 or even 15,000, with perhaps as many active supporters. The estimated strength of the GIA's armed forces was some 2,500. Guerrillas were predominantly under twenty-five, unemployed and lived in towns or cities, though many were older and had long criminal records. The groups raised money among Islamist supporters in emigré Algerian communities in Europe and North America, particularly from wealthy Algerian businessmen with Islamist symphies. Armed robbery of banks was an additional source of finance; in March 1993, for instance, there was a five-day siege of a bank near Blida.

Iran and Sudan have often been demonised as the grand international patrons of Islamist organisations, and Algeria has repeatedly singled out the two countries as foremost among foreign governments that support its extremist groups. In March 1993 Algeria severed diplomatic ties with Tehran. Although the extent of Iran's support of Algeria's extremists has probably been exaggerated, there is considerable evidence pointing to official Iranian support as part of its policy of exporting the Islamic revolution throughout the Muslim world. There is reason to believe that Iran was involved in the Algiers airport bombing of August 1992 and there were occasional reports of Iranian 'agents' being deported from Algeria. The Algerian press described the Iranian embassy in Algiers as a 'nest of spies' and claimed that Iran paid for a group of Algerian Islamists to travel to Lebanon to receive military training in Hezbollah camps. Evidence of Sudanese involvement, however, is less convincing and rests mainly on the established links between Islamists in Tehran and the Sudanese capital, Khartoum. Sudan's Islamist-backed military government has earned a reputation as a haven for numerous foreign Islamist groups, particularly Egyptians, and the Algerian authorities probably feel compelled to denounce Sudan as well as Iran.

A War on All Fronts

The Islamic extremist insurgency affected certain parts of northern Algeria to a far greater degree than other areas. Although the extremist groups enjoyed some support throughout the north, they tended to confine their activities to specific areas. These were the Algiers region, the Constantine hinterland, the Tellian Atlas (particularly around Blida), the Sid Bel Abbes area as far as the Moroccan border, and the central region around Djelfa. Greater Algiers and Blida province were by far the worst affected particularly the area known as the 'triangle of death'. Support for the FIS remained strong in the high-density, low-income districts of Algiers and terrorist killings and shoot-outs were a daily occurrence. Intensive security elsewhere in the city – the centre and those suburbs favoured by the nomenklatura, and the foreign enclaves, such as Hydra and Ben Aknoun – ensured that violence occurred much less frequently there.

Remote mountainous regions provided the ideal terrain for the extremist groups, as they did for the FLN and the followers of Bouyali before them. Both the MIA and GIA formed *maquis* groups in the mountains of the Tellian Atlas, from where they could mount ambushes on the security forces along roads and in nearby population centres. Official figures for terrorist-related incidents in the period February 1992 to April 1993 showed that of approximately 860 casualties, 315 were security-force personnel and soldiers; 370 presumed Islamic extremists; and 170 were civilians. The guerrillas would often terrorise the local population into concealing their whereabouts from the security forces. An operation in May 1992 provides a good illustration of the size and organisation of a typical guerrilla force. Five army battalions were mobilised against armed extremists who had installed themselves in the remote mountainous region near Lakhdaria, south-east of Algiers. The MIA-linked group had planned to use its remote base on Mount Zbarbar to attack the security forces and symbols of state authority in the area. Abdelkader Chebouti was also reported to have established a training camp on the mountain to shelter a number of Islamist army deserters. At least 150 would-be *maquisards* were arrested in the operation.

In the autumn of 1992 the extremists began an assassination campaign against their enemies. The motives behind the killings were a combination of classic terrorist tactics ('kill one to scare a thousand') and religious zeal. As Francis Ghillles has observed, the killings were often redolent of sacrificial acts. 'Honour can only be washed with blood, [and] witnesses must be present at the sacrifice.'[1] Cassette tapes of sermons in which extremist

---

[1] *Middle East International.*

imams ordered the faithful to kill anyone collaborating with the authorities began to appear in September 1992. Those under threat ranged from members of the government to civilians perceived as supporters of the regime in a wide range of professions and who were therefore enemies of the Islamist movement. This included civil servants, local government officials, *mudjahidine*, party politicians (particularly from the RCD and the FFS) and officials of state-run authorities. The assassinations were usually well planned and executed, and the periodic waves of attacks on particular targets were intended gradually to increase pressure on the regime. By 1995 most politicians and senior civil servants had been forced to flee their villas on the hills above Algiers to take refuge in the well-guarded seaside resort of Sidi Fredj to the west of the city, from where the most important travelled to work by helicopter. Such intense security prevented attempts being made on the lives of the most senior government figures, though one of the most audacious occurred in May 1992 when the defence minister, Khaled Nezzar, narrowly escaped a car bomb in the suburb of el-Biar as his convoy was passing. Members of Nezzar's élite protection squad were probably involved. In May 1995 the GIA managed to plant at least two bombs in the Aurassi Hotel timed to explode during a meeting attended by four government ministers and all forty-eight provincial governors, though the security forces managed to defuse all the devices.

In 1993 the extremists broadened their interpretation of their enemies to include relatives of government officials and 'anti-Islamist' civilians. While many victims had some family connection with the security forces, such as fathers or uncles in the gendarmerie or police, others had no apparent reason for being targeted. Scores of merchants, shopkeepers, engineers and labourers were knifed or shot to death. The assassins also struck at minor employees in local or central government. Although they were technically civilians, the MIA singled them out because of their vulnerability and their connection to the state. In March 1995 the GIA issued a warning that it would kill the wives, sisters and daughters of state functionaries, and followed it up with a spate of murders of women. In one such incident, a young secretary in a state-linked institution was shot in the back of the head as she entered her apartment. She died in her brother's arms. The extremists later imitated the tactics of the FLN by carrying out random bomb attacks in public places. In 1994 the GIA began to plant bombs with the aim of terrorising the population into pressing the authorities to negotiate with the Islamists. Among the most serious of these incidents was the blast outside Algiers central police station in March 1995, in which more than forty people lost their lives. In June 1995 the GIA began a campaign of suicide car bombings in Algiers.

The zealots also struck at journalists writing in 'anti-Islamist' publications and working for the state broadcasting corporation. The objective of this campaign, which was almost without precedent in the Muslim world, was simply to undermine the secular-nationalist state by removing its most distinguished and outspoken supporters, a class of people once referred to by former prime minister Belaïd Abdessalam as '*laïco-assimilationistes*'. The Kabyle journalist and writer Tahar Djaout was one of the earliest victims, fatally injured by gunmen near his home in the Algiers suburb of Bainem in late May 1993. Djaout was the editor-in-chief of the weekly magazine *Algérie Actualité*, and author of a prize-winning novel warning of the dangers of despotism and religious obscurantism. Almost every editor of Francophone newspapers received threatening letters, such as one printed in *Le Monde* in 1993, signed by the MIA: 'You are going to die; if not today, be sure that it will be tomorrow! And your death will be written in the glorious pages of the Islamic movement.' Another attacked its target as a 'Francophone extremist' and 'enemy of the language of the Koran'. The threats illustrated the enmity of the Islamists' for Francophones in general, and Kabyles in particular, on the ground that French-language newspapers were the vanguard of the secularist trend. By mid-1995 more than forty newspaper and broadcasting journalists had lost their lives. The campaign also targeted intellectuals and such academics as psychiatrists and sociologists, whose disciplines were seen by the extremists as 'un-Islamic'.

Infiltration of the armed forces was an important element in the extremists' armoury. Scores of incidents were planned with the knowledge and assistance of security-force personnel, acting either voluntarily or through direct or indirect intimidation. One of the worst examples occurred in March 1993, when an officer led six extremists dressed in genuine army uniforms in a raid on an army barracks near Algiers. After they had killed four sentries and disabled outside communications, twenty-nine other assailants drove into the barracks in a military truck, gunned down nineteen soldiers who were breaking the Ramadan fast, looted weapons and ammunition, and escaped. In a notable incident in 1994 prison guards helped more than 200 prisoners to escape from Tazoult-Lambèse jail. We have already seen how differing backgrounds resulted in contrary ideological orientations between officers trained in the French army (and who came late to the FLN cause) and those whose first military experiences were with the wartime ALN. This to some extent explained divergent attitudes among the military towards the Islamist movement. Furthermore, there was much published evidence and more of an unanecdotal character pointing to substantial sympathy for the Islamist cause among junior officers and conscripts. In February 1993 twenty-seven soldiers were condemned to death in absentia for failing to denounce 'crimes against state security' at a special military tribunal in the western town of Bechar. Such sympathies provided extremists with information on the selection of targets, on their movemets and on the layout of military premises. They furnished them with arms, ammunition and, despite official denials, deserted to join armed Islamist groups.

In September 1993 the GIA began to murder foreigners, and by mid-1997 more than 115 had died in Algeria, though, as with all other aspects of the post-Chadli crisis, there was a large degree of falsification in the reporting of the murders. We have seen how the GIA's loose structure allowed SM to infiltrate it; it is also entirely possible that certain elements within the ruling élite ordered some of the murders to focus world attention on the 'Islamic threat' and extract concessions from Western governments. The murders had two principal motivations. First, the extremists wanted to persuade actual and potential foreign investors that Algeria was unsafe, to suspend their operations and therefore undermine the regime's efforts at investment-led economic revival. Second, the extremists were acting out of xenophobia formed under French colonial rule and given fresh impetus by the anti-Western and anti-socialist polemic of radical Islam.

The wave of attacks against foreign nationals began on 21 September 1993 when militants abducted and subsequently killed two French surveyors driving to work on the Sidi Bel Abbès-Oued Tlelat road in western Algeria. In the following month the GIA kidnapped three French consular officials in central Algiers. In a letter handed to one of the hostages shortly before her release on 31 October, the GIA ordered foreigners to 'leave the country. We are giving you one month. Anyone who exceeds that period will be responsible for his own sudden death. There will be no kidnapping and it will be more violent than in Egypt.' The extremists sent similar messages on a videotape to the Algerian authorities and in a letter in French and Arabic to the Paris office of the Agence France Presse. The last letter warned foreign firms in Algeria of the dangers facing their employees and accused France of being an accomplice of the Algerian regime. A further threat was later issued by Moussa Kraouche, the detained spokesman of the main FIS-linked organisation in France, the Fraternité Algérien en France (FAF), who warned foreigners to expect 'much tougher acts of reprisal because you cannot play with the freedom of the people.' It is possible that the Algerian security forces were involved in the abduction of the consular officials; the authorities seemed to know when the two remaining male hostages would be freed, and it is significant that the three were the first foreigners to survive an Islamic extremist kidnap.

The GIA staged more attacks on foreigners across Algeria over the years that followed. The incidents were a combination of opportunism and sophistication. Most victims were long-term expatriates with no security and thus easy to target. Other victims were nationals of socialist or former socialist countries (such as Vietnam) with which Algeria had cemented cooperative alliances. In one of the most notorious incidents, twelve Croats were killed at Tamezguida, a town to the south-west of Algiers, in December 1993. The ritualistic details of the incident typify some of the more savage murders: the guerrillas snatched the Croats from their living quarters, tied their hands with steel wire, forced them to strip naked and herded them into an empty swimming pool where they slit their throats or beat them to death. Four technicians saved their lives by pretending to be Muslims and were locked up along with some Algerian workers, who were unharmed. The GIA stated that the attack was intended to underline its deadline and to avenge the deaths of Muslims in Bosnia.

By 1995 the leading Western countries, particularly the United States, had identified Islamic extremists as the most significant threat to Western interests worldwide, citing Algeria as the most visible 'proof' of this development. The threat of terrorist attack decimated Algeria's foreign business community, and those expatriates who remained did so from the safety of a guarded company compound, or were likely to be long-established residents who refused to leave Algeria and were unable to afford any protection.

Conclusion

Islamic extremist 'terrorism' was clearly one of the central determining factors in Algeria's post-Chadli crisis. More than five years after the MIA first resorted to armed attacks to persuade the state to lift the ban on the FIS, the Algerian authorities remained unable fully to eradicate a disparate coalition of crudely armed guerrillas and urban militants whose combined strength amounted to perhaps less than 10 per cent of its own military. Successive increments in the number of troops deployed had little effect against the *maquis* until desertions undermined their strength in 1995. The AIS never considered itself capable of overthrowing the state, but did succeed in undermining it by forcing the regime to resort to brutality and repression in its anti-militant campaign. Under the state of emergency regulations passed in February 1992, the interior ministry could order the searching of residences at any time of the day or night, ban marches, close public buildings and compel strikers to return to work.

The actions of the security forces did nothing to win over public opinion. Although torture of detainees had all but died out by 1991, it reappeared and became widespread, and in some areas routine, after the spring of 1992. In 1993 Amnesty International claimed that the security forces frequently resorted to administrative detention without charge and forms of torture such as beatings, burnings and near-suffocations. According to many reports, the use of the 'chiffon' method – forcing the detainee to swallow water so that he almost suffocates – was widespread. The prospect of a fair trial at the special anti-terrorist courts was remote and the death penalty was resorted to with increasing frequency. By late 1997, neither side could claim a victory, either military or moral.

9

THE BERBER QUESTION

Algeria's quest for a 'national' identity has been a constant theme in Algerian politics since independence. In the 1930s Muslim Algerians seeking to end the French occupation and establish an order based on the country's pre-existing Arab-Islamic character employed Arab nationalism as the channel for their struggle. One key objective was to raise a standard which would unite the various ethnic, geographical, family, tribal and military clans which constitute Algerian society. Ironically, the geographical area claimed by the early Muslim nationalists as their 'homeland' corresponded to the areas defined as 'l'Algérie' by the occupying power, and ignored the historical connections of the west with eastern Morocco and of the east with Tunisia. The nationalists also insisted on the Islamic basis of the new nation-state, whose official national language was to be Arabic, but the drive to create a unified, Arabo-Islamic Algerian state resulted in many casualties. As we have seen, the Arabisation programme created in Algeria a unique linguistic situation where language is a live political and social issue. It has also alienated a sizeable proportion of the country's population – loosely grouped together for convenience under the name of Berbers.

The country's large Berber minority is one of the obstacles to an Islamist conception of Algeria. The Kabyles are the most sizeable, politically best organised and most sophisticated of the various Berber groups. Their rugged mountain homeland has historically allowed them to preserve their separate identity and language, and the region's two main cities, Tizi Ouzou and Bejaia, have long been considered different from other Algerian towns. The post-Chadli crisis has accentuated these differences, and both towns are permissive and liberal oases in a sea of violence and intolerance. Tizi Ouzou is one of a few places where where alcohol is freely available in bars, restaurants and hotels and its university is the only one in Algeria to use French as the medium of instruction. A slogan often seen scrawled on walls in the town sums up the position of most Kabyles regarding the post-Chadli crisis: 'Neither a police state nor an Islamic republic'.

The Berber question, or more precisely the Kabyle question, has haunted Algerian politics since before independence. Kabyles and other Berbers articulate their demands for official recognition of their culture and language through the channel of 'Berberism'. In the mid-1990s two political parties, the FFS and the RCD, as well as the culturally-oriented MCB, constituted the wider Berberist movement. The movement itself preferred the term 'Berberist' to 'Berber nationalist' since the latter, though not incorrect, refers more to the idea of pan-Berberist unity incorporating Berber communities throughout the North African states. The Berberist movement's main demand is that the Algerian state recognise the Kabyle language 'Amazigh' alongside and in equality with Algerian Arabic. The Algerians have developed the word *Amazighité* to describe the speaking of Amazigh. Some Berberists argue that French should also be designated an official language. The other significant elements of Berberism refer to the cultural rather than political aspects of Kabyle identity, revealing the popularity of European political concepts such as civil society among educated Kabyles. However, separatism and nationalism are not dominant elements in Berberism and only a minority of activists favour total independence for Kabylia.

The Kabyles have always played a role in the country's history disproportionate to their number. Kabyles were among the most committed and active members of the the early nationalist movement and of the wartime FLN, including two of the organisation's most influential members, Abane Ramdane and Krim Belkacem, who headed the Muslim delegation in the 1961-2 talks with France. Since independence there have been scores of Kabyle ministers, senior civil servants and opposition politicians, such as Kasdi Merbah and Mohamed Said. Despite this, successive regimes did nothing towards recognising the Kabyles' particular linguistic and cultural identity – that is, until 1995.

Language

The question of the Berber language is the cornerstone of the Berberist movement and of many other aspects of Algerian politics. In Algeria the term 'Berber' is often used interchangeably to refer to the Kabyle dialect, known as Amazigh, though there are numerous other Berber dialects. Until the nineteenth century Amazigh was primarily a spoken language with a rich vocabulary of over 500,000 words. French scholars later stimulated the alphabetisation of Amazigh into a written form known as Tamazigh, Tamazight or Thamazighth, but most often referred to as Tamazigh. This alphabetisation has historically been a source of controversy. Berber purists insist on the use of Tifinagh, the elegant ideographic script used to write the Touareg dialect, Tamanhaq, but as this is not ideally suited to modern Amazigh, users of the language tend to favour a modified version of the Latin script. This created conflict with the proponents of Arabisation: in the 1980s President Chadli and the FIS argued that the Kabyles should write their language in the Arabic rather than the 'imperialist' Latin script.

The Berberists' demand for Tamazigh to be designated alongside Algerian Arabic as the national language of Algeria excites political passions among all Algerians. Salem Mezhoud has written:

While recognising the dual character of North Africa's people and culture, the Berberists still reject arabisation on the ground that it is based on false premises. To them, two languages are spoken in Algeria: Berber and Algerian Arabic, the latter being a very different idiom from what was made the official language of the country. ...The Berberists advocate, therefore, the abolition of this official language and its replacement, on equal terms, by the two truly national languages of Algeria: Berber and Algerian Arabic.[1]

Furthermore, the issue is closely implicated in the debate over Algeria's own identity, and in the determination of successive regimes to Arabise the country as a means of forging a nation and consolidating state power – a policy which is a legacy from the 'external' wing of the FLN. Kabyles typically view the victory of Ben Bella over other elements of the Algerian nationalist movement in 1962-3 as the victory of the 'externals' (that is,. those who fought the war from outside the country) over the 'internals'. The Boumedienne and Chadli regimes defended their refusal of the Berberists' demands on the grounds that to concede would risk further fuelling Kabyle regional separatism. This is an important consideration in a country in which regional suspicions and tribal feuds have traditionally played such a large role.

Historically, Algerian regimes have dismissed both Tamazigh and Algerian Arabic as mere dialects. This is nothing unusual in the Arab world, as virtually all its regimes subordinate local dialectal forms of Arabic to Modern Standard and Classical Arabic (the only exception is Morocco). The *arabisant*-dominated regimes of Boumedienne, Chadli and the HCE have all claimed that Berbers are descended from Arabs and that therefore there is no justification for special status being given to Berber languages. Salem Chaker[2] has described this policy as 'the synthesis of marginalisation and negation'. The resurgence of Islamism from the late 1980s has further strengthened the state's resolve to impose Modern Standard Arabic as the national language, with Arabic and Berber dialects confined to the home.

However, Tamazigh media and literature has undermined the state's policy. In the late 1980s Kabyles began to publish a wide range of Tamazigh newspapers, maga-

[1] 'Glasnost the Algerian Way' in George Joffé (ed.), *North Africa: Nation, State and Region*, London: Routledge, 1993.
[2] 'De quelques constantes du discours dominant sur les langues populaires en Algérie', *Annuaire de l'Afrique du Nord* (1981).

zines and books. There also developed a vigorous Kabyle music industry based both among the Kabyle immigrant community in France and in Algeria itself. The periodic efforts made by Islamists to prevent concerts by leading Kabyles from taking place, particularly during the Muslim holy fasting month of Ramadan, demonstrated its potency. Islamic extremists have also staged bomb attacks during concerts of Kabyle music. Despite the efforts of the state and the Islamists to restrict Berber dialects, an unofficial co-existence between Arabic and Berber dialects has prevailed in the 1990s, with Tamazigh restricted as a regional language.

The Roots of Berber Activism

There are two factors which gave birth to early Berber cultural awareness and later to its political activism: the work of numerous European ethnographers in the late nineteenth century and the French colonial authorities' policy of distinguishing Kabyle communities from the Arab population in order to impose their own control. As one contemporary French colonial officer remarked, 'The Kabyles have an advantage over the Arabs in that they have demonstrated a particular aptitude for education, particularly in the speaking and writing of French.' In 1907 the first Kabyle migrants arrived in France to break strikes by Italians in the port of Marseille. The thousands who followed them gradually developed into a small French-speaking educated class which, encouraged by exposure to European ideas of nationalism and national culture, began to reassess their own Kabyle cultural inheritance. One of the first significant examples of modern Kabyle literature was a collection of the Amazigh oral poetry of the revered Si Mohand, edited in 1925 by a Kabyle Christian convert, Si Saïd Boulifa. However, it was not until 1954 that Kabyle émigrés established the Association for the Development of the Berber Language (*Tiwizi i tmazit*) in Paris.

France was also the stage for the first glimmerings of Kabyle political consciousness among the émigré community. Kabyles played a major part in the establishment of the first Algerian nationalist movement, the Étoile Nord-Africaine, which later became the PPA. Here Kabyles were further exposed to modern European political ideas, particularly nationalism and socialism, and to techniques of resistance. In the late 1940s Kabyle militants within the PPA-MTLD created the so-called 'Berberist crisis' when they called on the party leadership to clarify its stance on the relationship between Islam and democracy. Awareness of the Kabyles' plight also grew at home, as illustrated by a ground-breaking series of articles entitled 'The Misery of Kabylia' by the *pied noir* writer Albert Camus which appeared in the daily *Alger Républicain* in 1939. However, the early flowerings of Berberism were cut short in 1952 when the French section of the PPA-MTLD was dissolved. As the nationalist struggle against the French intensified and the FLN gradually established its domination, the Arabo-Islamic tendency subordinated Kabyle conciousness and then marginalised or expelled many figures perceived to be Berberists. At the same time the *ulema* rejected Berberism as a 'reactionary doctine born of imperialism'. After independence many FLN commanders feared that their colleagues of Kabyle origin would exploit their positions to create a Kabyle state. To prevent this, Boumedienne's 'frontier army' was tasked with suppressing any signs of separatist ambitions in Kabylia.

Although Krim Belkacem was the first nationalist leader to call for the official recognition of the Kabyle language during the war of independence, Hocine Aït Ahmed assumed the unofficial leadership of the Kabyle minority after 1962. At independence Aït Ahmed immediately opposed Ben Bella's moves to concentrate power in his own hands, a process which he denounced as 'progressive fascisation and the regime's authoritarian drift'. Increasingly aware of the futility of trying to mount effective opposition to Ben Bella from within the Assembly, Aït Ahmed resigned from the FLN and established the Front des Forces Socialistes (FFS) in September 1963. Although the front grouped together many of the anti-Ben Bella forces in the FLN, the FFS was primarily a Kabyle-based political organisation. Aït Ahmed was arrested in October 1964 and sentenced to death for organising an insurrection earlier that year, though Ben Bella commuted his sentence to life imprisonment three months later in a bid to gain Kabyle support against Boumedienne and the Oujda clan. Aït Ahmed escaped from prison in el-Harrach in south-east Algiers in May 1966 and fled into exile in France and later Switzerland. He joined with Ben Bella's Mouvement pour la Démocratie en Algérie (MDA) in December 1985 in the short-lived alliance known as the 'London Declaration'.

Aït Ahmed's defeat in 1965 was a severe setback for Kabyle aspirations inside Algeria, and for the next fifteen years the focus of Kabyle activism shifted to the Kabyle community in France. Unable publicly to discuss Berberist ideas in their homeland, young Kabyles held meetings in France to discuss their agenda and began to publish prose and poetry in Tamazigh. In 1967 France-based Kabyle activists established the Académie Berbère de l'Échange et de la Recherche Culturel (ABERC) in Paris. The constant flow of immigrants' families between France and Algeria constituted a channel for the transmission of news of these activities, inspiring hundreds of young frustrated Kabyles. Many joined the clandestine FFS, which was at the time the sole Berberist political organisation in existence. In its manifesto, the FFS based itself itself on loosely-defined European 'social-democratic' principles and rejected both the dictatorship of the proletariat and the formalised power of the bourgeoisie. Despite this, Algerians have always identified the party with the Kabyles, and it has made little impact outside that community.

Berberism continued to develop underground during the Boumedienne years despite the strength of the state apparatus. A second Algeria-based Kabyle organisation, the Mouvement Culturel Berbère (MCB), emerged during the anti-Boumedienne unrest of 1968. The movement's objectives were the establishment of political pluralism and the thwarting of the state's plans to wage 'genocide' against the Berbers. The MCB attempted to appeal to Berbers across the political, ideological and social class spectrum by placing an emphasis on cultural and linguistic concerns, and it was rewarded as various Kabyle opponents of the ruling regime during the 1970s gravitated towards the movement as the most realistic and most radical channel for dissident activities. Many Kabyles drifted to the MCB in protest at Boumedienne's Arabisation programme. This was conceived not only further to reinforce the authority of the state and encourage uniformity, but also to suppress the regionalism, including Berberism, which the state feared would undermine those objectives.

The gradual radicalisation of Kabyle activism inevitably led to violence. The authorities arrested several Kabyle activists following protests in 1976-8 against moves to reduce the air time of Kabyle Radio (a legacy of French rule with which independent Algerian regimes had never been comfortable). In 1976 a group of young Berberists received death sentences and long prison terms for a bomb attack on the headquarters of the FLN newspaper *El Moudjahid* which had resulted in only minor damage. The regime capitalised on this episode by claiming that the perpetrators' alleged links with the Académie Française in Paris were proof of the foreign manipulation of the Berberist movement.

The events of April 1980 – the 'Tizi Ouzou Spring' – were the first serious outbreak of Berberist frustration in independent Algeria. Observers so nicknamed the unrest because of the perceived similarities with the Prague Spring twelve years earlier in what was then Czechoslovakia. The cumulative effects of twenty years of state repression was the principal underlying cause, though there were other contributing factors: the still unresolved conflict between the francisants and the arabisants in which the Kabyles were key players; the death in 1978 of Boumedienne, rightly feared by the Kabyles as a committed anti-Berberist, which unconsciously acted as an impetus to the Berberists; the subsequent accession of Chadli Bendjedid and the resulting hopes for liberalisation; and the growing strength of the MCB in Kabylia. Kabyle emigrants in France who were increasingly aware of and exposed to Kabyle literature and culture also played a part. Lastly, Kabyles had begun to look upon Tizi Ouzou as their 'capital'. The town, which had become prosperous due to remittances sent from Kabyles abroad, was the only real urban centre among the predominantly rural villages of Kabylia. A University Centre had been established in the 1970s and had developed as the cultural heart of Berberism. The first signs of trouble came in early 1980 when rumours – probably justified – began to circulate that the government was considering closing down Kabyle Radio. Later, there was a wave of strikes at various universities, including the centre at Tizi Ouzou, in protest at a sudden acceleration of the government's Arabisation policies. The last straw was the attempt to ban the lecture by the foremost Berber actrvist, Mouloud Mammeri: more than thirty people were killed and nearly 200 injured in the weeks of unrest which followed.

At first it seemed that the unrest would galvanise the state into making concessions. In May 1980 the minister of higher education and scientific research pledged to create a chair of Kabyle Studies at the University Centre in Tizi Ouzou and to re-establish the chair of Berber Studies at Algiers University which had been abolished in October 1962. Later, Chadli promised to appoint a commission to launch a thorough review of all cultural policy and draw up a Cultural Charter to be debated by a FLN commission. However, these glimmerings of hope were soon dashed when the government announced that the convinced *arabisant* information and culture minister, Abdelhamid Mehri, was to head the commission. These promises did not impress the Berberists, who proceeded with their campaign outside established channels, and sporadic but usually peaceful protests continued into 1981. In May a mob, reportedly swollen by extreme leftists, attacked public buildings and cars and clashed with the security forces. Aware that the unrest would harm the Berberist cause, Kabyle leaders denounced the unrest, and they were vindicated when around twenty activists were arrested for public order offences later in the month. Furthermore, the FLN Central Committee meeting in June-July finally passed a Cultural Charter which, while reaffirming Algeria's 'popular cultural heritage', made no direct mention of the Kabyles or other Algerian Berber communities. The government also began to renege on its promised list of academic reforms. Officially for 'technical reasons', Tizi Ouzou and Batna were omitted from a list of higher educational establishments in four cities where departments of popular literature and culture, with special reference to the Berber and modern Algerian dialects, were to be established. Furthermore, the plan projected that these courses would be taught in Classical Arabic, a good illustration of the regime's conception of Berber languages as a 'folklore product'. Meanwhile, the official media claimed that 'external influences', particularly France and Aït Ahmed's French-based FFS, had organised the unrest, and that the Berberists had intended to undermine the 'unity of the country'.

A weak response to the MCB's call for a general strike in September 1981 in protest against the Cultural Charter marked the high-water mark of Berberist agitation in the early 1980s. Subsequently the regime gradually and efficiently regained the upper hand by a systematic campaign of repression. Hundreds of young Berberist activists were detained, and released as soon as news of their arrest became public, only to be immediately replaced by the arrest of another activist. Although the regime periodically gave in to protests from both within and outside Algeria, the cycle of arrests, denials of travel rights and dismissals from state-run companies escalated in 1981-5. The Berberists responded by forming a number of unrecognised pressure groups, chief of which was the Comité des Enfants de Chouhada (CEC). The name (the 'Committee of the Children of the Martyrs') was a deliberate reference to the sacred institution of the war of independence and an implicit challenge to the FLN's self-appointed role as the embodiment of the spirit of the war.

Nevertheless, the Tizi Ouzou Spring was an important landmark in the development of the Berberist movement in Algeria even if it did little, if anything, to bring about the realisation of the MCB's objectives. The events prepared

the ground for the outbreak of anti-government sentiment in the riots of October 1988 and the resulting
doomed experiment with democratisation. They also
permanently ended the government's previous powerful
hold over the freedom of expression in Kabylia. Henceforth, the state was unable to exert the kind of authority
that it had enjoyed from 1965 to 1980. In the face of
official repression, the new cultural associations organised
occasional peaceful marches. In November 1984 the
CEC's Tizi Ouzou branch proposed the formation of an
association effectively to reappraise and re-write Algerian
history from a Berberist perspective, explicitly rejecting
the FLN's officially promoted Arab-Islamic view of
history. The movement also illegally and irregularly
published various cultural and linguistic journals such as
Tafsut.

From 1985 to 1988 the focus of the Berberist movement moved to the arena of human rights. The veteran
human rights lawyer Abdennour Ali Yahia founded the
Ligue Algérien pour la Défense des Droits de l'Homme
(LADDH) in July 1985, initially to press for the release of
twenty CEC members who had been arrested earlier that
month. The government rapidly realised the League's
ability to act as a channel though which its excesses of
power and anti-Berber policies could be exposed to the
international community, and Ali Yahia's involvement in
the League earned him numerous spells in detention. In a
bid to outflank the nascent human rights lobby, the
government in 1987 engineered a split within the the
ranks of the LADDH and sponsored the formation of an
'official' league with the same name although the International Human Rights Federation refused to recognise it.
Ali Yahia claimed that the government's actions represented a historic capitulation by the regime and an
implicit acknowledement that it no longer enjoyed the
monopoly on political life. For this the state arrested Ali
Yahia in July 1985 and sentenced him to eleven months'
imprisonment for forming an illegal organisation, despite
the fact that the League conformed with the terms of the
Algerian constitution. After further periods of jail and

house arrest Ali Yahia resumed criticism of the Chadli regime in 1987 from Paris and intensified these activities through the summer of 1988.

The MCB and the other Berberist associations had reassessed the focus of their activities by the time nationwide unrest erupted in October 1988. Despite the popularity and tenacity of Kabyle cultural expression in the mid-1980s, the constant repression of Berberist activists had allowed the state to regain the upper hand. Berberists were well aware of the Chadli regime's un-shakeable adherence to its Arab-Islamic conception of Algeria and the determination among certain elements of the regime to resolve the Berber problem once and for all by force. The leaders of the MCB consequently urged their supporters not to participate in protests or other acts which the regime could use as a pretext for intervention and further rounds of arrests and repression. This in part explains the peripheral role of Kabylia in the October 1988 riots. What unrest did occur in Kabylia, eight days after the beginning of the riots on 12 October, appears to have been a spontaneous and angry response to official pro-Chadli demonstrations, resulting in the deaths of up to ten people. The leaders of the Berberist movement had also wanted to establish a wider context for the Berberist movement by persuading non-Berber Algerians to adopt the agenda for political pluralism and democracy. It was felt that this would both spread the load of pro-democracy and anti-regime dissidence more evenly among all Algerians and help to neutralise anti-Kabyle propaganda disseminated by the regime.

The Kabyles and the Post-Chadli Crisis

The October riots were a turning point for the Berberists, as for the entire Algerian 'nation'. In many respects they would have been impossible without the precedent established by the Tizi Ouzou Spring eight years earlier and the subsequent removal of the state's control of all freedom of thought and the gradual erosion of the FLN's self-claimed legitimacy. The MCB was among the very few organisations within Algeria which were sufficiently organised and mobilised to take immediate advantage of the lifting of restrictions on political parties in 1989.

After 1988 the Berberist movement gradually became prey to the polarisation present in many other political movements and tendencies in Algeria. A young Tizi Ouzou psychiatrist, Said Saadi, began to attract support during the late 1980s. Saadi had drifted away from Aït Ahmed in the late 1980s and in February 1989 was the principal founder of the Rassemblement pour la Culture et la Démocratie (RCD) which was based very much on membership of the MCB. Initially the RCD's programme in the election years of 1990 and 1991 resembled that of the FFS in most respects – an emphasis on secularism and joint national language status for Tamazigh – and apart from a continuing public quarrel between Aït Ahmed and Saadi there was little to differentiate between them ideologically. However, there were some differences in their support base in that the RCD tended to enjoy marginally greater support among the young urban Kabyle intelligentsia, particularly in Algiers. The party's obstinate refusal to support any dialogue with the Islamist tendency during the crisis years of 1993 and 1994 earned it a reputation as the most hardline element in the 'eradicationist' tendency.

However, the RCD never seriously challenged the political pre-eminence of Aït Ahmed and the FFS. The regime had granted a pardon to Aït Ahmed in November 1984 on the thirtieth anniversary of the war of independence, and he had returned to Algeria on 15 December 1989, a month after the official legalisation of the FFS. It was clear, however, that the FFS remained a Kabyle-based political party despite its attempts to build a nationwide constituency. Most of its supporters and virtually all its members were Kabyles. Although the front's programme proposed a mixed economy and social-democratic policies, there was a strong emphasis on cultural and language rights for the Kabyles, such as the official recognition of Tamazigh and Kabyle access to the state-controlled media.

Unlike the other secularist opposition parties, the FFS and the RCD enjoyed a genuinely popular regional base between 1988 and 1992. Although they both developed relatively sophisticated national political manifestos, their main point of attraction to the Algerian voter was their tacit claim to represent the Kabyles. This was demonstrated by the parties' performance in the June 1990 municipal and provincial elections and the December 1991 parliamentary elections. The FFS's decision to boycott the June 1990 elections on the ground that it had had insufficient time to prepare left the way open for the RCD, which won virtually all the seats in Kabylia. Both parties, however, fielded candidates in the December 1991 parliamentary polls. The FFS won all twenty-five parliamentary seats in Kabylia, making it the second largest political party nationwide after the FIS, though almost entirely dependent on the Kabyle vote. The RCD attracted a meagre 2.9 per cent of the vote and failed to win a single seat.

The different actions and attitudes of Aït Ahmed and Saadi during the post-Chadli crisis underlined the ideological differences between the FFS and the RCD. During the tension of early January 1992 Aït Ahmed played a high-profile role in the formation of the 'Committee to Save Algeria', an *ad hoc* alliance of anti-FIS 'democrats' determined to prevent what it saw as the double fatality of an Islamist government and a police state. In contrast, Saadi formed links with the main backers of the January coup and openly supported it. In March 1992 Aït Ahmed refused Boudiaf's invitation to serve as chairman of the toothless CCN and in the following July he went back into voluntary exile in Switzerland in protest at the assassination of Boudiaf and the growing influence of the military. From exile Aït Ahmed kept up the pressure on the generals' regimes in Algiers by continually calling for a genuine national dialogue and playing a central role in successive peace initiatives. In January 1995 he participated in the peace talks with the FLN and FIS organised by the Sant' Egidio Community in Rome. By this time the RCD had evolved as one of the leading political supporters of the pro-Lamari tendency within the military and the state.

Islamists are the third element in the Kabyle political landscape. Although the FIS received a tiny proportion of the Kabyle vote in June 1990 and December 1991, significant numbers of Kabyles supported the front, usually in rural villages. The explanation for this was mainly historical and can be traced to the period immediately after independence, when the modernist trend eclipsed the more conservative and traditionalist population. In Kabylia this affected villages where marabout traditions remained strong. However, this traditionalist element re-emerged in 1992-3 after three decades of quiescence and gradually began to ally itself with extremist groups such as the GIA and the AIS. It is also noteworthy that many figures within the Islamist movement were of Kabyle origin, for instance the GIA's 'prime minister', Mohamed Said. The Islamic extremist insurgency properly began to affect Kabylia in the spring of 1993 when militants began to single out prominent Kabyles for assassination, the most prominent being the journalist and writer Tahar Djaout in 1993. These killings were intended in part '*pour encourager les autres*' either to accept Arabisation in a fundamentalist Islamic context or leave the country, and recalled the ruthless tactics of the FLN *mudjahidine* against their opponents – Muslims as well as *pieds noirs* – during the war of independence. The very existence of a people identifying itself primarily as Berber is anathema to most Islamists. To them Algeria is unequivocably Muslim and Arab. By 1994 the state faced a serious challenge in many remote parts of Kabylia, most notably the hinterland of Djidjel. The regime responded by distributing arms to improvised village *autodéfense* militias.

However, the Berberists have derived some benefit from the post-Chadli crisis. Although divided between the 'eradicator' stance of the RCD and the moderation of the FFS, the HCE and Zeroual regimes look upon the Kabyle constituency as a valuable 'modernist' ally against the 'obscurantism' of the FIS. This policy is one born of necessity, and the post-Chadli regimes in Algiers have been as opposed as their predecessors to the idea of Berber cultural and language rights. This has offered the Berberists their best opportunity since the early 1980s to pressure the regime and extract concessions, though the Kabyle political organisations remain as suspicious of the intentions of the regime as they are of the FIS. After two years of relative quiescence, the MCB in April 1993 revived its campaign for language rights by defying bans on public gatherings with demonstrations in Tizi Ouzou and Bejaia. In the following year the MCB intensified its campaign and replaced the Berber question near the top of the national agenda. The movement in September called on its supporters to boycott schools and colleges in support of its demands for the official recognition of Tamazigh and its introduction into school curricula, and organised a series of peaceful demonstrations in Tizi Ouzou, Bejaia and Algiers. The government responded by forming a commission to investigate the possibility but a crisis point was reached soon after when the GIA kidnapped the popular Kabyle singer Matoub Lounes, prompting the MCB to threaten a 'total war' against those responsible. Lounes, a prominent Berberist who had controversially told the Kabyle newspaper *Le Pays* that he was 'neither Arab nor Muslim', was released unharmed soon after.

The sudden rise in tensions caused by the Matoub Lounes kidnapping well illustrate the precarious and complex position in which the Kabyles have found themselves in the post-Chadli crisis. Most 'modernist' Kabyle villages have established their own armed militias and the MCB and its supporters have stockpiled arms and ammunition in readiness for a 'total war' against the Islamists. But the Islamists are not the only enemy and the Berberists have little faith in the state as a bulwark against the encroaching 'savage horde'. Indeed, such are the complexities of Algerian politics during the years of the post-Chadli crisis that it is not difficult to conceive of state elements deliberately fomenting confrontation between the Islamists and the Kabyles.

The mid-1990s are a crossroads for Algeria's Berbers. The Berberist cause apparently scored its first significant success in January 1995 when the signatories of the Sant' Egidio document explicitly recognised the 'Amazigh' as equal to the Arab character of Algeria. This was the first occasion on which the Arab nationalist FLN and the Islamist FIS had publicly done this. Even allowing for the strong possibility that neither party had genuinely abandoned its previous rejection of Berber identity, and had signed the document as a ruse to undermine the authority of the regime, the wording of the document must be considered a landmark in the history of Algeria. In early 1995 the MCB split into two factions when the government agreed to investigate the logistics of introducing Tamazigh into state educational establishments in response to the schools boycott. While Berberists who supported the RCD argued that the boycott should be ended, their FFS-supporting brothers favoured its continuation. In the first instance of intra-Berberist strife since the early 1980s, supporters of the rival camps clashed in Tizi Ouzou and Bejaia, and the MCB leadership divided into two rival committees with almost identical names. Soon after, however, President Zeroual clinched his apparent deal with the RCD by officially recognising the Berber character of Algeria and creating another commission to define the country's Amazighité.

Until that moment, the regime had denied Algeria's partial Berber identity so as to answer the imperatives of shoring up a deteriorating 'nation-state' in the face of the Islamic extremist insurgency. After having decided to opt for a single official language and a state religion, the state had become trapped by its own logic, obliged to deny any Berber and Kabyle dimension to Algerian culture. Expanding the hypothesis that the Islamism of the FIS is a logical continuation of the independence movement before 1962, it is strange that the movement in which wartime Kabyles had played such an important role should have denied the Berber dimension of the Algerian 'nation'. Perhaps the answer to the Berber conundrum is another question: what is Algeria?

10

THE ALGERIANS AND THE FRENCH

The relationship between France and Algeria is crucial to an understanding of contemporary Algeria. Thirty years after the departure of he French the links between the two countries remain · close, complex and fraught with contradictions. To the Anglo-Saxon observer Algeria can appear very much an invisible French sphere of linguistic and commercial influence. Many Algerian cities retain the air of slightly seedy French provincial towns and, despite the efforts of the Algerian government, few Algerians speak any foreign language other than French. Despite the rhetoric, the French dimension has always tempered and balanced Algerian foreign policy, even though France ceased to be Algeria's principal foreign trading partner in the 1970s. Although the links are likely to weaken over time – particularly as the so-called 'Party of France', the *Hizb Fransa*, dies out – the sociological and psychological ties between the two countries deserve particular examination. This chapter examines the Algerian Muslim community in France and the increasingly important question of its infiltration by exiled Algerian Islamists. After briefly examining the Harkis, this chapter concludes with the issue of language. Algerian foreign policy towards France is examined in the following chapter.

Algerian Emigration to France

The presence of around one million Muslims of Algerian origin in France constitutes the strongest of all the various links between France and Algeria. The effects of the French colonisation of Algeria from 1830 until 1962 have provided the principal reason for the drift of subject Algerians towards the land of their conquerors. From the 1840s to the 1860s the French authorities passed a series of laws intended to establish a European-style economic order in a land still dominated by traditional agrarian production. This resulted in the wholesale dispossession of countless thousands of Muslims from their farms, homes and villages. By means of the policy of cantonisation the French authorities allocated to their *colons* the most fertile and best irrigated agricultural land and allowed the Muslims to keep the rest, usually mountainous and ill-irrigated areas. This uprooted thousands of families from their villages in search of work, often forcing them to migrate to the growing cities of Algiers, Constantine and Oran, and to new settlements on the edge of the colonial *domaines*. As the traditional structure of Algerian society was seriously undermined, and *the pieds noirs* gradually attained control of the available agricultural land, the indigenous Muslims over time evolved into an agrarian working class. The colonial administration's introduction of a monetary economy, which subverted traditional distribution systems, and the resulting frequent food shortages and famines of the second half of the nineteenth century were additional factors that prompted Muslims to emigrate to France.

Kabyles have been disproportionately represented among the Algerian community in France since the first wave of immigration in the 1870s. The prime reason was geographical. The first migrants usually originated from the areas which benefitted least from colonisation, such as the mountainous and remote parts where the inhospitable terrain discouraged the *colons* from appropriating the available land for settlement: Kabylia, the Aurès, the Nementcha and the Ouarsenais. The colonial authorities' education policy was a second factor. France believed that Kabyles would be more receptive than the more Arabised to Christianity and European culture due to their seemingly weak adherence to Islam within their own particular social organisation. Thus the authorities decided that Kabyle children would be educated primarily in French, while Algerian children outside the region would be taught in classical Arabic. This resulted in the Kabyles being the best educated in the French language of all the Algerian Muslims.

Initially, the small Algerian emigrant community, which in 1912 numbered 5,000, was based in the large cities, principally Paris and Marseille. The emigrants usually stayed alone for three or five years and a close family member would often take their place on their return. Most took the lowest-paid employment and lived in poor and unsanitary conditions. Later the emigrants began to settle in small communities in French towns on the basis of their village or town of origin in Algeria. The flow of Algerian immigration to France increased significantly after the end of the First World War. This was largely to replace the hundreds of thousands of French skilled and unskilled industrial and agricultural workers killed in the war. When immigration from Algeria began to exceed that from other European countries in 1923, the proportion of migrants from regions of Algeria other than Kabylia, such as Algiers, Constantine and Oran, rose also. Even so, around 25 per cent of all Kabyle families had at least one family member working in France by 1939, by far the highest proportion of any Algerian region. This situation persisted into the 1980s, when approximately 46 per cent of Algerian immigrants in France originated from the Kabyle provinces of Sétif and Tizi Ouzou, as opposed to 16 per cent from Constantine and 6 per cent from Algiers.

Between 1954 and 1962 there was an almost 100 per cent increase in the number of Algerians in France (see Table), despite the growing strength of Algerian nationalism during this period. Many emigrants left their homeland for France for political as much as economic reasons, and during these years the numerous Maghrebi cultural and nationalist associations that had first emerged in the 1920s and 1930s became increasingly important politically. Thousands of young Algerians were exposed to the ideas of communism and other Western political ideologies which played the greatest role in the formation of political groups such as the FLN, PCA and PAGS. Indeed, the close contact of Algeria with France through emigration continued to exert a powerful influence on Algerian politics in the mid-1990s. French-based Algerians played a key role in the war of independence itself, raising funds, sheltering fugitives and trying to maintain pressure on the French government.

The greatest period of Algerian emigration to France took place during the first thirteen years of Algerian independence from 1962 to around 1975. Despite the psychological scars of the war and the widespread expectation in France that most immigrants would return to their homeland on independence, the numbers of Algerians in France actually increased throughout the 1960s. The main centres of Algerian immigration were Paris, Marseille, Lille, Roubaix and Nancy. From a total of around 22,000 in 1946, representing no more than 7,000 families, the number rose to 350,000 by 1966, of whom 202,000 were economically active. By 1975 the community had grown almost threefold to an official total of 710,000, with the real figure estimated at more than 900,000.

There were three main factors behind this rapid increase in migration. The primary one was that the adverse economic and social situation prevailing in Algeria immediately after independence prompted thousands to leave. The departure of virtually the entire European managerial and professional classes, and the havoc wrought by OAS sabotage, had aggravated the ravages of seven years of civil war and deepened economic difficulties. The demobilisation of thousands of former ALN soldiers massively increased the already high level of unemployment. The second reason was the omission in the Evian Accords of 1962 of any effective controls on immigration from Algeria to France. Paris had agreed to such liberal freedom of movement regulations in the erroneous belief that a far greater proportion of the *pieds noirs* would stay in Algeria; in the event thousands of families of workers who had already gone to France departed. The third reason was the actual shortage of labour in France during the country's economic boom of the 1960s. Promises of well-paid jobs, free housing, medical care and frequent subsidised trips home attracted many thousands. The reality proved depressingly different, however: in the early 1990s around half the immigrants were unemployed, with the remainder in poorly-paid *travaux pénibles*, the unpleasant jobs rejected by the French. There was a small group of Algerian immigrants working as doctors, lawyers and academics, often travelling back and forth between Algiers and Paris or other French cities, and their numbers were swollen following the breakdown of the democratisation experiment in January 1992. Between 1989 and 1993 the number of Algerian asylum-seekers in France multiplied tenfold, from 101 to 1,099.

Immigration was one of the main problem areas in relations between the Algerian and French governments during the 1970s and 1980s. Violent incidents between immigrant Algerian and French communities began to erupt in the port city of Marseilles in the early 1970s. After a wave of murders of Algerians in the city, the Algerian government in September 1973 suspended all emigration of its citizens to France. The fatal shooting of an Algerian schoolteacher, who himself had recently served a prison sentence for stabbing a Frenchman, was the climax of a steady increase in tensions during 1975. The violence, however, did not slow the rate of migration. By 1982 Algerians constituted the largest single immigrant group in France, though by 1990 they had fallen into second position behind the Portuguese. Despite over ten years of French government efforts to reduce the proportion of immigrant workers, there were some 800,000 Algerians legally residing in France in the mid 1990s (the real figure was estimated at 1.5 million, if one takes into account Algerians who had taken full French nationality).

Although the situation improved during the 1980s, the vast majority of Algerian immigrants in the 1970s were illiterate and unskilled. After leaving their families, young Algerian men frequently ended up in squalid, overcrowded tenement rooms in run-down inner-city ghettoes, or *bidonvilles*, on the edge of towns. The previously high proportion of Algerians employed in French agriculture has largely been reversed in recent years and

Algerian communities tend to provide the workforce for steel plants and factories. Construction, mining, car manufacture and road building are other industrial sectors with high proportions of Algerians in the workforce.

ALGERIANS IN FRANCE

	Number	As % of total population
1946*	22,114	1.3
1954*	211,675	12
1962	350,812	16.2
1975	710,690	20.6
1982	805,116	21.7
1990	614,207	17.1

* Number of Muslims of Algerian origin - Algerian nationality was introduced at independence in 1962.
Source: French censuses

By the mid-1990s the presence in France of such a large community of people of Algerian origin, both naturalised French citizens and those retaining their Algerian citizenship, was a key issue in both Algerian and French politics. France has a long and frequently honourable tradition of accepting foreigners into its midst, but the particularlities of Franco-Algerian history, most notably the colonial experience, afforded Algerians a specific place in French popular perceptions and therefore in politics. There are two historic and cultural factors that explain this. First, the unfortunate experiences of many Algerian Muslims at the hands of French civilians during the 1950s and, on occasion, French officialdom sealed the persistence of the coloniser/colonised where Algerian immigrants in France are concerned. Second, French culture has historically included a perception and rejection of 'otherness'. In the modern context, this is manifested in the widespread belief that Islam represents a threat to French culture. Unlike previous groups of usually Christian immigrants, Algerians are adherents to a visibly different religion and this considerably reduces their ability to integrate into the dominant culture. Uniquely among other Western European countries with large Muslim minorities, such as the United Kingdom,

Germany and Italy, the French state seeks to circumvent Muslims' freedom of religion. A ban on the wearing of the Muslim veil in French state schools was one of the most notorious recent instances of this policy. While such moves are intended to protect the cherished secularity of the French state, they serve to marginalise France's Muslim community and discourage integration. Indeed, French public opinion since the 1960s has shown a marked rejection of the Algerian community in the country. Although this was against the background of significantly generalised anti immigrant feeling, Algerians were perceived differently from other foreigners, even from other North Africans.

France's experience in Algeria is essentially unique, and attempts to draw parallels with its own and the United States' experience in Vietnam and even the British involvement in India inevitably fail. Successive French governments have tried to erase memories of the war from the national consciousness and veterans of the war have been treated with indifference. However, the post-Chadli crisis has stimulated a deeper reappraisal of the experience on both sides than at any time in the previous thirty years, notably in the film *La Guerre sans Nom* by the eminent French director Bertrand Tavernier, which was first shown in 1992. The film included interviews with twenty-eight conscripts who had served in the French forces in Algeria, many of whom admitted that they had never been able to discuss their wartime experiences, even within their own families. Many former soldiers had been traumatised by them, and most had not received any treatment.

Similarly, the presence of so many of its citizens in the land of its former colonisers is an ideological, political and logistical problem for the Algerian state. Algeria has been obliged to tolerate thousands of its best-educated sons and daughters leaving their homeland to work in France due to economic problems that, initially at least, were a result of the war of independence. The Algerian state defined its position on the situation in the National Charter of 1976 by determining emigrants as an integral part of the Algerian nation who continue to contribute to the national struggle for economic development. The Boumedienne and Chadli regimes actively promoted the view, shared by many of the 1960s immigrants to France, that their period abroad was temporary: the 'myth of return'. Algiers also passed laws trying to prevent the emigrants from losing their identity as Muslims and Algerians. Algeria discouraged the migrants from actively participating in French politics and Algerian law considers all children of its nationals born abroad as full Algerian citizens.

The full complexities and contradictions of the emigrants' position became clearer in the early 1980s. By this point the second generation of Algerian immigrants had reached the age at which both Algeria and France required them to carry out their military service, and the attitude of those eligible revealed the extent of split loyalties. After the Algerian authorities had detained many young French nationals of Algerian parentage on a visit to Algeria in 1981-2, the governments of the two countries in 1983 drew up an agreement allowing the young men in question to do their military service in either country. Some 80 per cent of men eligible for both French and Algerian nationality chose to do their service in France. Meanwhile, French Algerians were beginning to organise themselves politically along French secular lines, resulting in a series of demonstrations such as the '*Beurs*' march for legality and against racism in 1983. The communities also established several pressure groups to act as a mouthpiece of Algerian and other immigrants' views and to encourage the immigrants to register as voters, for instance *SOS Racisme, France-Plus* and *Repères.*

The foundation of the pressure groups was the logical response to the increasing exploitation of the race and immigration issue by both the right and left of French politics. For the right the very presence of such large numbers of foreigners subverted French traditional cultural values and for years it tried to subvert the privileged legal rights of Algerians in France. In the 1970s the seven-year presidential administration of Valéry Giscard d'Estaing repeatedly tried to encourage large numbers of Algerians to return home. The government of

Prime Minister Jacques Chirac between 1986 and 1988 made the first serious attempt to remove Algerians' right to French nationality, though the regulations were not finally changed until the government of Prime Minister Edouard Balladur in 1993. The new regulations removed the right of any child born on French soil automatically to receive French nationality if their parents were French, either native or naturalised; in its place the new legislation required any child born in France of parents whose own original nationality was not French formally to request French nationality on reaching the age of majority. Although the left has consistently championed the rights of French Algerians and prioritised initiatives to eradicate substandard immigrant housing, particularly the *bidonvilles*, its record in power has been equivocal.

The post-Chadli crisis reinforced the complexities of the position of the Algerian community in France. Many Frenchmen had long viewed the Algerian immigrant community as a Trojan horse determined to undermine the sacred culture and customs of France. While this is largely erroneous, the rise of fundamentalism and Islamism in Algeria provided a new focus for anti-Algerian racism and prejudice. Although the community reflected the diverse origins of French Algerians, comprising religious zealots as well as confirmed secularists, it did not deserve the '*vague verte*' (green wave) label current in the French media and in the discourse of the far right. The fears expressed in the French press of an Algerian 'fifth column' during the 1991 Gulf War were in no way realised.

There were, however, clear parallels between the role of the Algerian community in France in 1954-62 and after 1992. The vast majority of long-established members of the community in the post-Chadli years were indifferent to both sides in the conflict, favouring neither what they perceived as the corruption of the regime nor the radicalism of the FIS and the extremists. However, radical Islam did hold many attractions for a minority among the dispossessed of the younger generation. This assisted in the development between 1991 and 1993 of a clandestine network of groups sympathetic to the Algerian Islamists in France. Hundreds of FIS exiles had fled to France after January 1992 and sheltered behind membership of innocuously named FIS front organisations, such as the Fraternité Algérienne en France (FAF) which had been established in June 1990 by the Paris-based mathematics student Djafar el-Houari, and the Union des Organisations Islamiques de France (UOIF). The French authorities kept such individuals and institutions under surveillance and from time to time raided FAF offices and the residences of its members on the pretext that they were involved in terrorism. In November 1993 eighty-eight of the approximately one hundred Islamist leaders in France were arrested in raids on locations from Britanny to Provence. The French government realised that the moves were generally popular with the French public and carried out similar operations in 1994. There were more arrests and closures of FIS and GIA newspapers following the GIA hijack of an Air France aircraft on the tarmac at Algiers airport in December 1994.

Other exiled Islamists took up posts as teachers in mosques or mosque-related institutions, where many preached armed insurrection against the Algerian regime, some advocating the use of terrorism against French targets as a means of exerting pressure on Algiers. The most famous of these was the elderly Abdelbaki Sahraoui, one of the founders of the FIS. Sahraoui became imam of the mosque in the Rue Myrha in central Paris, where he established a large following among Islamists from Algeria and other Muslim minority communities. In July 1995 Sahraoui was assassinated inside his mosque during Friday prayers. Both the GIA and the 'eradicator' faction within the Algerian regime were suspected.

The Harkis

The Harkis can claim to have received the worst treatment of all Algerian Muslims living in France. The term *harka* was first used to describe local Muslims who volunteered to defend their villages against the FLN in the early stages of the war of independence, and it was later extended to other Muslim functionaries such as civil servants and minor politicians. The Harkis were estimated to number around 58,000 men at the end of the war in 1962, though this referred only to former soldiers, and the number of pro-French Muslims is likely to have been more than 150,000. The fate of the Harkis at the end of the war of independence is one of the most ignominious episodes in both Algerian and French history. De Gaulle made no particular provision for their protection in the Evian Accords as a reward for their pro-colonial stance during the war and this prompted some 12,500 to flee to France, many with the first Harka leader, Bachaga Boualem. The remaining 100,000 or so faced fates ranging from humiliation at best to torture and execution at worst. Although French troops were forbidden from intervening by the terms of the Evian Accords, there are numerous reports of French units disarming the unfortunate Harkis and then leaving them to their fate.

France did not provide the safe and welcoming refuge for which the Harkis had been hoping. Initially the authorities housed the refugees in makeshift accommodation in disused army camps, but later they gradually created cohesive communities in run-down areas of southern French cities such as Narbonne and Toulouse, but also in northern industrial centres such as Amiens. In the mid 1990s the number of Harkis and their children was estimated at around 450,000. However, as no Harki ever took Algerian nationality, this figure can be added to the estimated 1.5 million people of Algerian origin to produce a total of close to two million citizens of Algerian descent in France. Less than 50 per cent of the Harkis have been integrated into French society, with the remainder still living in sub-standard state housing such as the infamous purpose-built Cité des Oliviers in Narbonne, while others are still in military camps such as Bias. Around 80 per cent of them were unemployed and many had drifted into delinquency after receiving second-rate education. Successive French governments promised to solve '*le problème harki*', but the lack of decisive action has led to widespread dissatisfaction and alienation among the community.

Although the constant hostility between the Harkis and their non-Harki compatriots has occasionally led to intercommunal violence, the French state has more often been the focus of Harki discontent. The first eruption occured in 1978 when a Harki group took hostage the director of a nearby camp in the town hall of Saint-Laurent-des-Arbres. After an operation to free the hostage, President Giscard d'Estaing's government proposed the first Harki 'plan', but little was actually done. Subsequent hostage-taking operations at Pechiney in 1978 also failed to result in any concrete action, and triggered off more demonstrations to demand the Harkis' 'recognition'. Eleven years later, in 1989, young Harkis for the first time turned to the traditional French protest of blockading the roads and selected the RN 580. Disturbances erupted in June 1991 at the Cité des Oliviers when police arrested four young Harkis for rioting during protests about the high level of unemployment among their community. This sparked off a two-month wave of protests across the Midi, from Narbonne to Carcassonne, Nîmes, Toulouse, Avignon and scores of other southern towns. Hundreds of young Harkis occupied government buildings, threw petrol bombs at police, took over *péages* (tolls) on motorways and organised protest marches. '*Harkis, trente ans d'oubli, ça suffit!*' (Harkis, thirty years of ignorance is enough) and '*Nous sommes français, pas des beurs!*' (We're French, not French-Algerians) were their slogans.

The disturbances of 1991 for the first time drew national and international attention to the problem. The unrest subsided by mid-August when the minister of social affairs and integration, Jean-Louis Bianco, himself the son of Italian immigrants, pledged initiatives to increase employment opportunities and improve housing and pensions for the Harkis. Moreover, the minister for the first time acknowledged that France owed a 'blood debt' to the community and promised that part of the memorial in Marseilles to the repatriated French was to be dedicated to the Harkis. Few people believed Bianco's denials that millions of francs set aside to help the Harkis under the auspices of the Office National à l'Action

Sociale et Culturelle (ONASEC) had been diverted to immigrant organisations close to the Socialist Party, such as *SOS-Racisme* and *Recours*. Despite the pledges of jobs and better housing, the Harkis remain marginalised and resentful. They continue to face hostility and violence from non-Harki Algerians and even other North Africans, though the younger generations are likely to be increasingly integrated as they combat what they perceive as generalised injustice, racism, resentment and provocation. The very small steps towards the improvement of their lot remain insufficient to prevent possible repeats of the revolt of summer 1991.

11

ALGERIA'S FOREIGN POLICY

Independent Algeria has played a major role in international affairs in multiple arenas: the Arab world, the whole developing world, and the Non-Aligned Movement. This chapter examines the course of Algerian foreign relations over two chronological sections: a period of revolutionary policy, from 1962 to 1988, and a period of self-preservation, from 1988 onwards. As a country that had emerged from seven years of brutal war, Algeria at independence in 1962 perceived itself as a revolutionary state with a duty to spread revolt against colonialism and imperialism throughout the Arab and developing worlds. The Algerians' first-hand experience of colonial oppression, and the popular consensus that their nation had been forged in war, dominated and shaped its foreign policy throughout the first three decades of its existence.

As with almost all political and institutional aspects of independent Algeria, the roots of the country's foreign policy from 1962 until 1988 can be traced back to the experience of the wartime FLN. Throughout the war the organisation maintained relations with its newly independent neighbours of Tunisia and Morocco, and with the Arab nationalist regime of President Nasser in Egypt. Fourteen sovereign states recognised the provisional government in 1958, including most Arab and communist states such as China, North Vietnam and North Korea. By independence the number had reached more than thirty. The political and material support extended by these countries, most of which considered themselves as 'revolutionary', and the indifference of the West, particularly the United States, towards Algeria's struggle against the French imbued the state with a deep distrust for the prevailing world order. In the following twenty or so years, Algeria's foreign policy was instrumental in articulating the concerns of much of the Third World and the Non-Aligned Movement. In the post-Chadli crisis, domestic concerns have primarily shaped foreign policy: the need to win sufficient international support to assist financially and otherwise against the extremists, and to deny the Islamist movement a foreign base.

Exporting Revolution

Many Algerian nationalist politicians believed that their revolution did not take place in a vacuum, but rather was played out against a wider, global struggle between the underdeveloped world and the forces of imperialism. Algeria in the 1976 National Charter proclaimed its 'solidarity with the countries of the Third World in their struggle for political and economic liberation'. This steadfast adherence to principle and its expression through Algeria's participation in the Non-Aligned Movement won the respect of the Third World and, ironically, of the West. Algerian diplomats are respected as the among the best in the developing world, winning praise for their skills in mediation and conciliation. Algeria's mediation in negotiations between Iran and the United States in 1980-1 was the most noteworthy instance of this.

This 'revolutionary' stance was played out in Algeria's support for numerous and varied liberation movements throughout the non-aligned developing world: in Africa, the Middle East, Asia and Latin America. Combined, these four geographical areas constituted the most important of the three arenas for Algerian foreign policy, the other two being the Maghreb and the West. The advent of Algerian independence reinvigorated the Non-Aligned Movement along the lines of a more radically pragmatic view of national interests. Ahmed Ben Bella established the precedent of backing revolutionary groups that often openly advocated the use of terrorism.

Driven by his self-image as a revolutionary leader, and as part of his efforts to subvert the Western-dominated order in the developing world, Ben Bella made numerous passionate rhetorical speeches with frequent references to the war of independence. Later, Boumedienne attempted to promote a concept of a new world economic order. His campaign reached a climax in April 1974 when the United Nations incorporated the idea in its Charter, though without taking any concrete action. By the late 1960s Algiers had become the unofficial capital of the world's liberation movements, even playing host at one time to the American Black Panthers.

The Palestinian movement was a major focus and beneficiary of the Algerian policy of exporting revolution. Algerians have always drawn parallels between the Israeli/Palestinian dispute and their own struggle to expel the French settler-colonialists; to them, Zionism and Israel are agents of colonialism and imperialism and the Palestinian *intifada* was a just war of liberation against a colonial power. Adopting a hardline position in the 1967 Arab-Israeli war, Algeria extended military assistance to Egypt and was deeply shocked by the defeat of the Arab side in that conflict. Despite growing support in Arab states for peace with Israel, the Boumedienne and Chadli governments remained intractably committed to the view that a Palestinian insurgency was the only means of resolving the dispute. Algeria supplied military and financial aid to Palestinian guerrilla groups during the 1970s, and it was an enthusiastic participant in oil supply sanctions against countries deemed to be opposed to the Arab cause. In common with virtually all Arab states, Algeria severed ties with Egypt in 1978 in protest at the Camp David Agreement (though ties were resumed in November 1988). Algiers was the venue for the first high-profile meeting of the Palestine 'parliament', the Palestine National Council (PNC), in 1983 and the official declaration of Palestinian statehood in June 1988. Similarly, Chadli and his successors, Mohamed Boudiaf and Ali Kafi, acted with caution towards the American-Russian-sponsored Middle East peace process launched in October 1991, though the HCE gave a qualified welcome to the Israel/PLO mutual recognition agreement signed in September 1993.

Algeria's relations with Iran must also come under the heading of exporting revolution. Both Boumedienne and Chadli supported radical movements opposed to the Shah's regime, mainly to undermine his position as one of the United States' strongest allies in the Middle East. Despite Algeria's avowed 'socialist' orientation, the Algerian support extended to Ayatollah Khomeini during his years in exile in Paris prepared the ground for the special relationship with the Islamic Republic in the early 1980s. This close relationship changed after the events of January 1992; whatever the truth behind allegations of Iranian support for Algerian Islamist extremists, successive post-Chadli regimes have viewed Iran as a principal sponsor of the AIS and the GIA. Algeria severed ties with Iran in March 1993 after months of worsening relations.

During the 1960s and early 1970s Algeria directed much energy at exporting revolution in sub-Saharan Africa. This was in part due to the fact that many newly-independent African states were among the first to recognise the sovereignty of the GPRA and provide them with material assistance. This African policy reached its height under Ben Bella, giving rise to criticism that he was more concerned with pan-Africanism than pan-Arabism, a movement at the time led by the Egyptian President, Gamal Abdel Nasser. Algeria was among the founding members of the Organisation of African Unity (OAU) in May 1963, and Ben Bella overtly or otherwise extended financial and military assistance to liberation movements in South Africa, Mozambique, Angola and Rhodesia (later Zimbabwe). The Afro-Asian conference scheduled to take place in Algiers from 29 June 1965, marking the tenth anniversary of the historic Bandung Conference of Non-Aligned Nations, was to have been a major milestone of this policy, but the overthrow of Ben Bella during the preparations derailed the plan. Boumedienne continued support for African revolutionary movements in Southern Africa, Chad and Eritrea (which achieved independence in 1993). He broke off relations with Britain in 1965 over its perceived equivocation when faced with the white putsch in Rhodesia. However, from 1965 there was a definite shift in Algerian foreign policy towards emphasis on the Arab world, in particular, the Maghreb.

The idea of a unified Great Arab Maghreb, from Morocco to Libya, is rooted in the early Islamic era. It first re-emerged in the modern age during the French occupation and again in the 1960s. For Algerians this idea is connected with the desire to extirpate the vestiges of European colonialism and to re-establish their traditional cultural identity as much as to create a Muslim-Arab superstate in north-west Africa. The pre-existing culture underwent much greater subversion and dilution in Algeria than in the other countries of the region that also experienced colonisation. Initially the idea contained strong resonances of pan-Arabism and Islamism but in the 1980s and 1990s it increasingly became perceived as an effective and necessary response by the countries of the southern Mediterranean to the growing isolationism of the European Union, particularly with regard to the employment situation of people of Maghrebi origin in France, Italy and Spain.

Algeria's relationship with its Maghrebian neighbours – primarily Morocco and Tunisia, but also including for political purposes Libya, Mauritania and the Western Sahara – has been a cyclical history of détente and dispute, the explanation of which lies in cultural, political and geographic factors. To a large extent Morocco, Tunisia and Algeria share a common linguistic and cultural heritage that colonisation subverted to differing degrees in each country. At independence, this process was by far the most advanced in Algeria and each country approached the advent of full independence differently. Morocco restored a conservative traditional monarchy, while Tunisia under Habib Bourguiba opted for a more moderate version of socialism than Algeria. The political boundaries of the three countries were inhererited from the French who had – in many cases arbitarily but often for commercial reasons – decided the region's frontiers. Lastly, the governments of Morocco, Algeria and Tunisia always competed for special attention from France.

The often troubled relationship between Algeria and Morocco remains the fulcrum of the Maghreb. Both states aspire to political and economic leadership of the region and on many occasions have attempted to undermine the efforts of the other by supporting its domestic opponents. Traditionally there have been two main areas of contention, the definition of the mutual border and the Western Sahara issue, though the former was by and large resolved by the mid-1990s. Nevertheless, it is ironic that Algeria has only ever fought an international war to protect a legacy from French imperialism: the vast Saharan provinces that, before the coming of the French, had been little more than remote provinces of the northern cities. Morocco had assisted the GPRA during the war of independence on the tacit understanding that the eventual government of independent Algeria would be prepared to negotiate adjustments to their common frontier. However, the presence of iron-ore deposits at Ghara Djebillet, near Tindouf, to which Morocco had some legitimate historical claim, made the area more appealing and further complicated the situation. The enormous expense of transporting the ore to a Mediterranean port had prevented the mines from being properly exploited. In October 1963 Algeria and Morocco fought a brief border war over sovereignty of the area, though the following years were characterised by a cycle of rapprochement and renewed crisis.

The Western Sahara issue was the second area of contention. Morocco occupied the former Spanish colony in 1975 on the ground that the territory was part of the medieval Moroccan empire. Boumedienne was concerned that Moroccan control of the Western Sahara, which is rich in phosphate deposits, would undermine Algeria's developing economic, diplomatic and military pre-eminence in the Maghreb. He roundly denounced the occupation and rapidly extended assistance to the Sahrawi separatist Polisario front. Boumedienne made much of Algeria's own anti-colonial past in arguing for Sahrawi self-determination, though he also clearly was attracted by the prospect of a weak pro-Algerian state on his south-western border. Some commentators have also suggested that the Algerians extended support to Polisario to provide a shorter and thus cheaper transport route for iron ore produced at Ghara Djeibillet. Tensions over the issue grew to such an extent that in early 1976 Algerian and Moroccan forces clashed on the border. In March of that year Algeria formally recognised the self-styled Saharan Arab Democratic Republic (SADR), which established its headquarters in Algiers. Polisario was also allowed to establish refugee and military camps at Tindouf. Relations with both Morocco and Mauritania (which initially occupied the southern half of the disputed territory) were severed. However, wise counsels in the Algerian government prevailed and the dispute never constituted a pretext for outright war.

Although Chadli maintained support for Polisario, in general Algeria softened its line towards Morocco through a series of summits in the early 1980s. Chadli's objectives were to promote the elusive dream of a Great Arab Maghreb as well as to respond to improved relations between Libya and Morocco. In 1981 Foreign Minister Taleb Ibrahimi proposed Maghrebi unity as a peaceful solution to the Western Sahara problem, thereby for the first time putting it on the international political agenda. Chadli met King Hassan at a surprise summit at the Algerian-Moroccan town of Akid-Lotsi in 1983, though no real progress towards reconciliation was achieved despite offers of economic incentives to Morocco from oil-rich Algeria. Relations worsened again in 1984, however, as the entire dynamics of intra-Maghreb relations became caught up in the Algeria-Morocco dispute. To retaliate for an accord signed in the spring between Algeria and Tunisia (and subsequently Mauritania), Morocco and Libya in August signed the Arab-African Federation agreement in the eastern Moroccan city of Oujda. Outraged, Algeria reversed its previous policy of pressuring Polisario to maintain a low profile at the OAU, and Algiers was instrumental in the 'SADR' entering the organisation later that year.

The coincidence of a deteriorating economic situation in Algeria with a gradual improvement in the Moroccan economy turned the tables and led to a new period of détente between the two countries in the mid to late 1980s. While preparing for an Arab League summit in June 1988, Chadli attempted to persuade Libya to sign the Maghreb Fraternity and Co-operation Treaty in a bid to isolate Morocco and thus oblige it to resolve the Western Sahara issue. However Chadli abandoned this strategy when Libya refused to sign. To save face and to increase the number of moderate states at the Arab League summit, Chadli suddenly decided to restore diplomatic ties with Morocco in return for quietly dropping his insistence that King Hassan negotiate with Polisario. The rapprochement with Morocco continued throughout 1989-91 and culminated in the historic meeting in May 1991 between Chadli and King Hassan at Oujda.

The historic rivalry between Algeria and Morocco was the main reason for the failure of the Maghreb Arab Union (UMA) in June 1988. The need for north-west African countries to form a unified and coherent response to the EU single market in 1992, particularly in the case of Algeria, Tunisia and Morocco, was the main stimulus for the establishment of the union. However, Algeria resented the way in which the terms of the organisation were forced upon it and interpreted it as a policy defeat. This resentment undermined any optimism surrounding the birth of the organisation, and cracks soon appeared. Once again the prime split was between Algiers and Rabat, and relations were on a more or less continuously downward for some years after 1991. Despite the onset of the post-Chadli crisis and the increasingly strong clampdown against the armed Islamist movement, Rabat has become increasingly concerned by the prospect of Islamic extremist 'contamination' from Algeria. Two years of steadily growing tensions reached crisis point in August 1994 when two Spanish tourists were killed in a luxury hotel in Marrakech by a group of French Islamic extremists of Algerian and Moroccan origin. When Morocco responded by imposing entry visas (against the terms of a UMA waiver on internal visas), Algeria did the same and closed the border. Although it made no public accusations, the Moroccan government made it clear that

it believed some unnamed elements of the Algerian
government had been involved in the Marrakech attack
in an attempt to damage the Moroccan economy by
undermining the valuable tourist sector.

Relations with France

Algeria's relationship with France, the former colonial
power, has always been complex. According to Bruno
Étienne, it is 'paranoid and schizophrenic'. As with most
aspects of politics in Algeria, the relationship is closely
connected with the country's perpetual quest for a
national identity and with its conception of its own
identity. France, despite its systematic attempt to impose
its own 'superior' culture on Algeria and to create in the
country a mirror-image of itself on the southern shores of
the Mediterranean, remains in the mid 1990s the closest
non-Muslim state to Algeria – culturally, psychologically
and politically. It is also one of Algeria's principal trading
partners and, notwithstanding the European Union's
efforts to clamp down on immigration, as many as 1.5
million people of Algerian origin continue to live and
work there. These realities, however, obscured the
intricate and often strained nature of relations between
the two countries.

The war of independence shaped the French public's
perception of Algeria and the Algerians well into the
1990s. The eight-year war, which on some levels was
fought to preserve French 'civilisation' in Algeria, cost the
lives of more than 27,000 French soldiers. It also
precipitated important political change in France, at one
point pushing the country to the brink of civil war. Unlike
France's other former colonial possessions in North
Africa, Algeria was technically an overseas department of
metropolitan France, and to many French people its
independence represented a loss of part of France. The
flight of the *pieds noirs* to France in 1962 was one of the
largest single movements of refugees in the twentieth
century, and with them much of the unique Mediterranean civilisation that was French Algeria disappeared

overnight. In its place developed an equally unique hybrid of Maghrebian and European cultures, though the younger generation is increasingly unfamiliar with it.

The historical relationship and close economic links with France have left a lasting legacy where Algeria's foreign affairs are concerned. Despite the lingering resentments rooted in the colonial past and different political philosophies, the two governments remain closely bound to each other to a much greater degree than is the case with other West European states and their former colonial possessions. The Evian Accords guaranteed French co-operation with Algeria, and the close economic, cultural and linguistic ties between the two have always strictly limited the Algerian regime's freedom of action. Despite Algeria's determination to erase the French language and replace it with Arabic, French remains the day-to-day language of government and commerce. Few members of the new administration have a respectable knowledge of Modern Standard Arabic, and most of the small élite have been educated in France or at least in French medium schools in Algeria. Economically, France is dominant and for a long time remained the country's leading trading partner. It continues to provide most consumer exports and French firms dominate the hydrocarbons industry.

Despite the deliberate ambiguity shown by the Ben Bella regime towards the government in Paris, it was both unable and unwilling to reduce its dependence on it. France was also unable and very disinclined to withdraw completely from its former colony. Many French companies had grown to rely on Algerian markets, and thus the initial relationship between the two countries was often characterised by compromise. Paris viewed Algeria as its sphere of influence, a key commercial and political entrepot for the Maghreb and Africa, and even in the mid-1990s jealously guarded its leading position regarding the country within the EU.

President de Gaulle continually extended preferential treatment to Algeria and, according to Nicole Grimaud, 'made it a point of honour that there should not be a rupture in the two countries' relations'. His policy was aimed at both sustaining France's enormous remaining interests in Algeria and expunging memories of the war. France was the first foreign state to extend substantial assistance to Algeria after independence. In the climate of confusion and tension prevailing in Algeria at the time, de Gaulle arranged for large loans and technical assistance in a bid to offset the disastrous economic effects of the departure of some 90 per cent of the *pieds noirs*. During 1964, the year in which Ben Bella and de Gaulle first met on equal terms, co-operation in economic and other areas was intensified. Despite persistent disagreements over oil, the future of the remaining French military bases and Algerian immigrant workers in France, Ben Bella forbore to include France among the targets of his anti-imperialist rhetoric, reflecting the spirit of compromise then prevailing as much as the realities of the dynamics of bilateral relations.

This pragmatic attitude towards France only survived the first two years of the Boumedienne regime. The two countries signed a fifteen-year agreement regulating oil production soon after the coup of July 1965 and in the following year signed further economic and technical aid agreements. However a collision between the two became increasingly likely as Boumedienne invited in military and economic advisers from the Soviet Union as part of his plan to reorient his regime towards socialism and establish closer links with the communist world. Alarmed by the reorientation and rumours that the Soviet Union would be allowed to use the Mers el-Kebir naval base that had been handed over to Algeria in January 1968, France signed agreements cancelling Algeria's pre-independence debts and rescheduling Algeria's debt to France to 400 million dinars. It also agreed to provide technical and educational aid to Algeria for twenty years and to maintain military assistance.

Franco-Algerian relations deteriorated sharply when Boumedienne began to nationalise French interests. In line with the ideologies that were later used to justify the agrarian revolution, Boumedienne complained in 1969 that Algeria was not receiving a fair share of revenues from the exploitation of its hydrocarbon resources from

French firms, which he criticised as 'neo-colonialist'. Despite the bilateral agreement of 1965, and after almost two years of unsuccessful negotiations, the Boumedienne government in February 1971 unilaterally acquired 51 per cent of two French oil companies: CFP-Total and ERAP. Between them, the companies accounted for the major part of Algeria's oil production. The move effectively nationalised both firms and led to an immediate deterioration in relations. Paris strongly objected and rejected the insulting Algerian offer of compensation. When subsequent negotiations foundered the following April, France responded by withdrawing many French *co-opérant* teachers and technicians from Algeria and imposed a boycott of Algerian oil (trying, unsuccessfully, to persuade other countries to follow suit). However, CFP, ERAP and the Algerian state oil monopoly Sonatrach reached agreements in June and September whereby the French firms became minority partners with Algeria in return for guaranteed supplies of oil. The final agreement, which Boumedienne hailed as a significant step in the reduction of the 'last bastion of imperialism' in Algeria, was signed in December 1971.

The nationalisation episode coincided with a policy shift in Paris that clouded Franco-Algerian relations throughout the 1970s. On his succession to de Gaulle in 1969, President George Pompidou determined that France henceforth would treat Algeria as part of the Maghreb rather than as a privileged former French colony. His successor Valéry Giscard d'Estaing maintained the approach after 1975. Hopes that Giscard's visit to Algiers in April 1975, the first-ever by a French head of state to independent Algeria, would herald the beginning of improved ties and the 'final reconciliation between the French and the Algerian peoples' proved unfounded as a result of Boumedienne's pressure for the revival of the special privileged relationship between the two countries.

There was a slight improvement in relations between 1975 and 1981, though the emergence of the Western Sahara dispute placed new strains on the association. Algeria was angered by France's support for the partition of the former Spanish colony between Morocco and

Mauritania as a way of undermining Algeria's military and economic predominance in North Africa. Algeria and France signed an agreement providing incentives for the repatriation of 36,000 Algerian immigrants following Chadli Bendjedid's accession in 1978, though the Algerians had no intention of honouring their pledge. The same year Algeria lifted restrictions on a number of French bank accounts that had been frozen since independence. However, the slight improvement in relations was due more to the efforts of the government in Paris than a change of policy on Chadli's part. Against this background, though not directly connected to it, the United States had overtaken France as Algeria's main trading partner in 1977.

Algeria hoped that the election in 1981 of François Mitterrand as president of France would lead to an improved relationship. Despite Mitterrand's somewhat questionable personal record on Algeria (while interior minister in the 1950s he had played a key role in sending French troops to quell FLN insurgents in Algeria), the Algerians welcomed the election of a president from the Socialist party, which was committed to a radical policy in the Third World. As this appeared to coincide with Algeria's own foreign policy objectives, Chadli hoped that Paris would re-estabish the special political – and, more important, economic – relationship that had existed under de Gaulle. Mitterrand visited Algiers in December 1981 and Chadli returned the visit twelve months later – the first-ever to France by an Algerian head of state.

Economic cooperation and immigration were the two principal areas at issue between Paris and Algiers in the early and mid-1980s. The two countries signed a new protocol of economic cooperation in June 1982 when Mitterrand finally dropped France's long-held refusal to accept the gas price set by Sonatrach, which was higher than the prevailing world market rate. The French government also stopped the expulsion of Algerian immigrants from France. But the steady improvement in the relationship lost momentum in 1984-5 in response to France's increasing pragmatism in foreign policy, the failure of bilateral economic cooperation to measure up to expectations, and France's apparent support for the Moroccan stance in the Western Sahara dispute.

France tried to counter this deterioration by moving against Algerian dissidents. It suppressed the publications of Ben Bella's Mouvement pour la Démocratie en Algérie (MDA) and on one occasion expelled its members. In recognition, Algeria unfroze the assets of former French settlers and allowed them to sell their property to the Algerian government. Later it resolved one of the most contentious issues that had dogged relations between the two countries over a long period when agreement was reached concerning the children of mixed Algerian-French marriages. There is also speculation that the French government was implicated in the assassination of the Algerian opposition leader Ali Mécili in Paris in April 1987, allegedly in return for further economic benefits from Algeria. The circumstances surrounding his death, however, have never been fully established.

The turmoil of 1988 and the subsequent democratisation process placed new strains on relations between France and Algeria. President Mitterrand at first welcomed Algeria's democratisation experiment as it corresponded with his policy of withholding aid from regimes deemed to have poor human rights records. However *realpolitik* prevailed when Paris became increasingly concerned for the security of French commerical interests in Algeria. France also wanted to prevent further serious instability in Algeria, which it feared would give rise to a new wave of immigration and possibly destabilise the country's already large Maghrebian community. Equally, the French government was anxious to discourage the creation of an Islamic state and merely paid lip-service to the idea of genuine political pluralism in Algeria. Despite the rapidly mounting unpaid debts to French firms, France injected Frs. 7 billion in February 1989 to shore up the Chadli regime. This was the result of skilful pleading by the then economy minister, Ghazi Hidouci, who made much of France's 'duty' to avert a FIS regime in Algiers.

The Gulf crisis of August 1990-March 1991 also severely tested bilateral relations. Despite the long history of conflict between the two countries, most Algerians had traditionally considered France to have a special under-standing of the Arab world by dint of is historically close association with the Maghreb. At first Algerians approved of President Mitterrand's attempts at international diplomacy, seemingly at variance with the uncompro-mising tone from Washington and London. A feeling of betrayal and frustration at France's position emerged, however, as the FLN and the FIS began to adopt a stance sympathetic to Iraq. This increased significantly during the Gulf war itself, and provoked a series of attacks on French property in Algeria. Meanwhile the Chadli regime tried to exploit this latest outbreak of anti-French sentiment to underline its own rather weak Arab and Islamic credentials.

The post-Chadli crisis in Algeria precipitated the most difficult phase in Franco-Algerian relations since inde-pendence. The official French understanding of the crisis was based on three premises: first, that the crisis was a simple conflict between the state on the one hand and the forces of the Islamic movement (represented principally by the FIS) on the other. Second, with its 'fundamentalism', the Islamic movement was determined to work for an undiluted Islamic republic and was totally opposed to the political traditions of the Algerian state which, if it was to preserve itself intact, should never be forced to come to a negotiated agreement with the FIS. Third, an Islamic republic would be an unmitigated disaster for Algeria – whence millions of anti-Islamist 'boat people' would make for the southern shores of France – and for the Maghrebian community in France, which would be thrown into turmoil by the arrival of these new immigrants. This is the view to which the French government encouraged the world to subscribe, one which was indeed convenient for the eradicators who controlled Algeria's government in 1994-5 and did nothing to promote the much-discussed 'third way', representing a compromise agreement between the state and the Islamist movement. The interior minister, Charles Pasqua, was the architect of the policy. France sustained it during the winter of 1994-5 with regard to the five-party

Sant' Egidio peace proposal of January 1995. Paris only publicly endorsed the platform after the Algerian government had rejected it, a superficially contradictory posture that in fact underlined France's previous implicit rejection of any compromise between the Algerian state and the Islamist movement.

Relations with the Communist World

Algeria's ties with the states of the Communist world, particularly the Soviet Union, were founded on Moscow's support for the GPRA during the late 1950s, and in Algeria's firm belief between 1962 and the late 1980s that non-alignment was the most reliable means to achieve enduring political and economic independence. However, non-alignment implied remaining distinct from the two former superpower blocs while trying to establish equally good relations with both, and the three Algerian regimes of the Cold War era interpreted this differently. For Ben Bella and Boumedienne, the communist world was the natural ally of Algeria: it appeared free of colonialism and imperialism, and its militant revolutionary stance coincided with their own. Boumedienne largely replaced Ben Bella's policy of positive non-alignment with militant anti-imperialism, and this was particularly marked in the area of Algeria's unwavering support for the Palestinians. The Soviet Union and the other leading communist states such as China and Cuba supplied arms and finance to militant Palestinians to fight what was depicted as the US-backed Zionist threat, and relations with Moscow were consequently bound to be warmer than those with Washington.

Close ties with communist states were always a source of fierce internal controversy within Algeria, and this was particularly true of the Ben Bella regime. Ben Bella established strong ties with Moscow as a counterbalance to the continuing necessity of economic dependence on France. Moscow extended substantial loans to Algeria in 1963-4 as a prelude to the relationship. Ben Bella responded by providing conspicuous political support to

Havana during the 1962 Cuban missile crisis, a move that led to a serious strain in relations with the United States. Ben Bella was even awarded the Lenin Peace Prize in 1964. However, although aware of the economic advantages, traditionalists such as Boumedienne distrusted Ben Bella's ideological courting of the Soviets. He used Ben Bella's increasing closeness to the communist bloc as one of the principal pretexts for the July 1965 military coup.

From 1965 until 1967 Boumedienne deliberately lowered Algeria's profile in internatational affairs as the new regime distanced itself from the confident, personality-based leadership of Ben Bella. John Ruedy has remarked that although the apparent policy shift has often been attributed to Boumedienne's more 'Arab' credentials, the changing political landscape and imperatives of the late 1960s – the growing profile of the Palestinian problem and of the oil-producing states – would probably in any case have made this inevitable.[1] Although the Algerian government maintained its public commitment to support anti-imperialist movements throughout the Third World, it thereafter pursued its foreign policy goals with greater caution.

Despite Boumedienne's greater interest in the Maghreb and the Arab east, Algeria's ties with the Soviet Union and other communist states grew deeper, not least because of the economic and defence benefits. After a short initial period of uncertainty, Boumedienne made an official visit to Moscow in December 1995; Soviet Premier Andrei Kosygin returned the visit in October 1971. The Soviet Union sent Algeria significant technical, military and economic assistance throughout the 1970s and 1980s. Soviet advisors and engineers played an important role in the development of mining and industry in Algiers, and Soviet military staff trained Algerians to use Soviet equipment throughout the Boumedienne era. But, in accordance with the policy of non-alignment, Algiers did not allow the Soviet Union to construct military bases on its territory.

[1] *Modern Algeria: The Origins and Development of a Nation*, Bloomington: Indiana University Press, 1992.

Algeria adopted a more balanced approach to the Soviet Union under Chadli Bendjedid even though it remained the predominant military supplier. This was a result of concern over the quality and reliability of Soviet-made weaponry, as well as a more literal interpretation of non-alignment. The perception among Algeria's Maghreb neighbours and the West of being pro-Soviet was a further factor and one that had occasionally adverse effects on economic relations. Some 4,000 Soviet citizens were resident in Algeria, engaged in military assistance in the final year of the Soviet Union's existence in 1991. In common with other Western countries, however, the Soviet Union was anxious to recover loans to Algeria that in 1991 were estimated to amount to $4 billion, 90 per cent of which was militarily-related. Most of this debt was inherited by the Russian Federation, with which Algerian regimes of the early 1990s remained on good terms.

Relations with the United States

As an enthusiastic participant in the Atlantic alliance, the United States – tacitly and on occasion – overtly supported France during the Algerian war of independence. The then Senator John F. Kennedy famously caused a stir in the late 1950s with his speeches in support of the Algerian nationalist cause. Ben Bella's support for Cuba in 1962 compounded the unpromising auguries for US-Algerian relations and subsequent Algerian criticism of America's actions in Vietnam and its relations with Israel made matters worse. In June 1967 Algeria severed diplomatic relations with Washington in protest at US involvement in the Six Day War and began a sustained official propaganda onslaught aimed at US foreign policy that was only slowed in the late 1980s. However, the increasingly important US role in the Algerian economy from the late 1960s onwards, particularly in the hydro-carbons sector, prompted the re-establishment of diplomatic relations in 1974.

US-Algerian ties improved noticeably in the 1980s. This was a result of the more pragmatic foreign policy pursued by Chadli, his desire to attract substantial American investment, and an attempt to diversify Algeria's supply of foreign arms. Algeria's long-proven role as mediator in the hostile relationship between Iran and the United States was the springboard for the improvement. In 1980-1 Algeria negotiated the release of the fifty-two hostages held at the US embassy in Tehran, and in 1982 acted as intermediary in the payment of funds by Iran to American companies formerly based there. Algeria's desire to improve the international standing of a fellow revolutionary state rather than a desire to assist the Americans lies behind the mediation. Nevertheless, in 1985 Chadli paid an official visit to Washington, the first by an Algerian head of state. As with France, the years of crisis after 1988 created a new framework for the US-Algerian relationship. Economic ties became closer as Chadli and his reformist prime ministers Hamrouche and Ghozali were well aware that the United States, as the key member of the IMF, played a determining role in Algeria's economic fortunes. By 1993 the relationship was based largely on the hydrocarbons industry: several major American oil and gas firms invested heavily in Algeria, and in the mid-1990s the United States was a major customer for Algerian gas. Politically Washington was an enthusiastic supporter of the introduction of political pluralism, but its condemnation of the January 1992 coup was weak. The US government appeared to support the HCE in spite of its lack of democratic legitimacy and was reluctant to criticise its questionable human rights record.

A clear shift in US policy took place in 1994-5, the main element of which was to pressure Algiers to negotiate with the FIS. Washington publicly welcomed the Sant' Egidio proposal of January 1995 as the best solution to date, and indicated approval of the apparent success of the November 1995 presidential elections and the parliamentary elections of June 1997. Even so, foreign policy under President Clinton has placed more importance on the Pacific region, and Middle East/North African objectives have been primarily focused on progess in the Israel/PLO peace process. Despite the growing importance of Algeria for American oil and gas companies, Algeria is once again on the periphery of the American global vision.

12

CONCLUSION:
THE AGONY OF ALGERIA

Much has been written on the crisis that developed in Algeria from 1988 onwards. Potential explanations have included the crisis of legitimacy that affected virtually all post-colonial and developing societies in the 1980s and 1990s; the societal changes resulting from the marked increase in the rate of population growth in Algeria; the rise of Islamism and decline of the left; and tensions between various factions, clans and experiential groups that developed during the war of independence and were left unresolved throughout the first thirty years of Algeria's existence as an independent state.

This book has emphasised the last of these theses. The disruption engendered by the French occupation created a hybrid society where the role of traditional determining factors, particularly Islam and the role of the country's Kablye minority, were undefined at independence. The successive regimes of Ahmed Ben Bella, Houari Boumedienne, Chadli Bendjedid, the HCE and Lamine Zeroual all failed to reconcile these two key elements with the needs of a post-colonial society with a history as traumatic as that of Algeria. It was inevitable that the various political factions and groupings in Algeria would exploit the unresolved position of Islam and the ambiguous position of the Kabyles within the country's constitution.

The question of the role played by Islam in the constitution came to a head when the political and social system that had prevailed since 1962 came to an end around 1988. The country had become much younger, the rapid industrial and economic developments funded by oil and gas revenues had levelled off, and the ruling élite had become fatally dislocated from the masses. Most Algerians, raised on a diet of state propaganda of mass politicisation, bitterly reproached the élite for reneging on its promises, squandering the country's wealth and putting their own interests first. In the years that followed, the state miscalculated, overreacted and made a series of mistakes that precipitated the military intervention of January 1992.

The crisis that had its origins in the riots of October 1988 was the result of a complex combination of factors that had been at work since Algerian independence, including some new elements. The state's progressive loss of legitimacy and authenticity since independence is a key theme that has been explored in this book, and was a central factor contributing to the post-Chadli crisis. Despite the internecine conflicts and ideological disagreements that dogged the regime of Ben Bella, both he and his successor derived their popular legitimacy from their roles in the liberation war. For a country that had undergone such widespread disruption during more than 130 years of foreign occupation, the independence war provided a reference point to which all the country's disparate ethnic, regional, tribal, political and class groups could relate.

The state justified its refusal to introduce political pluralism by invoking the liberation struggle and the requirements of an emerging nation-state. Assisted by strong central control and an efficient security apparatus, this strategy remained viable until fundamental social changes forced Chadli to act in 1989. By this time the three pillars of Algeria – the army, the party and the state – had become so tarnished by corruption and mismanagement that in the minds of most Algerians they had forfeited their 'right' to rule. The crushing defeats suffered by the FLN in the elections of June 1990 and December 1991 were principally the result of the Algerian people articulating their rejection of the myth of the state as the vessel of legitimacy conferred by the war of independence and the 'Algerian revolution'. The situation deterio rated still further as the army ruled unsupported through its puppet organisation, the HCE, though less so than during Zeroual's first, unelected presidency from January 1994 to November 1995.

Factionalism emerges from this study as a dominant theme. After the war of independence, suppressed factional tensions and conflicts re-emerged to undermine the efforts of the FLN to transform itself into a genuine political party. Subsequently, every Algerian leader, from Ben Bella to Zeroual, was obliged to navigate the dangerous waters of conflicting demands from the various factions and interest groups, however formed, to remain in power.

The military has always been the most powerful and important of all factions. From 1962 till the onset of the 1988 crisis, the armed forces derived their legitimacy from systematically mythologising the role of the ALN in the war, promoting themselves as the true guarantors of the principles and aspirations of the Algerian 'revolution' and statehood. This myth, however, was seriously subverted by the regime's use of the army to quell the uprisings of October 1988, and since 1992 it has never really succeeded in is efforts to project itself as the defender of the 'republican' ideals of the Algerian state against the barbarity represented by the FIS and the GIA. Popular acceptance of the army's repressive counter-terrorist methods has been very reluctant; the army's unconstitutional seizure of power in January 1992 and its clear direction of goverment during the HCE and Zeroual regimes only compounded this unpopularity.

Linked to the phenomenon of factionalism is the imperative of every Algerian head of state to consolidate his authority. Ben Bella, Chadli and Boudiaf are all examples of leaders who failed in this crucial task: their opponents within the military forcibly removed all three when they were perceived to endanger their own interests, or – admittedly of secondary importance – those of Algeria. In contrast, Boumedienne managed to remain in power and win a large degree of political legitimacy by deft manipulation and navigation of the interest groups, clans and factions of the Algerian political landscape. Chadli's attempt to recreate this situation was undermined by his over-reliance on his '*cercle présidentiel*'.

One of the key methods employed by successive regimes to counter factionalism was the co-opting of groups promoting competing ideological positions. These viewpoints existed at different but parallel levels: on one level, political – from left to right; on another, secularist or religious; on still another, Arabist or 'modernist' (i.e. oriented towards Europe). Ben Bella and Boumedienne both embraced the left as a means of mobilising the masses and isolating their opponents, culminating in the very limited success of the 'agrarian revolution'. In the early 1980s Chadli shifted direction by trying to enlist the support of the Arabists and the conservatives. The conflict continued under Zeroual in the mid-1990s, manifested in the debate between modernists and conservatives regarding economic reform.

This study has also illustrated the very mixed history of the concept of popular democracy in Algeria. Hopes that the FLN would, on independence, be transformed into a vehicle for the articulation of the popular authority of the newly-liberated masses and for the promotion of a limited form of democracy were not to be released; instead, successive leaders used the FLN as a rubber-stamp institution, an instrument for the politicisation of the masses, and a vehicle on which the president's own authority would rest. Even Chadli's decision, widely applauded internationally at the time, to establish a multi-party system and hold open elections in 1990 and 1991 was not born of a genuine democratic impulse. Rather he and his supporters resorted to democratisation as a means of outflanking their opponents and consolidating their own position.

However, Chadli fatally underestimated the challange posed by the opposition and overestimated the people's loyalty to the state. The prime beneficiary of these two miscalculations was the FIS, an organisation whose appeal rested as much on its distinction from the regimes in power since 1962 and its nationalist credentials as on its Islamist programme. The FIS was primarily a radical nationalist party that articulated its policies in the context of Islamism rather than a 'classically fundamentalist' organisation, and the perception of it as a revolutionary and corrective movement represented its greatest strength. The decline in the Front's popularity by the time that Lamine Zeroual began to set in train his remarkable political stabilisation programme in 1995 was in part a result of his shrewd policy of assuming the same political ground as the FIS. Politically he repositioned himself outside the state while at the same time standing at its centre.

The development of armed conflict between hardline supporters of the FIS and the state after 1992 was a reaction to the military and political élite's abandonment of the democratic experiment. The proliferation of armed guerrilla and urban terrorist cells in the years that followed drew on a long local tradition of criminality, evoking parallels between the wartime FLN and the Islamist movement of 1980s, as well as seeking justification in the Islamic injunction to *jihad*. There was, however, an important distinction between the two 'coalitions' of armed groups, the AIS and the GIA: the first used violence with the aim of persuading the state to readmit the FIS into the political process, while the latter was determined to overthrow the state through guerrilla warfare and terrorism.

Social and cultural factors also contributed to the crisis. The position of Algeria's ethnic minorities, most prominently the Kabyles, has always been important politically, especially since the Tizi Ouzou Spring of 1980. After decades of persistent though largely unsuccessful pressure on the government of the day to recognise Amazigh alongside Arabic as the national language, the Berberists finally won a victory of sorts in 1995 when the Zeroual government granted several substantial concessions. It was perhaps ironic that the government agreed largely to secure the support of the predominantly secularist Berbers as allies against the Islamists; a complete reversal of the situation ten years previously.

In Algeria, language is a primary political, ideological, social and psychological issue, closely connected with the country's search for its identity. The leaders of the FIS stressed their command of Arabic and eschewed expression in French at all opportunities, a strategy that once again underlined their nationalist as much as Islamist credentials. This provided the FIS with a ready-made audience which, unlike much of the Francophone older generation, was naturally proficient in Arabic due to the Arabisation of education since the 1970s.

France continues to hold a unique position in Algeria. Even thirty-five years after independence most of the Algerian intelligentsia and élite are educated in French, are familiar with French political and economic thinking, and spend much of their time in France. Other Western powers continue to regard Algeria as primarily a French economic and political sphere of influence though this perception has diminished somewhat in recent years. Decades of Arabisation and policy reorientations towards the Soviet Union and the Arab world have failed to dislodge France's close links with Algiers.

Finally, this study has outlined the efforts of successive governments first to develop an ambitious programme of industrial and agricultural development, and then to address the resulting problems, and those that evolved subsequently, through economic reform. These attempts at economic reform, combined with the unfortunate consequences of the decline in Algeria's hydrocarbons revenues, proved sufficiently destabilising to touch off the cycle of unrest and instability that began in 1985, to precipitate 'Black October' in 1988 and to pave the way for the Islamist opposition's rise to prominence between 1990 and 1992.

A New Republic?

The parliamentary elections of June 1997 marked the high water-mark of Lamine Zeroual's programme to stabilise the political situation and renew his regime's legitimacy. The three years between his first appointment in January 1994 and the successful completion of elections in June 1997 reflected the victory of the state and its supporters over the forces that had contributed to the successes of their opponents in 1988-92.

But this 'new republic' was nothing more than the latest though clearly the most successful mechanism to legitimise the power of the military-political élite by using the façade of democracy. Zeroual and his key advisers managed to engineer a situation where the party of the state, the hastily-formed RND, was able to project itself as the natural and sanitised heir of the FLN, an Algerian nationalist party for the 1990s, and thus sweep effortlessly to power.

The changes to the constitution which were overwhelmingly approved at the referendum in November 1996 were clearly designed to strengthen the power of the presidency (and, implicitly, the influence of the military élite over the presidency). The amended constitution required every party to remove all explicit manifesto references to religion and ethnicity, something which seven parties (including Ben Bella's MDA) refused to do, leading to their dissolution. The main purpose of the constitutional rules was as a punishment held in reserve by the regime for use against organisations that did not prove cooperative. A precedent for this decision existed: the state only banned the FIS in February 1992 on the grounds of its radical Islamist platform, despite the prohibition on religious-based parties in the 1989 constitution. The parliament elected in June 1997 was to have very limited legislative powers, and work under the unspoken veto imposed by the military, which could step in to remove any administration that ignored its wishes.

Even without some degree of electoral irregularities, the RND would probably have won the highest share of the vote in June 1997. The party, which had only been founded four months earlier, enjoyed the support of the two most powerful non-political organisations in Algeria: the trade unions confederation, UGTA, and the war veterans' organisation, the ONM. Almost all cabinet ministers in the last, non-elected cabinet of the post-Chadli era (under Ahmed Ouyahia) flocked to the RND's platform, ostensibly built on centre-left politics and nationalism. As such, the 'baby born with moustaches' easily fulfilled the role designed for it by its founders and silent supporters as a channel for public support for the state and to eclipse the FLN.

The regime also managed to further marginalise what remained of the FIS and co-opt the more pliable, moderate parts of the Islamist movement. Both Hamas and Ennahda agreed to expunge all overt Islamist references from their platforms and style themselves 'conservative', subsequently an acceptable code for moderate Islamist. Many of the other opposition elements participated in the election mainly to avoid being even more marginalised and overshadowed by the RND and the MSP.

The election results were exploited right across the political spectrum. The moderate majority claimed the RND's victory as proof that the Algerian people had rejected both the Islamist and secularist extremes that bedevilled Algerian politics, and had returned to their nationalist roots. The Islamists, however, claimed the polls showed that many Algerians remained attracted by conservative and traditional teachings, an interpretation borne out both by Nahnah's strong showing in the November 1995 presidential elections, and by the respectable scores won by the MSP and Ennahda in June 1997. As with most things in Algeria, the truth lies somewhere among all these interpretations.

Zeroual's projects marked an important change in the country's perception of itself and of its government. For the first time in Algerian history, both the head of state and his government enjoyed a measure of popular legitimacy – in many ways more than during the Ben Bella and Boumedienne regimes. This was largely what the military and administrative establishment – *le pouvoir* – had planned.

Despite the indications to the contrary, however, the military élite remained as powerful as ever. The principal change wrought by the elections lay in the military's willingness to exploit the constitutional process rather than resist it and, as in 1992, overturn it. The military decided to support Zeroual as their candidate in November 1995, even though the former prime minister, Redha

Malek, who had also announced his candidacy, more exactly represented the interests of its senior members. As such, the military's decision, which by all accounts was reached by consultation among senior officers, marked an important stage in that institution's conversion to at least some acceptance of democracy.

The legitimacy of the state and the role of democracy is one of the three principal challenges facing Algeria as it enters the twenty-first century. The election of Zeroual and of the RND-led coalition went some way towards a resolution of the crisis of legitimacy that had dogged all the post-Chadli regimes, even though the institutions that precipitated the crisis had imposed their solution by the manipulation of the Algerian people. The fact that there had been no doubt of the outcomes of the elections testified to the efficiency of *le pouvoir* in manipulating the environment in which the elections took place to its advantage, and few doubted that the military would have been prepared to intervene again had the voters chosen an unsuitable president or government. For the post-1962 political élite to remain predominant without suffering a permanent challenge from the marginalised opposition forces, such as the FIS and its allies, the state must foster the convergence of the constituent parts of that élite – the military, the modernists, the conservatives, the Berberists and the moderate Islamists, all of whom participated in the project of the FLN during the war of independence. A successful convergence would create a political landscape where the resumption of a genuine political pluralism would be more likely to succeed.

Islam and its role in the Algerian constitution is the second challenge. The success of the FIS in 1990 and 1991, and the respectable shares of the vote garnered by Mahfoudh Nahnah and Nourredine Boukrouh in the 1995 presidential election and of the MSP and Ennahda in the 1997 parliamentary elections illustrate the enduring appeal of Muslim conservatism to the Algerian people. However, it was Zeroual who more accurately represented the position of most Algerians regarding Islam and its role in the constitution and influence on society. Most urban Algerians are more than passive Muslims, usually respecting the most important Muslim tenets, such as Ramadan, but often adopting relatively liberal attitudes on questions such as the employment of women and the imposition of *sharia*. This relatively moderate position does not correspond with the Islamic republicanism of the FIS and the millenarianism of the GIA, and it was the former's nationalist rather than Islamist platform that explained its electoral successes. Nevertheless, the challange for the Algerian state is to reconcile the moderate conservative position of the majority of the country's population towards Islam with the minorities on either extreme – the radical Islamic extremists and the secularists. Lamine Zeroual was perhaps the first Algerian head of state to reflect more accurately the majority position.

The third challenge lies in the social and cultural questions posed by the position of the Kabyle minority within Algeria, and the continued, ambiguous role of the French language. The Kabyles, and to some extent their rejection of Arabic in favour of French, are the main impediment to the project fully to Arabise Algeria. Lacking the historical heterogeneity and continuity of Morocco, a country that has more successfully accommodated its Berber characteristics, Algeria has been unable to reconcile its Kabyle minority and the continued predominance of French in political and economic life. This contrasts with neighbouring Tunisia, where Habib Bourguiba and his successor, Zine el-Abidine Ben Ali created a functioning bilingual Arab-French society. The state will not realise its plan to forge an Algerian nation if it fails to recognise the specificity of the Kabyle minority and the contribution to *Algérianité* of the country's Berber heritage.

There is no doubt that the Algerian people are capable of meeting these three challenges. The horrific experience of the war for independence and the impressive advances of the 1960s and 1970s proved them to be a resilient and resourceful people who provided an inspiration for many in the Arab and developing worlds. History also teaches their enduring propensity to reject pragmatism and compromise in favour of dogmatism and confrontation. This has reinforced the fissures and factionalisms of a society that has repeatedly failed to realise its potential, for which all the ingredients are in place: assured wealth from oil and gas; an educated and youthful population; a fertile and varied land; and proximity to European markets. Whether the country finally capitalises on these advantages depends very much on the lessons it draws from the tragedy of the post-Chadli crisis.

SELECT BIBLIOGRAPHY

Addi, Lahouri, *L'Algérie et la démocratie*, Paris, 1994.

Ageron, C.-R., *Modern Algeria: A History from 1830 to the Present*, London: Hurst, 1991.

—, *Histoire de l'Algérie contemporaine (1871-1964)*, Paris: P.U.F., 1964.

Ahnaf, M., B. Botineau and F. Frégosi, *L'Algérie par ses Islamistes*, Paris: Karthala, 1991.

Amnesty International, *Algeria: Deteriorating Human Rights and the State of Emergency*, London, 1993.

Benissad, M.E., *L'économie algérienne contemporaine*, Paris: P.U.F., 1980.

Benoune, M., *The Making of Modern Algeria, 1830-1987*, Cambridge University Press, 1988.

Blin, Louis, 'Les élites politiques', *Les Cahiers de l'Orient*, 1992, pp. 237-57.

Burgat, François, *L'Islamisme au Maghreb*, Paris: Karthala, 1988.

Chaker, Salem, 'L'émergence du fait berbère', *Annuaire de l'Afrique du Nord* (1980), pp. 473-83.

—, 'De quelques constantes du discours dominant sur les langues populaires en Algérie', *Annuaire de l'Afrique du Nord* (1981), pp. 451 ff.

—, *Les Cahiers de L'Orient* (1992), p. 91.

—, *Les Kabyles: Elements pour la compréhension de l'identité Berbère en Algérie*, edited by Tassadit Yacine, Paris: GDM, 1992.

Corm, George, *La réforme économique algérienne démocratique et populaire*, Paris: P.U.F., 1979.

Cubertafond, Bernard, *La République algérienne démocratique et populaire*, Paris, P.U.F., 1979.

—, *L'Algérie contemporaine*, Paris, 1981.

Droz, Bernard, and Evelyne Lever, *Histoire de la guerre de l'Algérie, 1954-1962*, Paris: Seuil, 1982.

Entelis, John, 'Elite political culture and socialization in Algeria: tensions and discontinuities', *Middle East Journal* (1981), pp. 191-208.

—, *Algeria: The Revolution Institutionalised*, Boulder, CO: Westview Press, 1986.

Etienne, Bruno, *L'Algérie. Cultures et révolution*, Paris, 1977.

—, *L'Islamisme radical*, Paris: Hachette, 1992.

Gaid, Mouloud, *Les Berbères dans l'histoire*, Algiers: Editions Mimouni, 1990.

Gautier, Emile-Félix, *Le Passé de l'Afrique du Nord. Les Siècles obscure*, Paris: Payot, 1952.

Granghuillaume, Gilbert, *Arabisation et politiques linguistiques au Maghreb*, Paris: Larousse, 1983.

Grimaud, Nicole, *La Politique extérieure de l'Algérie (1962-1978)*, Paris: Karthala, 1984.

—, 'French policy towards Algeria', *Middle East Journal*, 1986, pp. 252-66.

Harbi, Mohamed, *Aux origines du FLN. Le Populisme révolutionnaire en Algérie*, Paris: Bourgois, 1975

—, *Nationalisme algérienne en France*, Paris: L'Harmattan, 1985.

Horne, Alistair, *A Savage War of Peace: Algeria, 1954-1962*, 2nd edn, London: Macmillan, 1987.

Humbaraci, A., *Algeria: A Revolution that Failed: A Political History since 1954*, London: Pall Mall Press, 1977.

Julien, Charles-André, *Histoire de l'Algérie contemporaine* (1827-1871), Paris: P.U.F., 1964.

Kepel, Gilles, *Le prophète et le pharaon. Aux sources des mouvements Islamistes*, rev. edn, Paris: Seuil, 1993.

Khelil, Mohand, *La Kabylie ou l'ancre sacrifié*, Paris: L'Harmattan, 1984.

Lawless, Richard, 'The contradictions of rapid industrialisation' in Richard Lawless and Allan Findlay (eds), *North Africa: Contemporary Politics and Economic Development*, London: Croom Helm, 1984, pp. 153-90.

Lamchichi, Aberrahim, *L'Algérie en crise*, Paris: L'Harmattan, 1991.

—, *L'Islamisme en Algérie*, Paris: L'Harmattan, 1992.

Leca, Jean, *L'Algérie politique. Institutions et régime*, Paris: Fondation Nationale des Sciences Politiques, 1975.

— and Jean-Claude Vatin, *L'Algérie politique. Institutions et régime*, Paris: Armand Colin, 1975.

Leveau, Rémy, *Le Sabre et le turban. L'Avenir au Maghreb*, Paris: Bourrin, 1993.

Marks, J., *Algeria: Towards Market Socialism*, London: Middle East Economic Digest, 1990.

Mezhoud, Salem, 'Glasnost the Algerian way' in George Joffé (ed.), *North Africa: Nation, State and Region*, London: Routledge, 1993.

Moore, Clement Henry, 'Political Parties' in *Polity and Society in Contemporary North Africa*, Boulder, CO: Westview Press, 1993.

Mortimer, Robert, 'Islam and multiparty politics in Algeria', *Middle East Journal*, 45, no.4 (autumn 1991), pp.161-4.

O'Ballance, Edgar, *The Algerian Insurrection*, London: Faber and Faber, 1967.

Ottaway, D. and M., *Algeria: The Politics of a Socialist Revolution*, Berkeley: University of California Press, 1970.

Pfeifer, Karen, *Agrarian Reform under State Capitalism in Algeria*, Boulder, CO: Westview Press, 1985.

Quandt, W.B., *Revolution and Political Leadership: Algeria, 1954-1968*, Cambridge, MA: MIT Press, 1969.

Reudy, John, *Modern Algeria: The Origins and Development of a Nation*, Bloomington, IN: Indiana University Press, 1992.

Roberts, Hugh, 'Towards an understanding of the Kabyle question in contemporary Algeria', *The Maghreb Review*, 5 (Sept.-Dec. 1980), pp. 115-24.

——, 'The politics of Algerian socialism' in Richard Lawless and Allen Findlay (eds), *North Africa: Contemporary Politics and Economic Development*, London: Croom Helm, 1984

——, 'Radical Islamism and the dilemma of Algerian nationalism: the embattled Arians of Algiers', *Third World Quarterly*, 10, no. 2 (April 1988), pp. 556-89.

——, 'The FLN: French occupation, Algerian realities' in George Joffé (ed.), *North Africa: Nation, State and Region*, London: Routledge, 1993.

——, 'Algeria between eradicators and conciliators', *Middle East Report*, 189 (July-Aug. 1994), pp. 24-7.

——, 'Algeria's ruinous impasse and the honourable way out', *International Affairs*, 71, no. 2 (1995), pp. 247-67.

Tlemçani, Rachid, *State and Revolution in Algeria*, London: Zed Books, 1986.

Vatin, Jean-Claude, *L'Algérie politique. Histoire et Société*, Paris: P.U.F., 1974.

——, 'Popular puritanism versus state reformism in Algeria' in J. P. Piscatori (ed.), *Islam in the Political Process*, Cambridge University Press, 1983.

Zartman, I. William, *Government and Politics in North Africa*, London: Methuen 1964.

--, 'The Algerian army in politics' in I. William Zartman (ed.), *Man, State and Society in the Contemporary Maghreb*, New York: Praeger, 1973.

-- and W.M. Habeeb (eds), *Polity and Society in Contemporary North Africa*, Boulder, CO: Westview Press, 1993.

Note on Newspapers and Periodicals

Newspapers published in France devote a great deal of space to news and comment concerning Algeria. I have relied heavily on *Le Monde*, *Le Figaro* and *Libération* for daily reporting on events and occasional analysis. I have also drawn upon newspapers published in Algiers, particularly *El Moudjahid*, *El Watan* and *La Tribune*.

There is much thorough analysis of Algeria in French journals, magazines and periodicals. The weekly magazine *Jeune Afrique* is consistently of good quality. Among the most comprehensive and reliable journals are *Le Monde Diplomatique*, *Les Cahiers de l'Orient*, *Peuples Méditerranéens*, *Maghreb Confidential* and *Maghreb-Machreq*. The annual *Annuaire de l'Afrique du Nord* is a valuable source of reference.

Algeria remains ill-served by the media and academia in the English-speaking world. In London *The Guardian*, *The Independent* and *The Times* are reliable as sources and, less often, for analysis. Of the American press, only the *Washington Post* and the *New York Times* (often reprinted in the *International Herald Tribune*) can be relied upon to report on Algeria.

Magazines, journals and periodicals published in English only rarely examine Algeria. I have drawn on occasional articles in *Africa Confidential*, *International Affairs*, *The World Today* and *Third World Quarterly* (published in London), and the *Washington Report on Middle East Affairs*, *MERIP Reports* and the *Middle East Journal*, published in the United States. For clear and regular analysis of the current Algerian situation readers should consult *Middle East International and Middle East Economic Digest*, both published in London. Two Arabic newspapers published in London are also useful: *al-Hayat* and *al-Sharq al-Awsat*.

INDEX

263